ADHD

A Survival Guide
for
Parents and Teachers

ADHD

A Survival Guide

for

Parents and Teachers

by

Richard A. Lougy, MFT

and

David K. Rosenthal, MD

HOPE PRESS
P.O.B. 188
Duarte, CA 91009-0188

Hope Press
P.O. Box 188
Duarte, CA 91009 U.S.A

For other books by Hope Press see:
www.hopepress.com

DSM-IV criteria for ADHD reprinted with permission from the *Diagnostic and Statistical Manual of Mental Disorders, Fourth Edition, Text Revision.* Copyright 2000 American Psychiatric Association.

Taking Charge of ADHD: A Complete Authoritative Guide for Parents, by Russell A. Barkley. Copyright 1995. Used with permission of The Guilford Press.

ADHD and the Nature of Self-Control, by Russell A. Barkley. Copyright 1997. Used with permission of The Guilford Press.

Managing Attention Disorders in Children, by Sam and Michael Goldstein. Copyright 1990 by John Wiley & Sons, Inc. This material is used by permission of John Wiley & Sons, Inc.

Turning Points: Treating Families in Transition and Crisis, by Frank S. Pittman, III. Copyright 1987 by Frank S. Pittman, III. Used by permission of W. W. Norton & Company, Inc.

How to Reach and Teach ADD/ADHD Children, by Sandra Rief. Copyright 1993. Reprinted with permission of Prentice Hall Direct.

Helping Your Hyperactive/ADD Child, Revised 3rd Ed., by John Taylor. Copyright 1994, 1999 by John Taylor. Used by permission of Random House, Inc.

Library of Congress Cataloging-in-Publication Data

Lougy, Richard A., 1994 -
    Adhd : A survival guide for parents and teachers / by Richard A. Lougy
and David K. Rosenthal.
        p. cm.
Includes bibliographic references and index.
    ISBN 1-878267-43-4
    I. Attention-deficit hyperactivity disorder—Popular works. 2.
Attention-deficit-disordered children—Care. I. Rosenthal, David K.,
1958- II. Title
    RJ506.H9 L68 2002
    618.92'8589—dc21

To my family, who has supported me through their encouragement
and belief in this book.
Richard Lougy

To Marci and Alex, with love...
David Rosenthal

Table of Contents

Table of Contents v

Foreword 1

Acknowledgements 5

Introduction 7

Chapter 1
I Am Confused—So What Is ADHD? 9

According to the Experts, What Is ADHD? 9

Definition and Symptoms 11

Are There Different Types of ADHD? 11

Inattention 13

Hyperactivity 15

Impulsivity 16

Other Behaviors Sometimes Associated with ADHD 17

ADHD Predominantly Inattentive Type (ADHD-I) 19

Developmental Stages of ADHD 21

Infants and Toddlers 21

School Age 22

Adolescents 23

Four Behaviors Worthy of Discussion 24

Inhibiting Behavior 24

Rule-Governed Behavior 27

Inconsistent Performance 29

Motivation 29

What Are the Roles of Biology and Environment? 31

Myth or Fact 32

Brain Injury 32

Diet 32

Sugar 32

Lead Poisoning 33

Medical Problems 33

Genetics 34

Neurotransmitters 34

Family 37

School 38

Summary 40

Chapter 2

How Can I Know for Sure My Child Has ADHD?.................................41

Who Can Make a Diagnosis of ADHD?...41

Can Other Factors Cause My Child to Look Like He Has ADHD? 42

Will My Child's ADHD Go Away As He Gets Older?....................................43

Why Are My Two Children with ADHD So Different? 44

My Child Can Sit in Front of the TV for Hours and Never Move. Does That

Mean He Doesn't Have ADHD? 45

My Friend's Child Has Tourette Syndrome but Acts Like He Has ADHD.....46

My Doctor Now Says My Child May Have Bipolar Disorder, Not ADHD.

What Is Bipolar Disorder? 48

Summary 50

Chapter 3

Am I to Blame?...51

Should I Blame Myself? 52

I Feel Guilty Spending So Much Time with My Child 52

My Doctor Doesn't Believe Me—He Says, "Take a Parenting Class"..............53

My Parents Say We Are Terrible for Putting Their Grandchild on

Medication 56

Sally-Next-Door Says I Am Not Strict Enough 57

I Am Losing My Child...59

The Hardest Time for Me Was When I Had to Place My Child in a

Psychiatric Hospital...62

I Feel Like Running Away..63

Sometimes I Don't Like My Child 65

Summary 66

Chapter 4

"Don't Blame Me—I Have ADHD!"..67

I Didn't Take My Pill—Don't Blame Me! 67

Counting to Five Silently..70

Talk to Yourself 70

Plan Ahead for Problem Areas 71

Medication 71

He Seldom Says He's Sorry 73

   Acknowledging Mistakes 75

   Making Amends 75

   Chart "I'm Sorry" Statements 75

   Time to Talk 75

He Is So Emotional—Is This Normal? 76

   Counting to Five Silently 77

   Stop, Look, Think, and Do 77

   Prepare Your Child for Changes 77

He Never Seems to Learn from His Mistakes......................................78

   Ideas to Help Your Child Learn Better from His Mistakes 79

What Scares Me the Most Is When He Gets Violent 81

   I C.A.R.E. 82

   Green, Yellow, Red 83

   Zip My Lip 83

   Know What Makes Your Child Angry 83

   Exercise 84

Is My Child Noncompliant or Just Incompetent? 84

   Positive Directions 85

   Incompetence 86

      Reminder Sheets 86

      One Direction at a Time and Be Specific...............................86

      Keep a Stopwatch Handy 87

   Noncompliance 87

      Commonsense Rules...87

      Be Firm 88

      Time-Out...88

      Changing Habits 89

   Be Preventative, Not Reactionary 90

   Summary 91

Chapter 5

Our Child Takes a Lot of Our Time **93**

   Reminders, Reminders, All the Time...94

      Reminder Sheets...95

      Mnemonic Reminders 95

      Kitchen Timer 96

Oral Directions 96

Make Eye Contact 96

Be Close to Him 96

Family Outings Can Be Overwhelming...............................97

Look Before You Leap 97

Waiting Is No Fun 98

Change Is Not Easy 99

Getting Ready for School—It's Never Enough Time 99

Sleep Time 100

Bathroom Time...101

Time-Keepers 101

Medication 101

Sitting Down for Breakfast Can Be World War III...............102

Table Rules 102

Time-Keepers 103

Catch Him Being Good 103

Medication 103

Getting Ready for Bed Can Be a Nightly Battle.................104

Pre-Bed Rituals 105

Insomnia 107

His Sister and Brother Want to Live Next Door 108

Find Special Time 108

No One Wants to Be Abused..109

Brothers and Sisters Need a Vacation, Too.......................110

He Minds His Dad Better Than Me..................................111

Homework Is a Family Mission 113

Don't Jeopardize Your Relationship with Your Child 113

You May Not Be Able to Be His Teacher 114

Parental Responsibility..114

The Homework May Be Too Hard or Long 115

Let's Not Talk about Going to the Store! 117

Have a Plan..118

Rules on a Card 118

Take a Photo of the "Time-Out" Chair..............................118

1–2–3 Magic 119

Reward Him for Being Good..120

Our Marriage Needs Some Attention...121

   Taking Care of You Is Important...121

   It's Okay to Say No 122

   Stop Trying to Control Things 123

   Don't Neglect Your Partner 123

   Try to Share Parenting..123

I Am a Single Parent—Help! 124

   I Can't Find a Baby-sitter 125

   Dating? Say That Word Again!..126

   Where Do I Go When I Want to Explode?.........................127

   My Partner Isn't Patient or Understanding 127

   Try to Be Supportive, Not Enabling 128

   I Feel Alone and Nobody Cares 128

Summary 131

Chapter 6

My Child's in School—Can I Tell You Some Stories!............................131

Should I Tell His Teacher He Has ADHD?..................................132

I Think I Should Get a Diploma, Too!...134

I Feel Like Hiring a Tutor..134

How Much Does the Teacher Know about ADHD?....................137

I Hate to Hear from My Child's School.......................................141

His School Says It's My Child's Responsibility to Remember to Take

   His Medication 144

Homework Takes Forever 145

   Distractibility 146

   Disorganization 148

Homework May Be Too Hard or Long...150

He Does His Homework and Then Forgets to Turn It In!...........151

Monitor Your Child's Homework 151

Communicate Regularly with the Teacher 153

He Doesn't Seem Motivated to Get Good Grades 154

My Neighbor Has a Child with ADHD, and He Is Doing Fine in School—

   Why's That?...158

He Did So Much Better in the Third Grade Than He's Doing in the

   Seventh Grade..158

   Behavioral Expectations 159

Academic Expectations 160

Writing Assignments Are Especially Difficult for My Child.........................161

Could My Child Have a Learning Disability?.....................................163

My Neighbor Says Schools Have a Legal Obligation to Accommodate My
Son's ADHD. Is This True? 164

    IDEA 165

    Section 504 165

My Child Has a Hard Time at Recess 167

    Impulsive Behavior 167

    Difficulty Modulating Emotions 167

    Noncompliant and Oppositional Behavior 168

    Impatience 168

Ideas to Help at Recess...168

    Don't Leave the Classroom without a Plan 168

    Green Card 169

    Time-Out Areas 169

My Child's School Asked for a Student Study Team—What's That?............170

I Worry My Child Will Be a School Dropout......................................171

Summary 173

Chapter 7

Even My Pharmacist's Wife Says She Wouldn't Put Her Child on Ritalin

Even My Pharmacist's Wife Says She Wouldn't Put Her Child
on Ritalin **175**

1) My child's teacher says that my child needs to be put on medication. 176

2) What medications are most commonly used to treat ADHD? 177

3) What changes can I expect to see in my child after giving Ritalin
or Dexedrine? 180

4) Do stimulants cure ADHD? How do these medications work?.................180

5) How long do I need to try stimulants to know if they work?....................181

6) How do I know when I am giving my child enough, versus too much,
of a stimulant medication? 182

7) If the medication works, does that confirm that the diagnosis is correct? 182

8) What side effects might I expect my child to have from stimulants?.........183

9) Can stimulants cause problems with growth? 185

10) I've heard that stimulants can cause twitches or Tourette syndrome......186

11) Are stimulants addictive? 188

12) Can stimulants lead to problems with abuse of other drugs?...................188

13) Are there particular children who would be expected to do poorly on stimulants?..189

14) My child's teacher says that my child should only be on Ritalin for school, and my doctor says he needs it daily. Whom should I believe? ...191

15) Are there problems with adverse drug interactions if my child is on a stimulant? 191

16) I've heard that kids can become psychotic on stimulants. 192

17) Can stimulants be used in children under age five?..........................193

18) My child seems to do better after drinking soda or a cup of coffee. Is there anything wrong with using caffeine instead of Ritalin? 193

19) Can stimulants bring out bipolar disorder (manic-depression)? 194

20) My child used to do well on Ritalin but now it doesn't work. What is going on?..195

21) Are there any good natural remedies available? 196

22) Are there medications used to treat ADHD other than the stimulants?.198

    Clonidine (Catapres) and guanfacine (Tenex) 199

    Tricyclic antidepressants..200

    Wellbutrin (bupropion) 200

    Neuroleptics 201

    Mood stabilizers..201

    New ADHD drugs on the horizon 201

23) When should drugs like Prozac be used? 202

24) Do medications help learning disabilities?........................202

25) My child is defiant. Will medication help with this? 202

26) My child with ADHD doesn't sleep well—what should I do about it? ...203

27) Are stimulants used to treat adults with ADHD?........................204

Summary 204

Chapter 8

If It Works, Try Again, but It Won't Work for Long 205

What Works for His Younger Brother Doesn't Work for My Child with ADHD 205

Medication Helps, but I Need More 207

There Will Be Good Moments and There Will Be Bad Moments........209

I Am Tired of Yelling..212

I Am Uncomfortable Bribing My Child to Be Good........................215

My Adolescent Is Too Old to Place in Time-Out 219

Summary 225

Chapter 9

**I Would Love to Help as a Teacher, but I have 35 Children
in My Classroom** **227**

I Have Too Many Other Responsibilities 228

The Challenge Presented Teachers 228

Blame Doesn't Help 228

Teachers Need Not Feel Guilty 229

My Students Find Some Curriculum Especially Difficult 230

Written Work 231

Arithmetic 232

Reading Comprehension 232

I'm Angry That I'm Responsible for His Medication 234

He Is on Medication, So Why Isn't He Doing Better Academically? 235

Stimulants 235

Short-Term Effects of Stimulants on Academic Performance 236

Long-Term Effects of Stimulants on Academic Performance 237

What Stimulants Cannot Do to Improve Academic Performance 237

Other Reasons Why He Is Not Doing Better 238

He Is Disrupting the Education of the Other Children—I Can't

Allow That 239

Have a Plan 239

Set Firm Limits and Follow Them 240

Pick Your Battles 240

Catch Him Being Good 241

What Interventions Seem to Work Best in the Classroom? 242

What Activities Give Students with ADHD Difficulty? 242

He Always Needs to Be Reminded 243

Primary Grades (Kindergarten through Sixth Grades) 243

Secondary Grades (Seventh through Twelfth Grades) 243

He Wastes Time During Class 244

Primary Grades 244

Secondary Grades 245

He Fails to Remember to Turn in His Schoolwork 245

Primary Grades 245

Secondary Grades 246

Written Work Seems Especially Difficult 246

Primary Grades 246

Secondary Grades 247

He Gets Out of His Seat Without Asking 248

Primary Grades 248

Secondary Grades 248

He Gets Angry and Upset Too Quickly 249

Primary Grades 249

Secondary Grades 250

He Turns in His Schoolwork, but It Is Sloppy 250

Primary Grades 250

Secondary Grades 251

Section 504 Worries Me 252

How Should I Tell Parents I Think Their Child Has ADHD? 254

How Can I Help the Doctor? 256

Summary 258

Chapter 10

From Frustration to Hope—a Summary 259

Appendices **265**

Appendix A—DSM-IV-TR Criteria for Attention-Deficit/Hyperactivity
Disorder 267

Appendix B—Developmental Stages of ADHD 269

Appendix C—Nerve Cell 271

Appendix D—Disorders That Can Mimic ADHD 273

Appendix E—Stimulant Medications Used in Treatment for ADHD 275

Appendix F—The Weekly Report 277

Appendix G—Daily Student Rating Card 279

Appendix H—Web sites offering information about ADHD 281

Appendix I—Recommended Reading 283

For Parents and Teachers 283

For Children 284

Reference List **287**

Index **297**

Foreword

This book provides sensible, heartfelt advice for a myriad of issues entangling family members in frustration, conflict, and disappointment. The authors have produced a very readable road map to guide you through the complexities of dealing with ADHD at home, in the community, and at school. While it is within the comfort zone of those who want to maintain a conservative approach to ADHD, it also stretches outside the box by providing hundreds of suggestions for preventing and resolving many of the problems that most of the other ADHD parenting books skim over or ignore completely. Congratulations on deciding to use this book as your guide. I deeply appreciate the privilege of being invited to write this foreword for your benefit.

The authors make the important assertion that our knowledge is in a constant state of expansion and that controversies abound within almost every aspect of this condition and its definition. They introduce it as a biologically based disorder with multiple facets, virtually every psychiatric symptom of which comes from the range of normal experience. My own surveys of the current research literature expand this notion somewhat to include the caveat that some of the physiological characteristics of many individuals with this disorder are not within normal limits. In that sense one can't truly separate the brain from the body, and ADHD is a multi-faceted condition reflecting not only abnormalities in brain structure and chemical functions, but also impaired functioning of other organ systems.

This book uses my "200 Cards" analogy to clarify the fact that no two children with ADHD will have an identical symptom array. These traits, correlates, indicators, and symptoms are constantly in flux, brought to levels of increased or decreased intensity by a host of factors, many of which are idiosyncratic to the individual. We are not dealing with a simple black-white entity, but with thousands of possible gray ones. The fact that executive functions such as planning and organizational skills are impaired adds further support for the authors' position that there are numerous subtypes and categories within the broad label of ADHD. One area often ignored in other parent guides is infancy, and another is adolescence. You will find some refreshing clarification in this book of what to expect at these age ranges.

The authors point out that much of the behavior-related difficulty in these children reflects brain chemistry abnormalities rather than a simple lack of willpower or desire to behave. The ultimate cause of ADHD probably has to do with abnormalities in brain metabolism. These authors cite the impairments shown by recent research to the prefrontal lobes and to the occasionally demonstrated brain lead toxicity found among children with ADHD as obvious sites of physiological impairment. They provide an excellent discussion of medication effects and options, all of which directly affect brain chemistry.

A cornerstone of intervening effectively to help a family involved with this condition is that ADHD issues be approached from at least three directions. The authors adhere strongly to the inspired principle of coordinating efforts between school, family, and medical-psychosocial professional helpers. Teachers typically feel underused as allies and left out of important decisions such as the effectiveness of prescribed medications. In fact, only about one in seven is ever asked by prescribing physicians to provide direct feedback about the results as reflected during school. These authors provide a refreshing and valid appeal, and several sage bits of guidance, for stronger ties between the physician and the teacher with the permission and assistance of the parent. Likewise they give encouragement and some practical techniques for maximizing the clarity of communication and the cooperation between teacher and parent.

About 80% of these children have a major academic difficulty of some sort, and one-third have a diagnosable learning disability. You will find a thought-provoking discussion of the various reasons why students with ADHD face so many academic difficulties, accompanied by numerous classroom and home-based interventions for various grade levels. Recess can represent special challenges for these students, and these authors provide some sensible preventative advice for you. It is important not to overwhelm the teacher with demands and lists of modifications to employ for your child. These authors recommend a simple booklet to clarify your child's needs to any teacher. I endorse their idea and would suggest that you could also own copies of video or audio classroom suggestions and perhaps some small books to lend to each teacher each year. I have produced these kinds of resources for years and have found them helpful for guiding cooperative teachers in assisting students who have ADHD.

Parents are most likely to have four major negative feelings, symbolized by the acronym *ACID*—angry, criticized, inadequate, and discouraged. This book discusses the bases for these emotional reactions and includes many suggestions for effective self-care to prevent their development. Frequently parents will try to overcompensate by pitying, nagging, or overprotecting the child who is facing special challenges. These authors clarify these kinds of reactions, as well as forms of marital stresses commonly found in these families, such as denial, overinvolvement, and one-upsmanship.

I concur with the authors' admonition to take a preventative approach to child discipline. They realize that after-the-fact retroactive discipline is not as beneficial to smooth family relationships or to building of conscience as proactive efforts such as organizing for success. I always recommend emphasizing prevention of misbehavior by children with ADHD, and these authors provide some strategies such as specialized reminders. Try to use touch as well as visual and auditory reminders. Pay special attention, as do these authors, to potentially high-stress daily times such as bedtimes, mornings, and shopping. Remaining positive, providing encouragement rather than criticism, and acknowledging effort will always help. As these authors indicate, wise discipline includes noticing the positive aspects of your child's or teen's daily behavior.

I advocate providing specific instruction to enhance targeted social skills known to be difficult for these children. In this book you'll find some suggestions along the lines of targeting social skills known to be difficult for these children, such as making amends, anger control techniques, acknowledging mistakes, and apologizing.

Sibling rivalry is often a major issue in these families, but few ADHD parent guides provide much help. You'll find some practical suggestions here, including the one I most strongly endorse and advocate—spending special time with each child on a regular basis. The most frequent complaint given by older siblings is that the child with ADHD gets into their rooms and their belongings. This intrusiveness into the siblings' privacy and living space is often a key issue fanning the flames of sibling conflict, as these authors point out.

You will enjoy perusing this book and you will refer to it often. I'm delighted to recommend it to you.

> John F. Taylor, Ph.D.
> Director, A.D.D. Plus
> Author of *The Hyperactive Child* and
> *Helping Your ADD Child*
> www.ADD-Plus.com
> PO Box 4326
> Salem, Oregon 97302

Acknowledgements

Even though we have found writing a book to be a solitary act, the successful completion of a book involves the support of many people. We first want to acknowledge the parents and children who have demonstrated dignity and courage in dealing with this difficult disorder, especially Lynelle Coates, Garren Stumpf, and Dabney Day, who are parents of children with ADHD. You are so knowledgeable about ADHD, and your commitment and dedication to children has made it a pleasure to know you.

We thank our colleagues who have given guidance and support, especially Dorothy Marshall and Teri Berke, who spent many hours reviewing the draft and giving us important advice. The many teachers and other professional staff throughout the San Juan Unified School District are remembered kindly for sharing their time and experiences with us.

A special acknowledgment goes to Debbie Forsyth—through your time and effort, the Colorado State University/Fort Collins graphics department became an important contributor to our book cover design.

We owe much to our families, especially our wives, who never lost faith in our goal.

Our thanks go to our editor, Theresa Mesa, for her support and patience in getting this book ready to print.

We offer a special thank you to David E. Comings, MD, owner and publisher of Hope Press—your commitment and belief in our book has been so much appreciated.

Introduction

Our hope is that you will gain more understanding and confidence in parenting your child through reading this book. Raising a child with ADHD is a very personal experience for each parent. No other parent can mirror your challenges and no other child is exactly like yours. No two families tell the same story, yet a common thread runs throughout their experiences.

The knowledge you gain through this book should give you the strength and confidence to outlast storms that come your way, and can free you from fear and anger, allowing hope to be part of your experience with your child. Your new awareness of your child's challenges, along with a knowledge of interventions to minimize these challenges, will give you respite from anxiety and feelings of hopelessness.

This book was written with the intent that it would be user-friendly. It can be read from cover to cover, or you can read individual sections that are of special interest. We encourage you to use it like a survival guide—a resource of interventions to deal with problem behaviors. However, we do recommend that you read chapter 1 first to better understand the reasoning that underlies the interventions presented in the book. You will find some repetition of information; however, we feel it is necessary in light of the book's format. The reader, remember, can jump from one interest area to another, so important points or themes appear more than once.

The term *Attention Deficit Hyperactivity Disorder (ADHD)* is used as the main descriptor of the primary population addressed in this book. However, as you will learn, ADHD is a spectrum disorder that presents itself in various ways. For example, some children present with ADHD behavior without hyperactivity. Notation is given to the specific descriptors ADHD-C, ADHD-HI, and ADHD-I (see page 11 for description) when deemed necessary for clarity and understanding.

For ease of reading, in most cases we have chosen to use the male gender for people with ADHD, and the female gender for caretakers (parents and teachers). We realize that many females have ADHD, and many caretakers are male, but we have tried to avoid possible confusion when discussing people with ADHD and their caretakers in the same paragraph. Feel free to mentally exchange gender references throughout the book as you read.

Some of the chapter headings and subtitles are comments made by parents and teachers. They represent common themes and issues that challenge families, caretakers, and teachers. They express the questions as well as frustrations that are associated with raising these children. You may identify with some while you find others too strong or not representative of your situation. That's okay. Attention Deficit Hyperactivity Disorder affects people to different degrees. We hope this book will address many of your unanswered concerns and provide useful information for parenting your child with ADHD.

I

I Am Confused—
So What Is ADHD?

Having ADHD is not just a matter of being inattentive or overactive, nor is it a stage a child goes through as he grows up. Poor parenting does not cause ADHD, and it is not the result of marital problems. It also does not necessarily signify a severe neurological abnormality. The child does not want to have ADHD, nor does the parent want her child to have ADHD. What makes this disorder so difficult to understand, and at times accept, is that this child in many ways is not significantly different from other children. One of the most difficult aspects of identifying ADHD is deciding how much of unusual is normal. A child with this disorder does not look physically different from other children, nor does he act differently most of the time. In fact, many characteristics of affected children are socially appropriate and desirable. They can be spontaneous, enthusiastic, stimulating, creative, and the life of the party, yet research finds that they have a neurodevelopmental disorder (related to the brain and neurological development) that can affect their day-to-day performance in school and their interactions with peers and caretakers.

New research has given both parents and clinicians working with these children promising ideas for success. Ongoing investigation and understanding has allowed better treatment and counseling for families dealing with ADHD. Most parents ask, "What is ADHD and how can I help my child?" No better questions can be asked or deserve to be answered. Our goal is twofold—to help you separate myth from current scientific understanding and to help you deal with your child's behaviors.

According to the Experts, What Is ADHD?

ADHD is one of the most studied of all psychological disorders in children, but our knowledge is still incomplete and the diagnosis remains a controversy in many public and private sectors. This confusion stems from the fact that so many experts are involved, and their opinions regarding the diagnosis and treatment of ADHD vary widely, resulting in uncertainty about the status of this disorder and whether it should or should not be treated and, if so, how. Adding to this confusion is inconsistent diagnosis, with the disorder sometimes being overdiagnosed or underdiagnosed. As a consequence, experts continue to debate both the cause and definitions that best describe ADHD.

Thousands of scientific papers and numerous books for teachers and parents have been written. It has become one of the conditions most frequently seen by child guidance personnel in this country. So much effort and study has been dedicated to ADHD because it has social and educational implications, and the cost to society for untreated ADHD is high. This population consumes a disproportionate share of resources and attention from the health care system, criminal justice system, schools, and other social agencies. These children usually have impairment across multiple settings—home, social, and school. Early diagnosis is critical, therefore, for minimizing problems they will encounter in academic activities and interactions with peers and adults. Unfortunately, ADHD has often been mishandled, leaving thousands of children, adolescents, and adults incorrectly diagnosed and thus denied the benefits of proper treatment.

The behavior patterns we associate with this disorder generally appear between the ages of three and five; however, some children do not display symptoms until late childhood or adolescence. The majority of children, contrary to popular belief, continue to have the full disorder into adulthood (Spencer 2000, 16). More boys are diagnosed than girls; however, when hyperactivity is not present, the ratio between boys and girls seems to be closer to equal. Girls, unfortunately, continue to be underdiagnosed and are not provided with preventative and early intervention strategies so important for their social, emotional, and academic success. This disorder affects 3% to 20% of the national population, depending on the information source. Most professionals accept 3% to 5% as the range of population diagnosed with ADHD; however, recent studies suggest 4% to 12% as the range of unscreened school-age population (six–12 years old) (Brunk 2000, 1, 5). One of the leading experts in this field, Russell Barkley (1995), proposes that more than two million school-age children may have ADHD. That averages out to one or two children in each classroom.

It is seen today as primarily a polygenic disorder (more than one gene contributes to it) that can often be minimized or exacerbated by environmental factors. It is a biologically determined spectrum disorder presenting a myriad of variables and distinctions, yet it's often best treated by environmental manipulation and medication. ADHD refers to several chronic neurobiological disorders that interfere with an individual's capacity to regulate age-appropriate activity level, inhibition, and attention; however, there is no blood test, brain scan, or definitive psychological test that can currently diagnose ADHD. This lack of tests is not unique to this disorder, but applies to most psychiatric disorders, such as schizophrenia and autism (NIMH 1999).

Research has not stopped, however, and more information may change the way we view this disorder. Currently, however, there are common characteristics that experts in the field generally accept.

Definition and Symptoms

"I do not assume everything that wiggles is ADHD"
Louis B. Cady, M.D.

Are There Different Types of ADHD?

Early attempts to define ADHD focused primarily on motor activities, hence the diagnosis of "hyperactivity." Since then, a broader and more inclusive definition has changed both its labels and our understanding of it. The core symptoms include developmentally inappropriate levels of attention, concentration, activity, distractibility, and impulsivity.

The current diagnosis is divided into three categories, ensuring that professionals use the same language and have the same understanding when they identify ADHD and communicate among each other about a patient or client. A child's diagnosis will fall under one of these categories, which depends upon the component that is most representative of the child's behavior: children having primarily inattention, called *Predominantly Inattentive Type (ADHD-I)*; children having primarily hyperactivity and impulsivity, called *Predominantly Hyperactive-Impulsive Type (ADHD-HI)*; and children having attention deficit and hyperactivity, called *Combined Type (ADHD-C)* (see Appendix A: *DSM-IV-TR*).

The primary symptoms currently associated with ADHD are *inattention, hyperactivity,* and *impulsivity.* These primary symptoms can be viewed as dimensional aspects of behavior rather than as categories. The relative degree and pattern of these primary symptoms help us better index this disorder for purposes of diagnosis. Not all children present these symptoms in the same way or to the same degree. Some will present only mild impairment, while others present moderate to severe impairment that can impact day-to-day interactions with others, and performance in school and on the job. Those whose symptoms show significant impairment will often be diagnosed with ADHD.

This disorder probably represents the extreme end of normal human traits, rather than a true pathological condition. Like other human traits, these traits probably undergo developmental changes as the individual matures. If ADHD represents one end of a continuum of traits, then the problem with diagnosis lies in determining the boundary between the unaffected population and those with ADHD. We all have ADHD traits, and those diagnosed with ADHD may simply represent the extreme. This disorder can be viewed like other traits, such as reading ability, height, weight, or intelligence. Where one falls on the continuum determines whether one's trait is considered normal or abnormal. Children with ADHD differ in how much they inherit the traits in much the same way we all differ in how much we inherit height or intelligence. No two children inherit or present similar behaviors.

John F. Taylor (1994, 13), an expert on ADHD, talks about this difference by using an analogy of a deck of cards. Imagine, he writes, every child being given a deck of 200 cards. On each card is a trait of ADHD, e.g., running around all the time, entering a sister's bedroom without permission, not following teacher's directions, or jumping from one activity to another, and its overlapping conditions, e.g., impulsivity, hyperactivity, distractibility, impulsivity, and inattention, to name a few. Each child receives cards that represent particular behaviors, but some children will receive only a few cards, and others will receive many. Those who receive many cards stand out from other children and are seen as different.

Also, even though two children may have the same number of cards, their collection of traits or behaviors may be different. One child may be inattentive without hyperactivity, another child predominantly impulsive and hyperactive. Your child may be inattentive and highly distractible, but less hyperactive than another. This variability in symptoms is one of the most confusing and frustrating factors for parents and caretakers. You know this if you have ever tried to explain to a teacher, grandparent, or doctor why your child has ADHD when he acts so differently from the child with ADHD down the street. This can especially be true if your child is not that particularly hyperactive but is definitely inattentive.

It would be a lot easier for parents and clinicians if children were like mathematical formulas—clear, consistent and tested true over time—but they're not. Each child comes with his own temperament, personality, bumps, and bruises that don't fit neatly into any category. All that any list of symptoms can do is give us an approximate idea of behaviors in a child, not an exact match. No child should be thought of as the poster child for ADHD. If you could line up 100 affected children on the street, you would find that they definitely don't look alike, generally don't act alike, and some will be more noticeable than others.

Let's briefly review the three core symptoms outlined in the *Diagnostic and Statistical Manual of Mental Disorders-Fourth Edition-Text Revision (DSM-IV-TR)* that professionals use in diagnosing ADHD.

Inattention

Have you asked your child to pay attention and then found that he still didn't remember what was asked of him? An important component of remembering is a factor called *attention*. An affected child often doesn't attend when given directions, so he may make decisions based on partial information, leading to incomplete or forgotten chores or schoolwork. Simple tasks such as remembering a small number of items to get at the grocery store can be embarrassing and frustrating for him. You are probably thinking to yourself, "Well, everybody forgets at times," and yes, that's true; however, people with ADHD forget more often, creating ongoing frustration and discord because of their *inability to remember to remember.*

They seem to have difficulty with focused and sustained attention when involved in laborious or routine activities. One authority suggests that when we say they have a short attention span, what we really mean to say is that they have a "short interest span" (Barkley 1995). They will show no noticeable problem when involved in high-interest activities. In fact, when involved in high-interest activities, they can be *hyperfocused*—so focused on what they're doing that they are oblivious to what is happening around them. Put an affected child in front of a computer, action movie, or video game, and he will probably not stand out as less attentive than other children around him.

When one or more of four particular characteristics are present—something new, interesting, intimidating, or one-on-one with an adult—you will often find that the child can pay attention as long as other children (Phelan 1996). We once took a group of affected boys to the movie *Raiders of the Lost Ark* and, we can assure you, they were glued to the screen and showed no indicators of boredom or "short interest span."

The affected child has great difficulty being attentive to one thing because he often pays attention to everything. He is constantly scanning the environment, distracted by all things around him except what he needs to attend to at the time. Where competing activities or distractions provide more immediate and meaningful gratification, he will often shift off-task to engage in those activities (Anastopoulos and Shelton 2001). In the classroom, he pays attention to a fly on a desk, the teacher's sparkling ring, or the custodian sweeping the sidewalk outside the classroom, and not listen to the teacher giving directions. At home, he leaves chores undone, forgets where he left his shoes, or loses hat or gloves when playing, because some other attraction gets his attention. Furthermore, inattention often affects his ability to engage in free play for long periods of time and to participate in organized sports, such as baseball and soccer. Finding it difficult to pay attention to what is important at the time can get him into trouble in the classroom and cause accidents at home, affecting both academic performance and social functioning.

Experts look at attention differently. Some emphasize one concept over another, but Sam and Michael Goldstein's (1990) discussion of attention is helpful because it relates to tasks that we have to do at home and school. A child having difficulty taking notes and paying attention to the teacher simultaneously would have a problem with *divided attention.* One who is described as a daydreamer, preoccupied with other activities instead of what is being talked about, would have a problem with *focused attention.* One who is distracted by outside noises, such as a door closing or a child walking down the aisle to the front of the room, would have a problem with *selective attention.* A child unable to remain on a task long enough to sufficiently complete that task would have a problem with *sustained attention,* or *persistence.* One who is unable to wait for the next spelling word to be presented by the teacher would have a problem with *vigilance,* or *readiness to respond.*

A child with the above difficulties would find everyday requirements surrounding following directions and finishing tasks difficult. Have you been disappointed in your child's seeming inability to consistently follow simple directions, or to remember to bring in the newspaper, feed the dog, or bring back his shoes from the bedroom? He will often find attending to directions difficult and this is not because of lack of desire, but because he has a neurodevelopmental disorder. All people sometimes choose not to listen or follow directions because they would rather do something else. Your great challenge is learning to know when your child is purposely ignoring you and when his seeming inattention is a symptom of his attention difficulties. Separating the two is not easy or foolproof, even for the most knowledgeable of parents.

Many of these children are not attentive to their body states. They may seem insensitive to pain, and when injured may not report it until much later. They may also seem inattentive to their internal body states—40% to 50% of hyperactive children have problems with bowel and bladder control. Daytime wetting and soiling of the pants occur because they don't seem aware they are about to have an accident (Taylor 1994). Sometimes they would rather not stop what they are doing than take the time to go to the bathroom, leading to embarrassing situations. Nighttime wetting, on the other hand, is more related to sleeping problems than to attention disorder. Very sound sleepers often have a history of bed-wetting.

Inattention is a core symptom and can present many problems. Your child would not have been diagnosed with ADHD unless he had difficulties with attention.

Hyperactivity

When people think of ADHD, they think of the hyperactive child in the neighborhood or in the classroom. He is known by everyone and, some would say, pesters everyone. Every teacher in an elementary school knows this child, and he becomes the topic of gossip of neighborhood mothers.

Hyperactivity is not just *high activity*, but *disorganized and purposeless activity*. Hyperactivity refers to a range of excessive body movements ranging from restless, incessant fidgeting while seated, to frantic running around the room for no apparent reason. The hyperactive child is often referred to as always "on the go" and "driven by a motor" (DSM-IV-TR 2000). He jumps, wiggles, squirms, runs, and hardly sits still or walks calmly from one place to another. He pokes, grabs, and touches things, especially where he shouldn't. He has difficulty playing or engaging in leisure activities, and is accident-prone. He can talk excessively, hang on the edge of a chair, or make excessive noises during quiet times. He is consistently loud and noisy when playing, making whistles, clicks, sounds, and producing an endless stream of chatter. In a nutshell, he has great difficulty managing his activity levels and is seemingly unable to stop without reminders.

Hyperactivity becomes a problem when he reaches the ages of two to four. Parents often feel they need to "batten down the hatches" when little Johnny gets out of bed. He's always on the go, getting into everything not locked up, screwed down, or put away or out of his reach. One mother said that simple tasks such as giving a morning bath to her toddler would turn into World War III. Hyperactive toddlers are difficult to handle even for the most energetic of parents. They take more time, more energy, and more patience to raise than unaffected children do. Parents describe going through a litany of interventions suggested by good neighbors, family members, and the child's doctor, but nothing seems to work consistently or for long.

This incessant motor activity and restlessness is especially troublesome when the child reaches school age. Staying seated in the school bus or in class can especially be challenging. Even when staying seated, he continues to be hyperactive, but in different forms, such as noisily tapping on a desk, rocking the desk chair, or swinging his feet to and fro.

Let's look at behaviors expected in the classroom to see why the hyperactive child has such great difficulty there. Children in a classroom are asked to sit quietly at their desks, follow the teacher's directions, not bother the children next to them, and not fidget or rattle things while working. It would be easier for many children we work with to lie on a bed of nails than to master these behaviors.

Thom Hartmann (1993) writes that schools were set up for *Farmer* types, not *Hunter* types, of learners. *Hunters* are constantly monitoring their environment, are totally focused on the moment and have incredible bursts of energy but not staying power. They love the hunt but are bored with mundane tasks and have a low frustration level for mistakes. *Farmers,* on the other hand, are not easily distracted or bored, they set long-term goals, and they're team players. *Farmers* are cautious and need to be patient with others. They attend to details and will sustain their efforts until the crop is ready for harvesting. Even though Hartmann points out that these characteristics are simplified for purpose of explanation, they can be useful in demonstrating the different behavior and learning styles between the two archetypes.

Children with ADHD are *Hunters,* not *Farmers.* They usually get bored easily, are not cautious, and are easily distracted by outside noises and events. Add the incessant running, excessive body movements, and general disruptive behaviors, and it's no wonder your hyperactive child is called down to the principal's office more than other children in his classroom.

Hyperactivity, unlike inattention, is not necessary for a diagnosis of ADHD. However, the hyperactive child seems to come to everyone's attention right away, leading to more children with hyperactivity seeing the doctor and being diagnosed than the inattentive-type child.

Impulsivity

Impulsivity is difficulty waiting one's turn, blurting out before thinking, and interrupting or intruding on others' time and space. This child can alienate others around him because of this difficulty with impulsive behavior. He may come across as demanding and inflexible, appearing selfish. He starts things before the directions are completed, takes things without thinking, and is often seen by others as difficult to be with for any length of time. He will often butt into line to get ahead of someone, or take another turn in a game because he can't wait until his turn comes again. He raises his hand in class, and then when called upon, won't know what to say. He starts writing on a test paper before being given permission or, when playing a board game, will not wait his turn or will move another child's piece without permission. He has trouble keeping playmates because of his impulsive behaviors. He's not invited to parties or asked to participate in recess games or to be partners in group activities in the classroom.

The impulsive child can greatly frustrate parents and cause them to lose their temper and sometimes think they will go crazy raising him. He seems driven by the moment, which can interfere with his relationships with peers, family, and school personnel. One parent described going to the grocery store with her child as an "embarrassing and frustrating experience." He would invariably grab a store item off the shelf, or run ahead and disappear around an aisle. She never looked forward to taking her child out in public and talked about her guilt and anger. She was a single mother without outside support, which made the situation even more stressful. Another parent described her third-grade child during a school recital as "doing everything but listening to the recital." While the other children were attending to the recital, he was turning around, waving to his mother, pushing a classmate next to him, and unable to attend for even a short period of time. His behavior, driven by the moment, made his mother feel embarrassed both for him and for herself.

The three symptoms of inattention, hyperactivity, and impulsivity are the primary and core behaviors of ADHD. Understand that in addition to these symptoms, clinicians have also found other behaviors sometimes associated with this disorder.

Other Behaviors Sometimes Associated with ADHD

Children with ADHD—especially those with strong hyperactive-impulsive behaviors—can often be *noncompliant* and *oppositional*. One-third diagnosed with ADHD also can qualify for a diagnosis of Oppositional Defiant Disorder (ODD). Research suggests that children diagnosed with ADHD-HI and ODD often present an earlier onset of ADHD when compared to those with ADHD alone. One study showed a mean age of 3.4 years for ADHD/ODD, versus 4.0 years for ADHD alone (Anastopoulos and Shelton 2001). The noncompliant and oppositional child with ADHD can be negativistic, hostile, and defiant towards peers and authority figures.

He is commonly argumentative with adults, frequently loses his temper, swears, is often angry or resentful, and is easily annoyed by others. Noncompliant and oppositional children are often in trouble with authority figures, and are at risk for engaging in thefts, getting expelled from school, and drifting into alcohol and drug use. They can also cause stressful and ongoing problems in the home.

Affected children often *crave high-stimulus situations,* which put them at risk for accidents. This can be seen in the reckless driving behaviors of teenagers or the eight-year-old child who decides to climb to the top of an 80-foot pine tree. The urge to experience risk, the desire for that adrenaline high, seems more common in these children than in others we professionally evaluate.

Another symptom sometimes associated with ADHD is *high anxiety.* The child can become very anxious about a number of activities, from test taking to staying overnight with a friend. He will fixate on a thought or fear, which sometimes leads to anxiety or avoidance of activities.

He may be very *compulsive,* which involves doing one behavior or ritual over and over, or he might refuse to change activities. One child we worked with would jump from one compulsion to another, from playing with computers to riding on his bike for hours on end. When in high school, he went through a period of time when he became obsessed with "Magic Cards," taking them with him everywhere. He would play with them and not do his homework, take notes in class, or study for tests. His behaviors were probably not representative of most children with ADHD, but there seems to be a subtype that do have this compulsive tendency.

The child can be *emotionally volatile,* his unpredictable moods going up and down in a heartbeat. He seems to wear his feelings on his sleeves, showing little restraint and not cushioning his emotions, which are often expressed in extreme and raw ways—which overwhelms and sometimes frightens those around them. He has low frustration tolerance, can be irritable, easily upset, and react viciously to others who irritate him. He cannot tolerate being teased. He will explode, and then a few moments later be happy and genuinely surprised that others won't play with him.

He can be *self-centered,* lacking awareness of his impact on others. Because he does not feel personally at fault when something goes wrong, he is quick to blame others for his own anger. His own needs and wants seem to be his dominant concern. He wants rules changed to satisfy his wants, and has an *I don't care* attitude if confronted for his selfishness.

The child can be *impatient* regarding others' space, feelings, or wishes. He'll start writing before listening to all the directions, push over a game board in anger, or shove a person ahead of him in line. He can't work for long periods of time without being rewarded and often seems to demand immediate attention from parents, teachers, and other caretakers. His impatience, combined with impulsivity, leads to a lack of respect for others' boundaries. He walks into a room without knocking, repeatedly rings a doorbell while waiting to enter, or borrows things without permission. He is too impatient to wait until he has permission to use a bike or toy.

Not all children present the above behaviors, but many do show a tendency towards some or many of them.

ADHD
Predominantly Inattentive Type
(ADHD-I)

Children without hyperactivity—that is, those who are predominantly inattentive (ADHD-I)—are often described as underachievers, anxious, less attentive, daydreamers, sluggish, disorganized, distractible, drowsy, and generally slow-moving compared to other children. Research, though limited, suggests that the attention disturbance of the ADHD-I child is different from that of the other affected children. Inattention may come in two different forms: one related to poor selective attention, passivity, and sluggish information processing—found in children with ADHD-I, and the other represented by difficulties with resistance to distraction, recall of previously learned information, and persistence of effort—seen in children with ADHD-HI and ADHD-C (Barkley 1997).

Both children with ADHD-I and ADHD-C face academic problems. The child with ADHD-I, however, may have more problems in math, as well as delays in language and reading. He can find day-to-day school activities difficult. You may find him sitting in the back of a classroom, being mentally all by himself and not attending to the teacher's directions or classroom activities. Consequently, he often fails to turn in schoolwork, hear what's being said, and he makes more mistakes than his classmates. Unlike the child with ADHD-HI, who is headstrong or impulsive, he seems to have difficulty sifting out relevant from irrelevant material. He may look like he's attentive and working, but mentally he's not there, not processing the task or instructions, so he often makes decisions based on misinformation or partial information. This leads to parental conflicts and teacher frustration.

Unlike the child with ADHD-C or ADHD-HI, the child with ADHD-I does not always get help from teachers and parents because he is seen as just immature or a child who doesn't try his best. He is often seen as a good student to have in class—he doesn't talk too much and he makes and keeps friends more easily than the other two types, and he is usually not impulsive or physically aggressive towards peers or adults. Unlike the hyperactive and impulsive dimensions of ADHD, which seem to decrease in severity over childhood, inattention can be problematic throughout a child's education.

This child can be very anxious. Research suggests that children with ADHD-I are more likely to have anxiety disorders and perhaps other mood disorders, and are often seen as socially withdrawn, shy, reticent, and more apprehensive than those with ADHD-HI. Their anxiety, unfortunately, is frequently hidden from others, and is not considered troublesome for these children. Yet the child with ADHD-I seems to have fewer psychiatric conditions than those often associated with ADHD-HI.

Studies show that these children do worse than others on tests involving motor speed and hand-eye coordination, so it may take them longer to complete written work. It is often appropriate to provide accommodations for written work to address this difficulty. Children with ADHD-HI, unlike children with ADHD-I, can have trouble synchronizing hand-eye movements with their fast-moving thoughts. While they can produce interesting ideas at a rapid rate, their poor motor ability prevents them from keeping pace with these thoughts; their writing is disorganized and does not represent their knowledge of the subject (Levine 1987). However, sometimes difficulties with handwriting tasks can be symptomatic of impatience, rather than representing a fine visual-motor coordination problem. If your child has significant difficulties with written language tasks, request a psychoeducational assessment to check for the possibility of a learning disability.

Children with ADHD-I can present challenges like those with other ADHD subtypes in social systems such as school. They also frustrate parents and caretakers because of their inconsistent performance in home activities such as chores. If your child has ADHD-I, be careful not to judge his forgetfulness as purposeful, when in fact, it may be a manifestation of his disorder.

Developmental Stages of ADHD

ADHD presents symptoms differently at different times, and the symptoms can change with age. Some symptoms are more of a problem at some ages than at other ages (see Appendix B: *Developmental Stages of ADHD*). For example, hyperactivity is generally more noticeable in a six-year-old child than in an adolescent, but inattention and impulsivity may be present throughout the child's life and continue into adulthood. A 52-year-old speech pathologist in therapy for ADHD had a history of impulsive buying, resulting in severe debt. With counseling and medication, she no longer bought things impulsively. "I'm a new woman, no longer depressed or anxious over my impulsive buying habits."

Infants and Toddlers

Some infants and toddlers with ADHD can present significant challenges for their parents. These children seem to have difficulty getting to sleep, staying asleep, and waking up in the morning refreshed, pleasant, and not cranky or irritable. The infant commonly has colic and feeding problems (difficulty nursing or accepting a formula), and is more irritable or cries excessively. One parent talked about taking midnight drives to get her infant to sleep. The infant can have health problems such as allergies, colds, asthma, or fluid in the ears, and unusual crib behavior such as foot thumping, excessive rocking, and head banging. He is often described as less cuddly.

The toddler may have difficulty staying on schedule, is always on the go, and is usually noncompliant, aggressive and reckless. He pushes, bites, pinches, grabs toys, and can't play cooperatively with others for any length of time. He is destructive, breaking, throwing, tearing, and destroying things either from curiosity or high activity level. Because he's always on the go, he may be clumsy and prone to accidents—many toddlers and young children are first identified after being seen in an emergency room. The toddler also has difficulties playing alone without frequently demanding the parents' attention. Raising him may be exhausting. He can run you ragged, and keeping him safe and pacified can be a 24-hour job.

Generally, it is only after the child reaches preschool age, three to five years old, that parents seek professional help. A child who develops hyperactivity after school age is rare, and the causes are often different. It is at this age that the hyperactive child enters daycare, preschool, or kindergarten. When the preschooler enters daycare, parents attend more conferences with other caretakers to discuss their misbehaving child who is often described as less attentive and cooperative during group activities. He is probably engaged in solitary play more often than he might like, and develops a negative reputation which can be long-lasting. It is also at this age that parents may compare their preschooler with ADHD with other children his age. Maybe you're thinking to yourself, yes, I remember my child. He did run around more, get into more accidents, and generally stand out from other children his age.

Not all infants or toddlers present similar problems or to the same degree, but you can usually find problems coming to the attention of others who work with these children. Your toddler may have been one of those who was described as "a misbehaving child," a child who would bring tears of frustration to your eyes and make you feel powerless. As you read further, you may better understand his frustrating behavior.

School Age

When a child with undiagnosed ADHD enters elementary school, school officials or other caretakers will tell the parents about their child's difficult behaviors. Parents, sometimes not familiar with age-appropriate behaviors, may not consider their child a problem. Families hold widely differing views about what is tolerable or not tolerable in their child's behavior. Some parents of a toddler with ADHD may not think his behavior that upsetting or unusual. Also, expectations for attention, following directions, and sitting still are more of a factor in school than in the home. "Thus," writes two experts on ADHD, "it is not just having AD/HD that determines the type of problems one might experience, it is the manner in which AD/HD makes it difficult to do what is expected at a given age" (Anastopoulos and Shelton 2001). Children, as a consequence, are often first diagnosed after entering school because this is the first setting where their particular developmental level is not a good fit with school expectations, and where psychosocial difficulties can arise.

Hyperactivity and impulsivity, the two symptoms that society most understands and associates with ADHD, are most elevated at school age. The child, because of lack of maturation and experience, has generally not developed coping skills to help minimize these behaviors, resulting over time in poor self-image, conflicts with others, and for many, school failure. Educationally, he has as many difficulties as children with learning disabilities do. He underachieves because of difficulty following instructions, and storing and retrieving information given in class. Even children with ADHD but without hyperactivity can perform poorly overall in school. Depending on the definition used, anywhere between 18 % and 53 % of the

ADHD population will be academic underachievers, performing significantly below their intelligence (Anastopoulos and Shelton 2001). One expert reports that 10% to 40% of affected children have a learning disability (Taylor 1994).

Early intervention and diagnosis identify and minimize behaviors that can be so much trouble. Late diagnosis can lead to needs for multilevel support, such as medical, educational and family counseling, and the cost can be high for the family and society.

Adolescents

For a number of years clinicians believed that children outgrew ADHD. Today we know this is not generally the case, and interventions, both medical and educational, are sometimes based on this mistaken belief. This can be partly understood and forgiven by the fact that by adolescence, the hyperactive component is less pronounced and often replaced with behavior described by parents and teachers as "fidgety." The adolescent is described as always moving his feet, knees, or having difficulty sitting through dinner or a movie without constantly getting up or moving around. The fidgety adolescent is sometimes no longer easily identified as being hyperactive.

Symptoms can change from predominantly hyperactive to impulsive. Blurting out answers before questions are asked or interrupting others are more common behaviors than hyperactivity. The adolescent continues to speak out of turn, and he intrudes on others' conversation without waiting his turn. His impulsivity can sometimes be irritating, costly, and dangerous. One teen, after getting his driver's license, received two tickets within a month. One was for parking in a handicapped zone while "I ran in to get a Coke." The other ticket was for making a U-turn against a red light. Both behaviors reflected poor impulse control—this young man didn't stop long enough to consider the possible consequences of his behavior. Like many affected adolescents, he continued to be driven by the moment.

In addition to being restless and impulsive, the adolescent can present high distractibility. He's distracted by both external activities and internal thoughts. He can continue to be a daydreamer, not attending to what's being said by his parents or teachers. Like his younger self, he'll be distracted by outside noises or activities and, in most situations, will need someone to get him back on track. The consequence of this continuing distractibility is that he may fail to turn in homework, daydream when he should be working in class, or forget to lock the front door before leaving the house.

Normal adolescent developmental issues are more pronounced with affected children. Like most teenagers, they want more freedom, but most are less ready for freedom than their peers without ADHD. They may have greater problems with relationships with parents and rules. Over time, most teenagers learn when to exert their newfound independence, but for affected teenagers, this lesson does not come easily. Because of difficulties pausing or contemplating the consequences of an act, they get in more trouble with parents, teachers, and other caretakers. They will often display more extreme forms of defiance and noncompliant behaviors than the unaffected teenager. Parents will usually be more verbal and use coercive tactics that lead to negative communication between the child and parent. Unfortunately for the parent, adolescents are better able to argue than younger children, making the conflicts more severe, which makes the parents feel helpless. Frustrated and feeling powerless, the parent may either give up or overreact.

Adolescence is difficult for unaffected children, but for a child with ADHD, it can be even more upsetting. He may have low self-esteem, poor social skills, learning problems, and conflicts in school with peers and staff. He often goes through a series of short-term relationships, and may be sad and depressed—many are treated for associated mental health problems such as depression and anxiety. However, adolescents with little history of problems at a younger age do not present any more problems than the unaffected teenager. Also, with appropriate educational and medical interventions, even those with a history of behavior and learning problems can be successful.

Four Behaviors Worthy of Discussion

When speaking to educators and groups of families, we like to discuss four kinds of behaviors that help them better understand these children: *inhibiting behavior, rule-governed behavior, inconsistent performance,* and *motivation.*

Inhibiting Behavior

Our ability to inhibit our behavior affects many areas of our life, from interacting with people to performing well on a job. Children with ADHD have great difficulty inhibiting their behavior. Russell Barkley (1997) proposes in a recent theory that ADHD is not a disorder of attention, per se, but rather a developmental delay in the brain circuitry that underlies inhibition and self-control. What we see as hyperactivity and impulsivity is a part of an underlying problem with inhibiting behavior. This impairment affects the ability to pay attention and to defer immediate rewards for future gain. The child will think, "I like to punch Johnny," and while thinking this thought, punches Johnny. The time between thought and action is short—sometimes nonexistent. He immediately responds without stopping to think about the consequences of what he is doing.

Behavioral inhibition, in broad terms, performs three interrelated neuropsychological functions:

(1) preventing an immediate response to a reward or punishment

(2) stopping or interrupting a response pattern that has proven to be ineffective

(3) shutting out interfering stimulation or thoughts (internal and external) while trying to complete a task

The proper performance of these three functions results in the protection and support of the "executive functions," essential for goal-directed behaviors (Barkley 1997).

The term *executive function* refers to an individual's self-directed actions that are used to help that person regulate his behavior, that is, actions we perform that help us exert more self-control and better reach our goals. It is, in some ways, a cognitive process that serves as a kind of "supervisor or scheduler, capable of selecting strategies and integrating information from different sources" (Baddeley 1986).

Barkley (1997) suggests that the executive functions, encompassing covert or internalized neuropsychological processes, seem to be impaired in the ADHD population. These executive functions fall under four areas:

(1) non-verbal working memory (holding events in mind, sense of time—helps us guide behavior across time towards a goal)

(2) internalization of speech (verbal working memory)

(3) self-regulation of affect, motivation, and arousal

(4) reconstitution (goal-directed behavior, flexibility, and creativity).

The executive functions represent the internalization of behavior that helps us anticipate changes in the environment and events that lie ahead in time. Barkley sees behavioral inhibition as the lead function in the chain of events provided by the executive functions. Without proper functioning in behavioral inhibition, according to Barkley, the executive functions cannot occur without interference (Barkley 1997).

The child's pattern of talking more than other children, whether to self or others, and making more vocal noises than others, may be taken as evidence of poor behavioral inhibition. He is slower to initiate inhibiting behaviors when asked by a parent or teacher and shows variance in compliance. Especially problematic at school is his tendency to not use the extra time when forced to wait to check his work and improve his classroom performance. This can sometimes be the result of *poor interference control,* that is, difficulty inhibiting responses to interferences while engaged in a task (Barkley 1997).

An example of poor inhibitory behavior is a high school student who was sent to the vice principal for throwing lighted matches at students in the classroom. When asked why he threw the matches, he sincerely and without hesitation admitted he didn't know why. We believe the answer lies in a number of factors encompassing, in part, *fixation on a thought, disinhibited behavior,* and *limited attention to consequences.* We find all three components common in the behavior and decision-making of the person with ADHD.

This young man, fixated on the thought of lighting the matches and throwing them, and having difficulty inhibiting this thought, acted out without processing the consequences of this dangerous behavior. His inability to inhibit his behavior resulted in suspension from school, and he had to face his peers when he returned to class. He said that his classmates thought he was stupid and they hoped he never came back to class. This young man had a history of poor choices, leading to underlying poor self-image and feelings of victimization.

Because of difficulty with inhibiting behavior, these children have problems with free time or exciting events like a birthday or Halloween party at school. Unfortunately, they may not be invited to birthday parties, sleepovers, or skating parties because of their behavior. They seem like children on the outside, not regular participants in normal childhood experiences. In talking to them, we find a general sense of sadness in their voices and stories. This sadness is sometimes expressed in anger or purposeful and mean-spirited behavior, and is not recognized for what it may be—the beginning of a long ongoing battle with depression. It may not be clinical depression as experts define it, but it surely can be an early sign of more serious problems that need to be addressed.

Difficulty with inhibiting behavior underlies internal and external distractibility. Affected children often have great difficulty resisting both internal and external distractions. Distracters will not interfere with all tasks, but are likely to do so when the task requires self-regulation (executive function). Classroom noises can be distracting, and unlike an unaffected child who can ignore such distractions or quickly return to his work if distracted, the child with ADHD is always in turmoil, unable to inhibit reacting to normal activities around him. He seems especially distracted when mental discipline and self-restraint are needed, such as is required in school. Sometimes, this distractibility has been compared to a faucet that keeps dripping, and as much as he wants to stop being distracted, he can't.

Not only is he distracted by outside noises and activities, he is also easily tempted by internal distractions. He may be described as a daydreamer, needing constant reminders to get back to work or "listen to me." His mind and body seem disconnected from events and people around him. He seems controlled by the moment, a prisoner of his own internal distractions. His mind dances with thoughts about what he has done or wants to do, and he's unable to stay focused for any length of time, jumping from one thought or action to another. He may head to his room to put his shoes away, and on the way is distracted by a toy in the bathroom. He may never reach his room, or he'll need repeated reminders to stop what he's doing and put his shoes away. As one woman with ADHD says, "You don't mean to do the things you do, and you don't do the things you mean to do" (Hallowell and Ratey 1994). Well said! The ADHD mantra could be, jokingly, *Do it, do it, do it!* The child's difficulty with behavioral inhibition seems, in the word of one expert, the "hallmark symptom of ADHD," and all three core symptoms associated with ADHD can be reduced to a delay in the ability to inhibit behavior (Barkley 1995).

Rule-Governed Behavior

Psychologists refer to *rule-governed behavior* as the ability to control future behavior. When people set goals and then do things to reach those goals, they are using rule-governed behavior. Rule-governed behavior appears to help the individual sustain behavior over a long period of time and provides a process for constructing novel and more organized responses that help the individual reach future goals. Affected children have great difficulty with this task. Some writers suggest that rule-governed behavior gives rise to moral reasoning and moral regulation of behavior.

This class of human behavior is initiated and sustained by rules and language. Privatization of language, Barkley (1997) suggests, has an important role to play not only in moral regulation, but also in motor behavior and development. These children seem to have difficulty developing internalized speech *(self-talk)* that assists them in following rules, instructions, and commands. Private speech provides a means for self-questioning through language, creating an important source of problem solving, as well as a way of generating rules and plans for action.

The development of internalized speech provides an important control over behavior by shifting an individual's response from the immediate external environment towards more internal sources of control. Internalized speech helps a child develop the capacity to comply with instructions that require delayed performance. He should be able to follow instructions or complete tasks without the need for immediate or frequent reinforcement. This difficulty with self-talk, along with other executive functions, affects his ability to comply with verbal instructions. So, internalized speech serves two functions, which seem to be problematic in this population: problem solving and control of motor responses (Barkley 1997).

Because of his difficulty with delaying actions, an affected child doesn't seem to develop a sense of the future and how present behaviors can affect it. One frustrated parent said, "No matter how often I've told him, he still can't stay out of his sister's closet." Because he has difficulty inhibiting or delaying his responses, he is less adept than other children in using rules or instructions to control himself, so he makes the same mistake over and over again. ADHD is in some ways a disorder of performance, and not acquired knowledge. The child generally knows what to do, he just has difficulty doing it.

Unaffected children, as they grow and mature, are not as controlled by immediate thoughts or feelings and are better able to reach future goals. They develop a sense of self-control, and outside events or internal distractions are not perceived as always controlling what they can accomplish. Their actions and plans can change what happens to them. In a child with ADHD, this lack of self-control can lead to feelings of victimization, and he can develop a mindset that the world is unfair and people are out to get him. An important goal when counseling is to help change this perception of victimization. One step in helping changing this perception is to teach him winning ways to reach goals. The result, when successful, is that they can begin to feel that they can change things that happen to them.

Inconsistent Performance

This child is a puzzle to teachers and parents because he can be productive one moment, and the next moment or day get nothing accomplished. There is a pattern of inconsistent performance both at home and in school. A parent or teacher may say, "If he did it one time, why can't he do it all the time?" Such admonitions cause pain and suffering to children with ADHD. This expectation, generally voiced in frustration, would be hard for any child or adult to live up to. No one does it well all the time!

The problem is not that this child cannot be productive; it's that he cannot maintain that level of productivity the way other children do. Consistency in work habits requires the ability to not be driven by momentary thoughts or distractions—an ability that he lacks. He is often described by teachers as being distracted, not turning in homework, and not using class time productively. Barkley (1998) writes that self-control, or the ability to inhibit or delay one's actions, is critical for completing any task. As children grow up, they gain the ability to engage in mental activities that help them "deflect distractions, recall goals and take the steps needed to reach them." To complete a task or goal, a person needs to remember the goal, keep his emotions under control, remind himself what he needs to do to reach that goal, and maintain a level of self-motivation to reach it. The affected child has great difficulty with these functions. It is not a matter of willpower, but a matter of the brain functioning poorly, where normal levels of self-control and willpower are nearly impossible.

Again, inconsistent performance is the hallmark of ADHD behavior. This may be explained in large part by developmental difficulties with inhibiting behavior; however, that's not to say that your child is not like millions of other children his age. All children will avoid doing things they don't like to do.

Motivation

A person with ADHD seems to have difficulty maintaining his interest in projects or activities for any length of time. He can be highly motivated with high-interest activities, but lose interest quickly with routine tasks. The result is that many projects or chores are started, but most are only partially or never completed. He gets bored quickly with routine activities and moves on to something else that attracts his attention. It's very difficult to keep him motivated. This pattern of low motivation is why interventions to help modify behavior with children with ADHD need to be changed frequently. We suggest that parents hang the following saying on the refrigerator and review it often: *Use whatever works, but it won't work for long.* We refer to this as the *W-W Theory. Use whatever works* does not mean child abuse, but acceptable forms of punishment and reinforcement that help minimize problematic ADHD behaviors in the child. *But it won't work for long* means the parent will need to change forms of behavior reinforcement regularly. You may have great success with a new behavioral intervention, but in a couple of weeks, oops, it's not working anymore—"Bobby's bored with it!" That's right, Bobby will get bored more quickly than other children his age, and you will need to find something new to motivate him.

Some writers suggest that part of the child's profile is a *motivational deficit.* Neuropsychological understanding helps explain in part this pattern of low motivation for routine activities and task completion. The child has difficulty with *goal-directed persistence.* Some theorists suggest that motivation, when coupled with other neuropsychological processes, helps an individual reach intended goals. Barkley offers that the proper functioning of these neuropsychological processes (executive functions) leads to "goal-directed persistence, characterized by willpower, self-discipline, determination, [and] single-mindedness of purpose. . ." (Barkley 1997).

There is strong documentation that these children have difficulties with self-regulation of motivation, particularly with persistence of effort. They seem to have more problems with tasks requiring repetitive responses that involve little or no reinforcement, e.g., arithmetic tasks where persistency of performance is important for success. Their poor motivation and self-regulation can help explain some research that shows their insensitivity to reinforcement. Unaffected children's behavior is superior to that of affected children when there are few or no rewards because unaffected children may be able to keep their goal in mind by talking to themselves (Barkley 1997).

This suggested motivational deficit found in the ADHD population can also be explained in part by briefly reviewing studies done on the brain. By using a kind of brain scan known as *positron emission tomography (PET),* studies completed on the ADHD population have found blood-flow patterns of underactivity in a part of the brain called the *prefrontal lobes.* Blood-flow patterns are measured by monitoring the rate of activity in certain parts of the brain when called upon to function. When parts of the brain are stimulated, the cells involved show an increased rate of metabolism. Research has found that the brain's prefrontal lobes are involved not only in functions related to paying attention and planning and execution of thoughtful behavior, but also in motivation. In the ADHD population, there may be underactivity in the prefrontal lobes, affecting motivation (Comings 1990).

The degree to which this suggested motivation deficit contributes to low motivation in getting good grades or completing home projects is probably not measurable. We all know that most children dislike doing homework, mowing the lawn, or cleaning up the room. Motivation is an important factor, but it is not the only factor that goes into decision-making and task completion; however, it should not be dismissed, even if it is difficult to measure or prove. The reader is referred to chapter 6, in "He Doesn't Seem Motivated to Get Good Grades," for further discussion.

To boost motivation, we must use methods that ensure success in maintaining productivity, such as breaking tasks into shorter periods of time, followed by immediate rewards for sticking to the task. Remember, in high-interest activities, these children seem to be as productive as other, so interventions need to address the more-routine tasks.

What Are the Roles of Biology and Environment?

Man's actions are influenced and directed by both biology and environment. Environment can help or hinder, but it's never neutral. It may not be as critical a component in understanding ADHD behaviors as biology, but it can have an influence on a child's life. Being raised in a chaotic and highly stimulating home or school setting will cause more problems than a child raised in a more structured and calming environment. In later chapters, you will learn ways to provide environmental settings that can promote more success for your child at home and school.

Understanding as well the role biology plays is an important step towards appreciating the complexity of your child's disorder. Professionals working with ADHD no longer accept that we are dealing merely with or only with poor parenting. Current research strongly suggests that it is a genetic neurodevelopmental disorder; however, scientists cannot definitively prove that any neurological abnormality directly causes ADHD. This applies to other psychiatric disorders, too, including disabling diseases such as schizophrenia (NIMH 1999). Research can give us highly suggestive evidence, but so far, no absolute proof. However, you can say with conviction to doubters, "Yes, my child has a biologically based disorder, and no, it is not caused by poor parenting." As a parent, you can now look to science to give you emotional ballast to fight off unfair and sometimes cruel criticism by teachers, relatives, and neighbors.

Myth or Fact

We will review common, but generally less significant or mild, contributors to ADHD. In talking with families and teaching staff, these topics are the most commonly misunderstood areas.

Brain Injury

ADHD was once conceptualized as *minimal brain damage*. Most people with ADHD, however, show no signs of brain injury. Research has shown that only a very small percentage (less than 5%) of children with ADHD have a history of brain injury (Anastopoulos and Shelton 2001) The reasoning behind the conceptualization of brain damage stems from the belief that a child could have a lesser degree of injury to the brain without noticeable signs of other brain injury. Through the 1950s ADHD was thought to be caused by mild brain injury resulting from some trauma to the brain through mishap in pregnancy or due to later illness or injury to the child.

Diet

One of the most popular and well-known diet theories related to ADHD was Benjamin Feingold's claim that eating foods containing additives and preservatives could exacerbate ADHD symptoms. However, there is no clear evidence implicating food additives as substantial contributors to ADHD. Studies have generally refuted the causal association between food additives and behavior disturbance in children (Wender 1986, 35–42).

However, some neurotoxic chemicals, such as chemical additives in foods and beverages (MSG or artificial sweeteners), and soaps, can be monitored and taken out of a child's diet. Taylor (1994) believes that for those children who he classifies as "sensitive-allergic," diets such as the Feingold Diet can prevent chemical exposures that lower the level of certain neurotransmitters. He believes that if offending molecules are no longer available, the neurotransmitters return to their correct levels and symptoms disappear.

Sugar

No credible studies have shown that sugar causes ADHD behavior in children. In fact, sugar has not been found to cause clinically significant or dramatic changes in *any* behaviors in children. Studies have shown that dietary sugar does not exacerbate symptoms in groups of children. Even though no study can prove that sugar doesn't worsen behavior in any *particular* child, controlled studies have failed to demonstrate that sugar is a significant contributor to ADHD symptoms. Research suggests that the power of psychological suggestion contributes to the perception that sugar is a culprit. Scientists have discovered that mothers who were told that their child received sugar rated their child as being more hyperactive than mothers who were told the truth, that their child was given aspartame, used as a placebo in the study. In fact, not only did the mothers who believed their child had been given sugar rate their child as more hyperactive, they also were more critical of their child's behavior, talking more frequently to, and hovering over, their child (Barkley 1995). When presenting this evidence to parent groups, we continue to encounter disbelief and difficulty accepting this evidence. We have come to the conclusion that no amount of scientific evidence is going to change most parents' minds about the effects of sugar on behavior.

One study, however, suggests that even though sugar does not cause hyperactivity, it may make symptoms worse in an affected child who eats high-carbohydrate, low-protein foods. Adding protein to a diet may help reduce the level of hyperactivity. This study offers that it is reasonable to conclude that eating protein at breakfast is even more important than for unaffected children (Connors 1988, 23–25).

Lead Poisoning

There is some evidence that high levels of lead in the bodies of young children increase the risk of hyperactivity and attention-based problems. High levels of lead in the body, especially at younger ages (12–36 months), have been reported to injure brain tissue. Some studies suggest that there may be a group of children whose attention-deficit or developmental symptoms are due at least in part to lead exposure (Barkley 1995). However, finding slightly above-average lead levels in either the blood or teeth was not helpful in diagnosing ADHD. What is disturbing is that there is stronger evidence that children exposed to high levels of lead can develop learning disabilities (Goldstein and Goldstein 1990).

Medical Problems

A medical evaluation must take place to ascertain whether the behavioral symptoms observed in the child are the result of a medically treatable illness. Some medications used in the treatment of seizure disorders can trigger hyperkinetic behavior, and illnesses such as hyperthyroidism, left temporal lobe seizures, pinworms, sleep apnea, and other illnesses can cause ADHD-like behaviors. However, even though any medical illness has the potential to cause some ADHD symptoms, it is not common for the primary symptoms to be triggered by a medical illness, but a medical evaluation is important to ensure other contributors are not present.

Genetics

Heredity, or a positive family history, appears to be the most common identifiable cause of ADHD. We work with families where a brother, sister, and one or both parents might have ADHD. In fact, the frequency of the disorder in siblings is much greater than in the general population. Studies of adopted children found that ADHD occurred more in the biological parents than in the foster parents. That these children develop the disorder despite being raised by unaffected foster parents, suggests that the transmission is by genetic, rather than environmental, factors.

Current research suggests that this is a *polygenic disorder,* meaning more than one gene contributes to it. Nongenetic factors that have been linked to ADHD are premature birth, maternal use of alcohol and tobacco, exposure to high levels of lead in early childhood, and brain injury, especially involving the prefrontal lobes. Nongenetic factors can account for 20% to 30% of ADHD in boys, and much less in girls (Barkley 1998, 69).

Understanding that this is primarily a genetic disorder helps prevent other siblings from being overlooked as possibly having ADHD. Sometimes parents and teachers ignore the child without hyperactivity because "he's nothing like his brother." He may be viewed as an underachiever or lazy, but he's not recognized as having ADHD, with its associated behaviors that can have social, educational, and emotional implications for the child.

Neurotransmitters

In order to understand the role of neurotransmitters in ADHD, you must understand the function of the nerve cell. The nerve cell is not only the holder of the neurotransmitters, but also the roadway on which messages pass through the *central nervous system* (see Appendix C: *Nerve Cell*). Communication *within* nerves is electrical, whereas communication *between* nerves is chemical. An electrical impulse traveling through one nerve (the *presynaptic nerve*) triggers the release of that nerve cell's neurotransmitter from the cell into the *synaptic cleft,* or space between that nerve cell's terminal end and adjacent nerve cells. These neurotransmitters then bind to receptor sites on adjacent nerve cells, and electrical impulses are generated in these nerves. In this way, information gets passed from one nerve cell to potentially millions of other cells in the central nervous system.

The movement of impulses across the synapse is the physiological mechanism by which we learn. Each activity we learn is the result of electrical impulses across nerve paths. Garber, Garber, and Spizman (1996) use the example of learning to play the piano. When we learn to play the piano, electrical impulses must make their way from the fingers to the brain and back again. With each practice, the pathway becomes better-established and we play the piano more fluently. They state, "Learning occurs after an electrical impulse produced by a stimulus is transmitted and moves across a neuronsynaptic course several times." This explains why repetition is so important. With practice and repetition, the pathway becomes automatic. "If in ADHD these neural bridges are blocked or incomplete, whatever is being learned does not become automatic." (Garber, Garber, and Spizman 1996).

In recent years, many neurotransmitter systems have been identified in the central nervous system, although the exact number has yet to be determined. Each system uses its own unique neurotransmitter to transmit messages within that system, although separate systems are able to communicate with each other. The three neurotransmitters most directly related to ADHD are dopamine, norepinephrine, and serotonin. Abnormalities in one or more of these neurotransmitter systems accounts for many of the signs and symptoms.

The medications used in treatment intervene by changing the regulation of the neurotransmitters. Brain chemistry is very complex, and the exact mechanisms by which some medications work are still debated; however, current thought suggests that medications such as Ritalin and Dexedrine, which are stimulants, elevate levels of norepinephrine and dopamine, helping the nerve cells to work more efficiently in areas of the brain that are underactive in those with ADHD. Medications such as stimulants increase the availability of neurotransmitters; other medications, such as antidepressants, reduce the rate of their removal from the synapse once the neurotransmitter gets used. The child is sometimes referred to as *stimulant starved.* Consequently, giving him a stimulant doesn't necessarily make him *more* hyperactive or distractible, and may actually have the opposite effect, helping him block out irrelevant thoughts and impulses, which in turn helps him focus on what is important. The child on medication is theoretically more appropriately inhibited and has more self-control. Medications stimulate a child's "brake pedal," thus providing support for some children whose feet are always on the "gas pedal" (Taylor 1994). These medications don't actually slow a child down or change his personality, but they help him to make better decisions. He is better able to *stop, look, think, and do,* and not act so impulsively.

Imaging techniques over the last decade indicate which brain regions might malfunction in this population. Research suggests the involvement of the *prefrontal cortex* (higher mental activities), *striatum,* the *vermis part of the cerebellum* (regulates muscular tone, coordination), and at least two of the clusters of nerve cells deep in the part of the brain known as *basal ganglia* (the brain's switching station for movement, memory, and emotion). Some research reports overall brain size is generally 5% smaller than in unaffected children; however, this average difference is too small to be useful in making a diagnosis in a particular individual (NIMH 1999). One author reports a study finding that the right prefrontal cortex and the two basal ganglia regions, as well as the vermis part of the cerebellum, are smaller in children with ADHD. The imaging findings showing that those areas are smaller are the very ones that regulate attention (Barkley 1998, 67–68). These areas of the brain are involved in impulse control, attention, organization, anger control, and motivation.

Regions of the brain involved in monitoring these tasks are reported to be less efficient because the neurotransmitter systems perform irregularly. Norepinephrine, for example, is important in allowing the body to filter out irrelevant stimuli and in stopping responses to stimuli that have been presented several times. Serotonin, another core neurotransmitter, is believed to suppress arousal and regulate hunger, temperature, sexual behavior, aggression, mood, and the onset of sleep (Brown 1998). Serotonin inhibits or stops the functioning of other nerves, and when serotonin levels are low, parts of the brain become disinhibited or overactive. Dopamine is closely linked to the prefrontal lobes and areas of the brain involved with paying attention, motivation, and planning and executing thoughtful behavior.

The prefrontal lobes, above the eye and behind the forehead, function like a giant switchboard that processes messages, performing the highest levels of integration in the brain and coordinating information coming in from the senses. It is one of the last parts of the brain to develop and mature. When the prefrontal lobes don't work properly, the ability to pay attention and make and change plans is diminished. The person lacks the motivation to stay with a plan and often experiences impulsive and thoughtless reactions to events. Normal behavior requires normally functioning prefrontal lobes. Again, when neurotransmitters, such as dopamine, are not balanced, the brain is not performing at its potential (Comings 1990). We sometimes tell parents and teachers that their child, like an eight-cylinder automobile, needs a tune-up because he is running on only six cylinders, rather than eight. The car can generally take you where you want to go, but the car is working harder and is not running as well as it could.

A basic knowledge of the biological components in ADHD helps parents to better understand both the neurodevelopmental issues associated with their child's disorder and the role medication plays in addressing those concerns. Your child has a neurodevelopmental disorder that affects his central nervous system. His difficulties in paying attention, sitting still, staying motivated, and controlling his impulses are in large part caused by abnormalities in brain chemistry, not by a lack of willpower.

Accepting that chemistry plays an important role in understanding ADHD does not negate the influence of environment in its development. Parents we counsel quickly learn that medication alone is often not enough to cause positive changes in their child's behaviors over a long period of time, but medication along with behavioral management can bring about positive changes in his behavior. They recognize, as recent data suggests, that medication, when properly monitored, is superior to behavioral treatments of core symptoms (inattention, hyperactivity, impulsivity), but that combining behavioral treatment with medication is superior to medication alone.

Family

There are no studies to support the idea that bad parenting or a chaotic family causes ADHD. Studies on twins suggest that shared environments, such as the home, contribute little if any explanation to individual differences in the core symptoms. Shared environments, such as social class, family education/occupation, family nutrition, child-rearing practices, and general home environment, account for less than 5% of the differences among individuals, that is, whether one child will be more impulsive than another. However, shared environmental factors such as the home environment may contribute to the persistence of behavior problems during the development of a child, so even though environment does not cause ADHD, it may affect a child's level of functioning.

Nonshared environments, such as social environment, biological hazards, or neurologically injurious events, that can impact one child and not another, seem to suggest a higher variance (15% to 20%) in symptoms. Nonshared environmental hazards, such as maternal smoking or alcohol consumption during pregnancy and significant prematurity at birth and smallness for gestational age, may be important in some cases (Barkley 1997).

ADHD, as suggested by current research, is a genetically-based disorder for the majority of affected children, so there is a good possibility that one or both parents could have ADHD. About 15 % to 20 % of mothers and 20 % to 30 % of fathers have the disorder at the same time as their children. This can sometimes help explain the difficulty therapists have when working with these families. Parents too may be disorganized, impulsive, and inattentive. Their genes, like their children's, may be the culprit! Did you discover you had ADHD after taking your child to the doctor?

A family experiencing ongoing social and financial stresses will create a different experience for a child with ADHD than a more stable family. Education, social status, mental status, and age of the parents affect these children, as they do all children. Very young and very old parents are generally going to show different patterns of interacting with their children. The physical and mental status of a parent is going to have an influence on the levels of consistency in parenting. Those with health problems may not have the energy to be consistent in structuring their child's day. Parents with drug, alcohol, or mental health problems are often not physically and mentally available for their child, and the severity of the child's behaviors is found to influence the level of problems in the parent. If a parent has more than one child with the disorder, the problem can be even more involved; approximately 26 % of brothers and sisters can have this disorder (Barkley 1990).

Children don't grow up in a vacuum. Family and caretakers influence their behavior, and they in return can influence their parents' and caretakers' behavior. The family is the most important social support a child can have, and when this support is unstable, the child is affected. Consequently, any appropriate help needs to address and support the family unit. When we treat a child, we often work with the whole family, because his family will ultimately be his primary support.

School

These children generally have great difficulty in school. Roughly a third of them will be held back one grade in school, about one-third will not complete high school, and between 40 % to 50 % will receive special education services. More than half have an oppositional component to their behavior that gets them into serious trouble with school staff. Up to 15 % to 20 % will be suspended or expelled from school because of their behavior (Barkley 1995). Adolescents, because of the emphasis on independence and self-regulation, are often challenged by school, and are often underachievers and receive lower grades.

These are not pleasant facts. We did not include them to shock you, but to emphasize that school is often a difficult environment for these children. With more appropriate educational options, they would be more successful. Schools are currently struggling to find ways to deal with the active child. They're not easy to teach, and they can wear down even the most patient of teachers. The classroom experience can be even more difficult if there is a poor fit between teacher and child. Our experience is that most teachers want to help, but because of the number of children in their classroom and a lack of knowledge about ADHD, they may mishandle the child's behaviors and learning needs.

The child's success in school requires a number of factors that will be discussed in more detail in chapters 6 and 9. The school's environment should be as positive as possible—he will be spending about five to six hours a day in school, and it can have a major effect on his social and emotional development.

Environment, in summary, does not cause ADHD, but it can help to minimize or maximize problem behaviors. Family counseling and educational interventions can make a real difference in the child's development; however, no amount of environmental accommodation can completely make up for delayed or impaired neurogenetic development (Barkley 1997).

This chapter has given you knowledge that will help you make decisions based on fact and not fiction. The remaining chapters, except for chapter 2, will discuss environmental settings and medical interventions that have been found to be effective in treatment.

Review and Tips

- ADHD is a biochemical and developmental disorder that can present itself differently in different children and at different ages. Some children seem to be significantly affected by their disorder, while others present mild to moderate symptoms.

- ADHD is a biologically based disorder affecting the central nervous system. Nerve cells, because of genetic differences, seem to function differently in affected children than other children.

- Environment does not cause ADHD, but it can exacerbate or minimize problems. Accommodations in the home and school can make a big difference.

- Educate your child about this disorder, and share information that is appropriate for his age. He needs to understand that he is not stupid. He has a biochemically based disorder that can affect his day-to-day interactions with others. He can learn ways to find greater success in school and work.

- Be a supporter and not an enabler of your child. Understand and separate ADHD behaviors from normal developmental patterns. Society does not tolerate aggressive behavior towards others or behavior that interferes with the education of other children. The solution is not to make excuses but to communicate with schools and caretakers ways to work successfully with your child.

Summary

ADHD is a disorder that most experts feel is primarily caused by a genetic abnormality that affects the central nervous system. Weak will, a "bad seed," or poor parenting does not cause ADHD. Good parenting and a stable and secure environment in which to grow is good for all children. The disorder that can present itself differently in children, and it also can present itself differently at different ages. Behaviors that may be of concern for an eight-year-old child will not necessarily be of equal concern for that same child at 15. Environment, even though not the cause of ADHD, can be a factor in minimizing or maximizing some problem behaviors. Appropriate educational and home interventions can help stabilize a sometimes volatile child. Intermittent counseling by a knowledgeable person can help with appropriate parenting, as well as facilitate educational accommodations for the child. Proper treatment of a child requires close communication between the family, school, and doctor.

We encourage you to refer to this chapter from time to time because it's the flagship of the book, an important chapter that will provide more meaning and understanding to the interventions suggested in this book.

2

How Can I Know for Sure My Child Has ADHD?

Parents often come to our office asking for a second opinion about their child's diagnosis. They feel uncomfortable with the diagnosis and want to know, "How can I know for sure my child has ADHD?"

Often a diagnosis is made quickly and/or without much explanation, so the parent is unsure if the doctor or therapist did a thorough job. A parent may question a therapist's credentials and will seek out other professionals to confirm the child's diagnosis. Consequently, we feel it is important to review material that will help parents better evaluate their child's diagnosis, because any treatment plan needs parental support of professional recommendations.

Who Can Make a Diagnosis of ADHD?

The person most qualified to evaluate your child is the person who knows the most about the disorder. This person, whether a psychiatrist, neurologist, geneticist, clinical psychologist, school psychologist, marriage and family therapist, or licensed social worker, should be knowledgeable about ongoing ADHD research and literature (Barkley 1995).

Diagnosis requires a multidisciplinary approach; a proper assessment requires input from the child's parents, school staff, doctor, and other caretakers. A psychoeducational assessment is sometimes suggested to determine whether educational stressors or previously unidentified learning disabilities are contributing to the child's observed behaviors. Lastly, an evaluation of the child's behavioral and emotional interactions with significant caretakers should be completed.

Unfortunately, the diagnosis is often inconsistently made, with some children underdiagnosed and some overdiagnosed. Practitioners will often use some but not all the guidelines required for a diagnosis of ADHD. A clinician, for example, will rely solely on symptom frequency counts as the sole basis for establishing a diagnosis, not duration of symptoms and if they are maladaptive or inconsistent with the child's age. Some practitioners do not use structured parent/teacher questionnaires or rating scales in concert with a clinical interview (Anastopoulos and Shelton 2001). There also appears to be a "disconnect" between the medical and educational community, so the doctor or clinician evaluating the child has minimal contact with the school. Contributing to this barrier of communication between important parties involved in the child's diagnosis and treatment is lack of insurance coverage for "neuropsychological evaluations, behavior modification programs, school consultation, parent management training, and other specialized programs" (NIMH 1999). When parents pursue treatment for their child, they often face high out-of-pocket expenses because treatment is not covered by many insurance policies. Adding to parental frustration is that schools may not have programs available to provide social skills and behavior training.

Monitoring a child's progress may require extra time outside the office visit. Feedback from teachers, daycare staff, and sometimes grandparents and neighbors are needed if the child spends a lot of time with them. The mental health or medical professional must not only have knowledge about ADHD, but also the understanding that management of a child requires telephone conversations with caretakers, possible school visits and, at times, regular counseling for both the child and family. We never recommend a clinician go it alone when evaluating or managing children with ADHD. A professional needs the support of other professionals, both medical and educational, to provide proper assessment and treatment.

Questions you should remember when having your child evaluated or treated: 1) Does the mental health professional or child's doctor sound knowledgeable about ADHD? 2) Is he or she willing to communicate with your child's school and other professionals?

Can Other Factors Cause My Child to Look Like He Has ADHD?

Yes, there are other factors that could cause your child to look like he has ADHD (see Appendix D: *Disorders That Can Mimic ADHD*). School personnel will often tell a parent they think their child has ADHD when in fact he does not. A parent might think her child is affected when he is not. Medical disorders and environmental stresses can cause children to look like they have the disorder. Children who have moved into a new school or home, or whose parents are going through a divorce, can have symptoms that mimic ADHD. Children transitioning into a new grade or who have an unidentified learning disability can exhibit those behaviors, as can those who are on medication, depressed, or anxious because of home or school stresses. Children experiencing these situations can be distractible, inattentive, hyperactive, moody, and generally hard on themselves and others around them. These behaviors are usually brief and the child may return to his old ways in a relatively short period of time. The examples above are the most common reasons children are incorrectly diagnosed. The clinician diagnosing your child should be familiar with other behavioral and emotional disorders that can mimic ADHD.

Two less-common disorders that can be confused with ADHD are *Tourette syndrome (TS)* and *bipolar disorder* (*BD,* also known as *manic depression*). Both disorders are rarer than ADHD, but include behaviors that can mimic it. Both BD and TS include symptoms of elevated anger, hyperactivity, inattention, and impulsivity. Only with extensive family history and close monitoring by a qualified professional can subtle differences between TS or BD symptoms and ADHD be properly evaluated (see sections on Tourette syndrome and bipolar disorder for more detail).

If you doubt your child's diagnosis of ADHD, contact your doctor for more information. You may want another opinion or a more complete evaluation. Your child needs your confidence in his diagnosis and your reassurance, both of which are critical for ongoing treatment. If you have doubts, you may not be open to medications or suggestions given by professionals who work with your child.

Will My Child's ADHD Go Away As He Gets Older?

Contrary to popular belief, the majority of children will have a significant number of symptoms into adulthood. Fewer than 40 % show no symptoms as adults, and up to 25 % of adults exhibit more serious behavioral difficulties, including *antisocial personality disorder.* Approximately 12 % will complete college, but only 3 % will go on to receive graduate degrees (Anastopoulos and Shelton 2001).

One reason people have believed that ADHD goes away as children get older is that the hyperactive component is not so pronounced for most adolescents and adults. Symptoms frequently found in the older population are underachievement, poor initiative, procrastination, saying whatever comes to their mind, not following through on tasks, continuing distractibility, restlessness, and inattentiveness.

Impulsivity is exhibited in many adults by a tendency to say whatever comes to mind. Inattentiveness and disinhibiting behavior seems to be a major problem and can lead to ongoing difficulties with family, co-workers, and job performance. Adults will make careless errors and are poor at monitoring their work. They can quickly become bored, especially with repetitive and tedious job assignments, and will change jobs or be fired more often than co-workers. Like the younger population, they seem to have an intolerance for boredom, which may lead to high-risk behaviors such as gambling, sexual promiscuity, and drug and alcohol abuse, which in turn may cause marital and parenting discord.

An adult with ADHD oftens lacks adequate education and frequently ends up in lower-paying and nonprofessional jobs. To maximize academic and career potential, he often needs monitoring and educational accommodations. Major universities make accommodations under Section 504 of the Rehabilitation Act of 1973 and the Americans with Disabilities Act. These laws recognize ADHD as a disability, and federal legislation has mandated safeguards to protect children from discrimination. Both Section 504 and IDEA address this concern (see chapter 6, "My Neighbor Says Schools Have a Legal Obligation to Accommodate My Son's ADHD. Is This True?" for more details).

Why Are My Two Children with ADHD So Different?

This disorder can present itself differently in family members, and some siblings or family members will present no symptoms at all. If it is inherited, how is this possible?

The many genes responsible for symptoms and behaviors can manifest themselves in different ways in different people, depending upon their genetic background (Comings 1990). Any child comes into this world with his or her own temperament, personality, and some have special needs. Consequently, one of your children may present more problems than your other child. One child may be more oppositional, anxious, or moody than his brother or sister. A sibling may have ADHD without hyperactivity or impulsivity, and be better at making friends, staying out of trouble, and interacting more positively with adults and caretakers. A child may have a learning disability, a speech and language delay, or lower intellectual capacity, and the sibling may show few indicators of ADHD—and those symptoms may be milder. Some siblings may have *no* symptoms at all. Children in a family can display ADHD characteristics differently, so don't be surprised if one of your children is very different from others in your family.

My Child Can Sit in Front of the TV for Hours and Never Move. Does That Mean He Doesn't Have ADHD?

This question can be best answered by reviewing three observations. First, the child usually *is* moving, but the parent isn't always paying close attention. Parents will sometimes share that when their child's doctor asks, "Does he move around a lot when watching TV?" and they answer no, they are told he couldn't have ADHD. They leave the doctor's office puzzled and have a difficult time understanding or explaining their child's behavior. We've asked parents to observe their child more closely, and they will often back that he does move around a lot when watching TV, that he is being fidgety, rocking back and forth in a chair, playing with a toy, or tapping his fingers. One parent noted her child would crisscross his legs back and forth, squirm in his chair, and take more breaks to the kitchen for drinks or food than his unaffected brother.

Remember, these children can be as attentive as unaffected children when they are involved in high-interest activities. Your child may show great concentration when involved in a computer game, watching TV, or playing Nintendo. These activities are exciting, fast-moving, and make good entertainment for children with short attention spans. One could say that TV was set up for people with short attention spans. Cartoons, situation comedies, and adventure programs are action-oriented with high visual stimulation and timed interruptions for commercials on a regular basis. We wish school activities could be so perfectly matched for these children! The child can go to the bathroom, grab another toy, grab a snack, or fight with his sister while the commercial is on. Even commercials provide entertainment. No wonder TV makes such a great baby-sitter for many families.

Not only does TV provide high-interest entertainment for many children, but they are usually not having demands placed on them. With low-demand activities like TV, where children with ADHD can do what they please within limits, their behavior can be indistinguishable from that of other children. Symptoms, however, can return in group settings (even when watching TV), or where there is little feedback.

Third, these children have great difficulty staying motivated with routine and laborious activities like schoolwork. Symptoms are much more likely to present themselves where self-regulation is required and where repetitive, boring, or familiar activities like schoolwork is presented.

In conclusion, ADHD is not an all-or-none phenomenon. How a child watches TV is a poor assessment tool in evaluation. Remember that the core symptoms become a problem when he is asked to delay or attend to routine activities where self-regulation is important for success.

My Friend's Child Has Tourette Syndrome but Acts Like He Has ADHD

Your friend's child can have *Tourette syndrome (TS)* and manifest ADHD behaviors. TS is a complex neurobehavioral disorder whose diagnosis is based on the presence of motor and vocal tics (sometimes called "nervous habits"), present most days, for a period of at least one year. A variety of disorders are commonly found in individuals with TS, but ADHD and obsessive-compulsive disorder (OCD) are among the most common. In individuals who have both TS and ADHD, the ADHD behaviors tend to be more disruptive to a child than the presence of motor or vocal tics.

TS is also a polygenic disorder (involving multiple genes). It is commonly associated with making obscene gestures or yelling out four-letter words, but only a small percentage, less than one-fourth, of the TS population, has compulsive swearing known as *coprolalia*. The most common of the vocal tics seen in TS is throat clearing. Other common vocal tics include grunting, coughing, sniffing, barking, spitting, squeaking, and humming. We worked with one child who spit, so his mother gave him a cup or handkerchief to spit into. At one school meeting his spitting was especially pronounced, and the parents and school staff were very careful not to get hit! Motor tics are often not recognized by teachers or parents initially, unless the tics are brought to their attention. The most common motor tics are eye blinking, shoulder shrugging, head jerking as if moving hair out of the eyes, and opening of the eyes. One child would repeatedly lick his lips—redness around the lips was very noticeable—and when seen by a neurologist, the child was diagnosed with Tourette syndrome. Another child would grab at girls' breasts and crotch areas, eliciting disconcerting comments from staff and parents at his school (but this is an uncommon behavior in people with TS).

Emotional excitement or stress can increase the frequency and severity of tics. Yet what is puzzling to teachers and parents is that they may be able to be suppressed voluntarily for various periods of time, such as in school versus in the home. This can be partly explained by the fact that mental tasks often suppress tics; however, the voluntary suppression of the tics increase the need to provide relief by expressing the tics later. An analogy could be the need to scratch an itch. Experts label the urge to perform the tic action immediately preceding the movement as *sensory premonitions*. It is suggested that some of the medications used to treat the tics may "actually prevent them by eliminating the prior abnormal sensation" (Erenberg 1999, 49).

In some children with TS, the onset of tics can coincide with the ADHD behaviors, whereas with others, ADHD behaviors may be present five to 10 years prior to the onset of tics (Comings 1990).

Children with ADHD will often present with motor or vocal tics after being placed on stimulants, and the tics may continue after the medication has stopped. This raises concerns by the parents that the medication *caused* Tourette syndrome, when in fact it only lowered the neurological threshold at which the tics would be expressed. TS was already a part of the child's neurological make-up, but it was just unrevealed. Although stimulants may promote the early emergence of tics, studies suggest that tics associated with TS will emerge in any event, regardless of whether or not stimulants were used.

Don't be surprised if your friend's child with TS displays signs of ADHD, since these behaviors are commonly found in children with TS. Talk with your child's doctor if you see tic-like behaviors to assure yourself that your child is being accurately diagnosed.

Review and Tips

- Tourette syndrome (TS) and ADHD share similarities with respect to inattentiveness, impulsivity, and distractibility.

- Children with TS often present ADHD behaviors before the onset of motor or vocal tics.

- Stimulants do not cause TS but need to be used cautiously when medicating children with a history of tics ("nervous habits") and ADHD. In most situations, the stimulants didn't trigger the motor or vocal tics, since tics present themselves as part of the natural progression of TS.

- Regular monitoring of your child's medication by a physician is recommended to assess possible tic behaviors that can be associated with stimulants. Other medications for ADHD are available for children with suspected history of TS. There are monitoring scales to assess side effects for stimulants—speak with your child's doctor.

My Doctor Now Says My Child
May Have Bipolar Disorder, Not ADHD.
What Is Bipolar Disorder?

There is a tremendous overlap of symptoms in children with severe ADHD and those children with *bipolar disorder* (BD, or manic-depression). It is not uncommon for children to be initially diagnosed with ADHD and later with BD, but diagnosing a child with severe ADHD and possible BD is often difficult. In fact, because the symptoms of these disorders overlap so much, a child can sometimes meet the criteria for both diagnoses. A clinician must take a detailed family and developmental history, as well as document how the child's mood and behaviors have changed over time. Even with close collaboration between the family and doctor, it still is often difficult to distinguish between ADHD and BD.

Diagnosing BD in children is especially difficult because they often don't present classic bipolar symptoms. In adults with BD, symptoms often present themselves as moods that swing from overly high and irritable or euphoric, to sad and hopeless, and then back again, with periods of normality in between. An adult in a depressed state often has symptoms such as feelings of hopelessness and pessimism, decreased sex drive, sleep disturbances, and changes in appetite with weight gain or loss. They often have thoughts of suicide or death and may have a history of suicide attempts. When feeling high (manic), an adult will often have unrealistic grandiose beliefs in his abilities or powers, increased sex drive, and extreme irritability and distractibility, uncharacteristically poor judgment, abuse of drugs and alcohol, and denial that anything is wrong. However, not everyone with BD will present all bipolar symptoms.

Children may show some of the above symptoms, but it is uncommon for prepubertal children to have sustained periods of elation. Younger children more commonly present a mixed state, including both symptoms of mania and depression. Parents and professionals evaluating a child for BD generally see uncharacteristic behaviors of extreme enthusiasm, irritability, and anger. A child with manic symptoms is sometimes referred to as having "bad ADHD" because the most common disturbance in manic children is irritability and *affective storms,* with prolonged and aggressive outbursts. Thus, mania in children is often a mixed bag of atypical irritability.

Even though it has been known since the 1920s that BD can occur in childhood, there is a limited body of literature on this subject. One reason has been the confusion among clinicians between prepubertal mania and its symptomatic overlap with ADHD. Because one can find emotional lability, impulsivity, hyperactivity, and distractibility in both ADHD and BD, making a clear diagnosis is often difficult. Also, the predominant mood in prepubertal mania is severe irritability rather than euphoria, which complicates the diagnosis. Because the symptom of irritability can vary in degree and result from a number of causes, it can be mistaken for depression, a conduct disorder, or ADHD, so a BD diagnosis may often be missed.

If your child presents behaviors such as extreme irritability, moodiness, and extreme anger outbursts, consult with his doctor. Preferably, either a clinical psychologist or a child psychiatrist should evaluate him. The involvement of a psychiatrist is important, because for purposes of treatment, medicating for BD is usually different than for ADHD, and may be quite complicated. Many children with BD have life-threatening depressive states that require specialized training in psychopharmacology. A family physician or pediatrician generally does not have the training or may feel uncomfortable in treating children who need a combined pharmacotherapy approach (simultaneously taking more than one psychotropic drug).

In conclusion, some children with childhood-onset mania may also have ADHD. There is an overlap of symptoms between both BD and ADHD, so if your child presents symptoms that suggest possible manic-like behaviors, bring your concerns and observations to your child's doctor.

Review and Tips

- Children diagnosed with ADHD can present behaviors suggestive of bipolar disorder (BD). There is a tremendous overlap between symptoms of severe ADHD and BD, and a child can qualify for both diagnoses.

- BD often presents itself differently in children than in adults. Children often have chronic irritability, extreme enthusiasm, and affective storms with prolonged and aggressive outbursts.

- Have your child evaluated by a qualified professional (clinical psychologist or psychiatrist) if you feel your child presents many symptoms associated with BD.

- Children and adults with a BD diagnosis should have a treatment plan that includes both medication and psychotherapy.

- Children with a wide range of behaviors and emotional problems, such as presented in extreme ADHD and BD, need the support of a psychiatrist trained in psychopharmacology.

Summary

We have suggested some guidelines to help you better gauge your child's diagnosis. A professional who is knowledgeable about ADHD, as well as associated disorders that can often mimic ADHD, should evaluate him. We encourage you to present any concerns to your child's doctor if you find suggested indicators for possible TS or BD. Even though social and behavioral interventions are similar for ADHD, TS, and BD, medications are sometimes different.

We have included a few sections covering concepts and issues that often are confusing to parents of children with ADHD, such as a doctor dismissing a diagnosis of ADHD because the child can sit and watch TV without running around, or parents discontinuing medication treatment for their adolescent because they were told one outgrows ADHD.

Hopefully the above information has given you more confidence in evaluating your child's diagnosis. Remember that a diagnosis is an involved procedure that must be left up to professionals. If you have doubts about your child's diagnosis, go back to his doctor or get a second opinion from a qualified professional. Parents may often be too emotionally involved with their children to be objective, even if they are trained in mental health disorders.

3

Am I to Blame?

We have often heard these words expressed or alluded to by parents of children with ADHD. Searching for some reason, some understanding, many times reaching back into some secret sin not shared, the parent tries to assign blame. The parent, often the mother, carries this blame, holding it close to her heart, not comfortable facing it or even revealing it to her most trusted friend. This sense of blame reaches into the deepest part of her being; it is not easy to talk about or remove, even with reassurance and therapy. Recalling what Frank Pittman calls *Bolts from the Blue,* or unexpected crises in families, there lies the danger of trying to assign blame, "the effort to find something someone could have done to prevent the crisis." (Pittman 1987) You may say to yourself, "My child has been a *Bolt from the Blue,* and he challenges my patience every day."

If you're a mother, have you cried in private, and yes, even openly, in front of the world, because of what your parent, husband, or neighbors have said about your child? Your relationship with him can be so full of conflict, so up and down, that you're at war with those around you, trying to find balance between the energy invested in your affected child and other family members. Dad, you too may wrestle with thoughts, feelings, and actions that trigger discomfort with your relationship with your child. You may see in him parts of yourself at that age, and know and fear the possible pain he may have to experience because of this disorder.

In this chapter, we will talk about a feeling that seems to be pervasive and associated with many parents of children with ADHD: blame. You may relate to some of the feelings covered in this chapter, and also discover some feelings are not a part of your experience. Although we cannot find words that describe your individual world, we hope this chapter gives you the comfort, reassurance, knowledge, and understanding to help you forgive yourself.

Should I Blame Myself?

You may ask yourself, have I done something wrong? You may compare yourself with other parents, finding fault in yourself, which leads to a spiral of unending self-criticism. What is important, and will be repeated throughout this book, is that raising your child is not easy. He has a neurodevelopment disorder that affects behavior and learning. This disorder, primarily genetic in origin, is passed on through family members, and is not the result of what you have or have not done. You should not take any more blame for passing on this disorder through your genes than you would the color of his hair. You did not plan it, so try to stop blaming yourself and begin to understand your child's disorder.

I Feel Guilty Spending So Much Time with My Child

Raising a child with ADHD does seem to take a considerable amount of time and energy. Parents may attend more school conferences and doctor appointments, resolve conflicts between their child and neighbors, policing sibling conflicts, and deal with ongoing spousal differences over parenting. One father, frustrated with his wife's continuing preoccupation with their child, shouted in frustration, "She has no other life, no time for me or the other children!" Everyday activities can sometimes become unbearably difficult and stressful. One family discovered that getting their nine-year-old child ready for school in the morning required considerable effort and planning. Reminder notes were posted for him on the bathroom mirror, bedroom door, and refrigerator outlining what activities that needed to be done before leaving for school. Each and every step in his morning activities had to be orchestrated.

These children require additional time and energy to raise. It's not your child's fault or yours, but part of the package. Our experience suggests that your child will need more supervision at home, more contacts with schools, and will be more emotional and prone to make poor decisions concerning day-to-day activities. Children with ADHD can grow up to become productive and responsible adults with proper parental support and early intervention, and yes, most families do survive this process without long-lasting scars or bruises. Many parents share the guilt you may carry at times, and guilt will probably be part of your experience from time to time in raising your child. Unfortunately, these children seem to stir within parents those tidal waves of emotional turmoil that bring to the surface feelings of guilt.

Hopefully, as you read on and become more knowledgeable about this disorder, you will be kinder to yourself.

Review and Tips

- There is "no one right way to raise your ADHD child" (Barkley 1995). Remember this, say it often to yourself, and be a critical reader and listener of others' suggestions.

- Affected children generally do take more of their parents' time.

- Block off time alone with siblings, spouse, and for yourself that does not involve conversations around or activities with your child with ADHD. Block time off on a calendar so other activities do not replace this time. We all need to refuel our emotional tanks, so don't let yours run empty. This time doesn't have to be for long periods, but needs to be on a regular basis— you may find yourself having more patience with your child.

You will make mistakes; all parents do. Making a mistake is not as important as how you deal with it afterwards. Model honesty for your child by admitting you made a mistake, and apologize. He will not necessarily see this as weakness, but will learn that even Mom and Dad are human.

My Doctor Doesn't Believe Me— He Says, "Take a Parenting Class"

The doctor's recommendation to take a parenting class can, on many occasions, be an appropriate suggestion, even for parents of children *without* ADHD. Classes can be helpful and supportive. Sometimes, however, with limited background information, the doctor's recommendation or advice can be wrong, parents' concerns are dismissed or minimized, and the child's behaviors are viewed as resulting from poor parenting skills or an overanxious parent.

Most parents describe their first trip to the doctor to have their child evaluated as a positive experience, but in some situations, it is a disappointing experience. They paint a picture of the doctor's insensitivity and judgmental behavior, and describe leaving his office feeling blamed, defensive, guilt-ridden, and unheard. Most doctors are caring and sensitive to the feelings and concerns of parents; however, like all of us, doctors have bad days and they do not always put their best foot forward. Also, time limits, personal bias, and limited knowledge about ADHD can affect a doctor's judgment. Doctors' schedules may leave little time for discussion during an assessment.

An assessment is multidimensional. A proper diagnosis should include a clinical evaluation, a physical examination, mental health evaluation, family history, and input from schools, parents, and other important caretakers in the child's life. If the doctor finds no suggested history or observations of ADHD, he may assume, and many times rightfully so, that the parent is overly anxious and a parenting program is in order. Many times a child will not show his "true self," as one parent described it, in a doctor's examining room. Affected children respond well to structure, novelty, and one-on-one attention, all of which you find in a doctor's examining room. A child is somewhat intimidated by the doctor's visit, so his ADHD symptoms may be less noticeable during the examination. In such cases, the doctor may not identify him as having ADHD, and the parent doesn't know what to do or think.

Doctors too can find their decisions influenced by personal bias that can affect judgment. Currently, ADHD is well-publicized—you can read about it in newspapers, magazines, and hear it discussed on the radio. Doctors don't live in a vacuum, and like their patients, they are privy to this information, too. One frustrated doctor said, "Parents think every kid who acts out has ADHD!" Like this doctor, we too feel that this new awareness and interest has led more parents to   think their child is affected. Reflecting current opinion, the doctor may mistakenly not identify the child as having ADHD.

Parents, seeing the doctor as the expert, may initially dismiss their private concerns as overanxiety, but with time and continuing conflict with the child, might begin to question the doctor's assessment or suggestions. One mother, having come from the doctor's office, unleashed her anger and frustration. "I told Bobby's doctor he didn't know what he was talking about! I told him it was more than a 'child who needs to grow up.'" Like many parents caught in the daily conflicts and frustrations of raising of their affected child, she was irritated with the lack of support offered by her child's doctor.

You may have been frustrated and angry in dealing with your child's doctor, and in moments of reflection, he has probably had similar feelings towards you. Raising this child can tax your patience, and you may have developed a low tolerance for perceived indifference to your concerns. Recognize, however, that the doctor will be a necessary partner in the treatment of your child's disorder. If you feel his doctor is not knowledgeable or sympathetic to your concerns, it may be time you found a new doctor. You may even discover that an outside support person such as a daycare provider or teacher can communicate to the doctor her observations of your child. Doctors sometimes put more weight on the observations of a professional who works with children than a parent's opinion, because a teacher, day-care provider, or mental health professional has seen a large number of children and can compare your child's behaviors to other children his age. Don't hesitate to take into your confidence others who can help your doctor better understand your situation. You don't need a private therapist to do this. We have found that teachers are generally willing and eager to help the doctor in assessing and monitoring the child's behaviors.

Blame has never helped anyone or solved many problems. It generally creates divisions and roadblocks to effective communication. Your child's doctor is a critical component in treatment, so try to provide additional information that can help him. If you are frustrated with your child's doctor, try to communicate some of your frustrations. You may find that he will be more receptive than you think.

Review and Tips

- Before seeing your child's doctor, write down on a piece of paper times and events when your child acted out. Drop this list off at the doctor's office a couple of days before your child's appointment, in order to give the doctor time to review your concerns.

- Give your doctor permission to talk with other caretakers involved in your child's upbringing (teachers, daycare workers, grandparents, etc.). If your doctor is very busy, include with your list the comments and observations of other adults who have contact with your child.

- Ask your child's doctor what his feelings are about ADHD. You may find that you are miles apart, so you might need to find a new doctor. Remember that doctors have specialties and biases; if you are uncomfortable with the his position, change doctors. You are your child's advocate, and your trust and faith in the doctor is critical to your child's treatment.

My Parents Say We Are Terrible
for Putting Their Grandchild on Medication

The use of medication in the treatment of ADHD seems to be viewed negatively by the general population. Parents who place their children on medication may feel defensive and guarded about their decision. A mother, after picking up her child's medication, was confronted by the pharmacist's wife who said, in an irritated voice, she "wouldn't put *her* child on Ritalin." The mother, embarrassed and feeling guilty, sheepishly turned and walked away, hoping others did not hear. Many parents we counsel have shared similar experiences. They tell stories about being lectured, sometimes by strangers, for putting their child on medication. There has been some improvement in attitude at schools, but our experience with the general public is that there continues to be some trepidation and disapproval surrounding medicating children for ADHD. However, being eternal optimists, we believe with time, the public will become more accepting.

Parents, sometimes without consulting the child's doctor, will take their child off medication after reading books and newspaper articles relating the negative effects of medication. One parent said that she "felt uncomfortable and guilty when picking up her child's Ritalin at the drugstore after hearing about its side effects on the radio." She would wait until the line was empty, then quietly pick up the order. How unfortunate that societal attitudes and misunderstandings created for this young mother an atmosphere of guilt and embarrassment about picking up a medication recommended by her child's doctor. If her child was diabetic, she would not have felt the same trepidation about her decision to place him on medication. ADHD is not life-threatening like diabetes, but if untreated, it can cause severe and long-term negative effects, educationally, emotionally, and socially. Sadly, exaggerated and misleading claims by groups opposed to psychiatry in general have caused much anguish for many parents whose children are being prudently treated by medication (Barkley 1989, 3).

No wonder one parent shared that she felt attacked by her parents for putting their grandchild on medication. These grandparents received information about medication and ADHD from newspapers, magazines, radio, and general conversations with friends and neighbors, and they feared that "Johnny would grow up to be a drug addict." Studies, however, find that children properly treated with medication for ADHD have a lower propensity for using illegal drugs than children not treated with medication (Comings 1990). This child's mother was obviously upset and felt guilty about her decision. Time and time again, parents have shared with us negative comments made by others about their decision to place their child on medication.

Your decision probably did not come easily or without doubts. We have met few parents who do not continue to have mixed feelings about their decision. Medication is a serious intervention. Guilt whispers, "Nature gave us all the parts, so why should we interfere?" Even though during rational moments you understand that medication can and does help, there still may be those moments when you feel guilty and question your choice. To help you through these moments, read as much as you can on the role medication plays in treating ADHD (see chapter 7). The doubters will always be there, but if you are knowledgeable and comfortable in your decision, we believe you can help change the feelings of those closest to you, even the grandparents! You will not be able to change the feelings of everyone, but you can work on your reaction to them. You can only provide an opportunity for them to learn about medication in the treatment of ADHD; you cannot ensure that they will accept your explanations.

Review and Tips

- Remember that *you* are your child's parent, no one else! You are responsible for his well-being and care. Your responsibility is not to make the world understand, but to have faith in your own judgment.

- If you are unsure about your decision, understand that most parents have mixed feelings about placing their child on medication. It is a serious intervention and it would be unnatural if you didn't question yourself at times.

- Read as much as necessary to better understand the role of medication in treating ADHD (chapter 7). Talk with your child's doctor and ask him to suggest reading materials that may be helpful.

Sally-Next-Door Says I Am Not Strict Enough

We can't remember a client who has not shared an experience about hearing someone say, "All you need to do is be stricter and he will not do those things." We're not saying that children don't benefit from structure and consistent parenting—children with ADHD definitely do—but to blame all the behaviors on poor parenting is unfair to the parent. If all it took to change your child's behavior were "being stricter," the families we have worked with would have been successful long ago.

It's disturbing that friends, family, or teachers will not hesitate to go to a CPA for tax advice or take their car to a mechanic rather than trust their own limited knowledge, but when giving advice to a parent about the raising of their child, they do not hesitate to give their opinions with little fore-thought or caution, as though they had great expertise. This advice is generally presented in a statement such as "Be stricter," making the parent feel unsupported and incompetent. The advice-givers must feel that all children, like most tax laws, can be approached in predictable and similar ways. If you have children both with and without ADHD, you know that in comparing their behavior, there is generally a significant difference in their compliance and consistency in performance. Proper parental skills and attitude can improve an affected child's behavior, but a lack of discipline is *not* the cause of this disorder.

Most parents we counsel understand that their child responds best when there is parental consistency and structure. However, they also know that just being strict or consistent has not solved all his behavioral problems, so they use a myriad of interventions—some of which are more successful than others. Running out of ideas, the parent becomes frustrated, loses patience with the child, and seeks outside help from mental health professionals to give her guidance, as well as help her deal with her guilt.

Raising a child with ADHD is not simple or easy, and parents will often feel inadequate. These children can learn to behave better, but developing better behavior requires more effort and energy from the parent than is generally needed in raising unaffected children. Don't measure your level of success by comparing your child to his unaffected playmate next door. These children do not learn from their mistakes as easily as others because they are often driven by the moment and do not take time to measure the consequences of their actions. What works for unaffected children will not work as consistently with affected children. Your lack of success with your child is often the result of his disorder, and not something you have or have not done. Your neighbor, relative, or child's teacher may mean well, but you don't have to accept their suggestions or blame yourself for not following their recommendations.

Review and Tips

- Read as much as you can about your child's disorder. Attend a local support group or find a professional you trust to share your ideas and concerns.

- Remember raising a child with ADHD is not simple or easy. Your neighbor, relative, or child's teacher may mean well, but you don't have to accept their suggestions or blame yourself for not following their recommendations.

- If you, your child, or your family is having significant difficulties, ask the doctor to refer you to a specialist who works with these families. A child psychiatrist is an appropriate referral, and you should not hesitate asking for these services.

I Am Losing My Child

"Help me, I'm losing my child" (Barkley 1995). These words, spoken by a mother of a child with ADHD, express the pain and fear that is sometimes experienced by parents on a daily basis. Out of the continuing discord between child and parent, there seems to develop a distancing that can be very painful to the parent. The parent senses the loss of her bond with her child. This *Bolt from the Blue,* the child who takes so much patience and understanding, can make her feel unloved.

The parent senses this loss but may not be able to put it into words. She knows, as opposed to her relationship with her other children, the exchanges with her affected child can make her feel empty and guilty. One mother said she didn't want her son having angry feelings about her like she had towards her father. She went on to say that, "He used to yell, scream, and make me feel terrible, and I feel I'm doing the same things to my son. He's only 10; wait until he's 14—he'll hate me." Another parent dealing with a very difficult daughter broke down in the therapist's office, pleading for some relief from their turbulent interchanges. Parents in pain, knowing that few understand their feelings of loss, blame themselves. They see only dark clouds on the horizon, with little faith or hope that the clouds will pass. They can become moody, agitated, and irritable towards the child and other family members. Unfortunately, the parent, in trying to compensate for her guilty feelings, can become overly involved with the child at the expense of herself and other family members.

The child, picking up on the parent's disappointment, can withdraw into himself, or become a child who feels victimized and unloved, taking out his unhappiness on others around him. Sometimes the negative interactions can become a family affair. Your family shouldn't form a mob attitude directed at the child with ADHD. There is a danger that "virtually anything that goes wrong in the family [will] be blamed on the ADHD child" (Hallowell and Ratey 1994).

An important first step in overcoming the fear of losing your child and improving your relationship with your child is for you to begin to give up the child you wanted and accept the child you have. It means giving up long-held dreams and expectations concerning him. Parents have dreams and expectations for their child even before he is born, dreams that become dear and important in a parent's mind, expectations not only for the child, but for the parent's relationship with him. Unfortunately, the affected child is hard to raise, and many of the expectations and hopes a parent had are tempered by the daily conflicts and personal sacrifices that result from raising him. A parent can become resentful and feel guilt and anger towards themselves and the child, who may not be a harbor of fulfilled expectations, but of lost dreams.

Your child has ADHD, which makes certain tasks more difficult, such as modulating his emotions, remembering to remember, waiting quietly in line, taking his turn, and stopping to knock before entering his sister's bedroom. As much as you would like your child's behaviors to be different, they will not generally change measurably. His impulsive behavior is driven by chemistry, not willful actions. To temper his impulsive behaviors takes not only great patience, but more guidance on your part.

An important step towards acknowledging the child you have is to not pity him. Yes, pity. He needs your guidance, not pity, and your honest feedback when his behavior is appropriate and inappropriate. Compliments should be honest and valid. A parent may try to compensate for her child's misbehaviors by being overly involved or enabling. A consequence is that she may feel uncomfortable about her decisions, and the child can become tyrannical.

It is human nature to pity someone who is experiencing difficulties. When one sees a child in a wheelchair or a blind child having difficulties opening a door or finding his place in a classroom, it is a natural reaction to want to help. Upon reflection, though, you may not necessarily be doing him a favor by helping. If you view your child's disorder as a problem he will have to learn to deal with and learn about, not something you can change, you will begin to view your responsibilities in a healthier way. Rather than focusing mainly on his mistakes, hoping that he will learn from them, you can comment on his strengths and how these behaviors can help him become a productive adult. Like Thom Hartmann (1996), you can view your child's *Hunter* archetype as neither a deficit nor a disorder, but as a set of skills, abilities, and personality tendencies that he can draw upon to be successful. Guide and counsel your child, providing age-appropriate information to help him understand his disorder and that his ADHD traits may someday be an asset and not a daily hindrance to his social and personal development.

Self-esteem comes from reaching personal goals and being successful, and a large part of that responsibility lies with the child, who can hopefully begin to identify and recognize that his traits can present both challenges and successes. A parent can provide an environment for success, but cannot ensure success will happen. You can try to give your child the "courage to be imperfect" (Dreikers 1964), and model that success generally comes with small steps, one at a time, and not in giant leaps. By adopting this attitude, you may find that you feel less anxious and less fearful of losing your child.

Review and Tips

- A relationship is the responsibility of both parties. Your child contributes to both the negative and positive patterns in your interactions.

- Walk away if the interactions become negative. A conflict, by definition, involves two parties; if you walk away, your child will be alone. Conflicts contribute to patterns of alienation between parent and child. This doesn't mean you walk away from your child completely, but only when the negative interactions between you and him become intense and destructive to the relationship. Continue to show him love and affection.

- Don't pity your child, but help him to recognize that some tasks will be more challenging than others. ADHD is a disorder that children generally don't outgrow, and they need to find successful ways to deal with its challenges.

- Most negative interactions between parent and child stem from the child wanting either attention or power. You don't have to play his game.

- Don't form a mob mentality directed at the child, blaming all family troubles on him. It's easy to fall into this trap, making him feel victimized and alienated from the family.

- The feelings and fear of losing your child can be changed, but will require changes on your part. No one says parenting is easy, especially in the raising of a child with ADHD.

- You have made many positive decisions, so don't get too down on yourself. You will continue to make mistakes—everyone does. Quoting Rudolf Dreikers (1964), "Perfection is an impossible goal, and striving for it seldom leads to improvement, but more often to giving up in despair."

The Hardest Time for Me Was When I Had to Place My Child in a Psychiatric Hospital

You may not have had to place your child in a psychiatric hospital, because most affected children do not have to be hospitalized. Those who are hospitalized generally have several diagnoses or problems apart from ADHD that present severe dysfunction in their life. The child's doctor may recommend hospitalization for purposes of monitoring a new medication, observing the child's behaviors outside the home when parental observations or behaviors are conflicting or confusing, and protecting children who may cause harm to themselves or others. Hospitalization is expensive and very intrusive for both the child and parent, and doctors tend to be very conservative with this intervention. Parents are often anxious and filled with feelings of guilt and blame when their child is hospitalized. The decision does not come easily for any parties involved.

Unfortunately, in our society, hospitalization for a mental health disorder seems to be much less acceptable to the general public than other medical conditions, which doesn't help the parent feel any better about hospitalization. As clinicians, we have found that most parents feel uncomfortable about their decision. The idea of giving permission to place their child in a psychiatric hospital is often very stressful and laden with guilt. They feel they've abandoned their child, that he will hate them even more, and they will lose what relationship they had. They often speak about these issues, especially their child's expressed anger towards them for allowing this to happen. Parents feel that they were probably the primary contributing factor in their child's unhappiness and acting-out behaviors, and this feeling of insecurity concerning their own abilities often leads to self-blame, or blaming other people or things. In most situations, however, they are hardest on themselves.

If you are a parent who has hospitalized your child, your feelings, including possible blame and guilt, are shared by many other parents who have preceded you in this decision. It's important to remember that this decision was not yours alone—your child's doctor, and possibly others, were consulted for their opinions. Your child has a condition that at times may require this level of intervention.

Review and Tips

- Your decision to hospitalize your child was a decision arrived at by both you and your   doctor. The intervention was a medical decision and was deemed necessary because of his condition.

- ADHD is a medical condition that may require a multitude of interventions during the child's lifetime. In most situations, outpatient care is enough, but some children need a more restrictive environment for monitoring and observation.

- If you continue to feel guilt or blame, reach out for support by counseling with your child's doctor or another professional knowledgeable about this disorder.

I Feel Like Running Away

Most parents have at one time or another wanted a vacation from their children. Raising children is not easy under the best of conditions, and raising children with ADHD is usually even more stressful and challenging. One parent described her situation as similar to a dog on a chain—she had some freedom of movement and choices, but the chain could be pulled at any time, whether she liked it or not. She saw herself as so closely connected to her child's life that she sometimes felt "choked by his problems." She felt that the child was in control and could pull her chain at will. Desperate for relief, this mother would fantasize about running away from home, leaving the family to the father's care. She knew she never would, but the thought often crossed her mind.

Maybe you too have imagined running away. An affected child can be demanding and sometimes unforgiving. He can test the best of a parent's patience and understanding, leaving the parent feeling emotionally drained. The parent, feeling her emotional tank near empty, has little energy for others or herself. Life can become one-dimensional, centered on the child's mishaps, transgressions, and tantrums. One parent, shortly before picking up her child at school, became tense and short-tempered with his toddler sister. She did not look forward to the long afternoon when things seemed to be the worst. She blamed herself, knowing it was wrong to feel this way, but she was at a loss for ways to change this feeling. Another mother, speaking of her seven-year-old daughter's physical aggression towards her, wondered aloud what was going to happen when her daughter was a teenager. She could only imagine the worst.

Parents do have moments when they feel they are in the eye of the storm and there is no relief in sight, and it is not unnatural or unusual to wish you were on another planet. At these moments you need what Rudolf Dreikers (1964) calls a "mental withdrawal-to-the-bathroom," to escape from your child or from angry telephone calls from neighbors and school staff. You know you cannot go in the bathroom and shut the world out forever, as much as that may sound comforting, but you need to find moments to be alone to refuel your emotional tank. If you don't take care of yourself, you can't take care of your child. Many suggestions in dealing with him will be introduced in later chapters.

Review and Tips

- If you feel like running away, you're not alone. This feeling is natural and common from time to time, and not only with parents of children with ADHD. The feeling generally doesn't last long.

- Try to block off on your calendar time to nurture yourself: coffee or lunch with a friend, a walk around the block, a matinee. Plan and mark these times so they are not replaced by other events. Try to block out a "mental withdrawal-to-the-bathroom" once a week or three times a month. If money is tight, brainstorm with relatives or friends things you can do to refuel your emotional tank.

- ADHD is a disorder that usually impacts a child throughout his childhood and, for some, into adulthood; therefore, there will be times when things don't go well, so plan on it. Your attitude and feelings about his disorder can and will affect how you will deal with it.

Sometimes I Don't Like My Child

Many parents have expressed this thought. They may admit it only to their mate, parent, or trusted friend, but generally it's their secret, shrouded in shame. These feelings are understandable—affected children can be very difficult to raise. They may fail to finish things on time, are moody, daydreamers, and even become enraged when interrupted or asked to stop what they're doing.

Your child may have characteristics that puzzle you, frustrate you, and add additional stress and conflict to your family. A child who presents, sometimes daily, behaviors that keep the soup boiling can and will trigger feelings of resentment and anger. He requires daily monitoring and orchestration around routine activities, unlike unaffected children. This endless feeling that you cannot let down your guard can make you resentful towards him. One parent rattled off a litany of complaints, commenting that, "He doesn't appreciate me, and he will do anything to make me mad." This mother, feeling alone and unsupported in the raising of her child, felt victimized by him, and she resented him for making her feel this way. You will have times when you don't like your child, but it's important that you talk with a professional familiar with this disorder if these feelings are long-lasting.

Unless parents have an understanding of ADHD, their relationship with their child will be more conflictual and heartbreaking. You are demonstrating your commitment to understanding by reading this book. There are many good books, videotapes, and audios available to assist you, and we encourage you to go to a local library or bookstore to find them. If there is a local CHADD (Children and Adults with Attention-Deficit/Hyperactivity Disorder) support group close to your home, participation can be helpful in directing you to reading and video materials.

Review and Tips

- You love your children, but they will do things that sometimes make you angry. Your child will do and say things more often that tests your patience and understanding.

- Not liking your child is a natural reaction at times to living and raising a child with ADHD, and this feeling is shared by most parents in your situation at one time or another. It is generally a feeling of the moment and passes with time, but if the feeling seems more permanent, seek professional help.

- Write down on a 3x5 card five positive behaviors you observed in your child during the day. Examples could be shutting the front door properly, taking a toy back to his room, and sitting down and helping his younger sister put a puzzle together. Catch him being good and then record it! In doing this, you may find the feeling of not liking your child will be less intense and less frequent.

- Remember that trying to be a perfect parent leads to despair. Be kind to yourself and work on those areas that trouble you. Change comes slowly. It's like climbing a slippery sand hill—you slip, fall back, and sometimes fall down. Progress may be slow, but you will make it to the top if you have a strong desire. By reading this book you show the desire; all that is left is the hard work, and we know you will be successful.

Summary

You can change your feelings about your relationship with your child. The first step is to accept that he has a neurodevelopment disorder that is not your fault or his. The second step is to accept that you are not perfect and you will make mistakes; all parents do. Raising a child with ADHD requires additional time, knowledge, and patience. These children are difficult to raise. Lastly, there are no magic formulas or words that will suddenly make things simpler, but there are proven ways that can make things go smoother in raising your child.

4

"Don't Blame Me—
I Have ADHD!"

"Don't blame me—I have ADHD!" shouted an angry and frustrated teenager to his parents as they entered the therapist's office. We have often heard these words shouted by children, and parents, confused and sometimes guilt ridden, don't know how to deal with this dilemma. "Is my child really to blame for his behavior and how much, if any, should he be disciplined?" Many parents in counseling ask this question. No parent wants to discipline a child for something the child can't control.

The dilemma presented is one of trying to balance what parents know society expects in terms of following rules with the recognition that their child's difficult behavior is the consequence of his disorder, and is not always willful or under his complete control. Most parents do not want to make excuses for their child, but are in constant turmoil over when he should or shouldn't be disciplined.

I Didn't Take My Pill—Don't Blame Me!

One eight-year-old boy, who was about to be punished for hitting his sister, yelled out to his mother while running down the hall, "I didn't take my pill—don't blame me!" His mother, crying in frustration, stopped in her tracks. She didn't know what was right or wrong when dealing with her son, Steven. She felt guilty most of the time because she was told that he had ADHD and he would do things without thinking. What was the right thing to do when he wasn't on his medication?

This question presents a common predicament for parents. All children are expected to follow rules. A clerk in a grocery store will not allow your child to run through the aisle and grab things off the shelf. Even though your child may do these things impulsively, society generally does not make exceptions for these kinds of behavior. Cooperativeness must be understood as the norm, and all children in general need to learn this rule.

Real-life choices are not black or white, and the answer should not be limited to punish or not punish. Most solutions are in the gray area. Some problems have easy answers, but most solutions leave us with doubt and anxiety. Decisions are often driven or influenced by outside forces that we have limited or no control over. You know that if your child hits another at school, he will be sent to the principal's office or suspended, ADHD or not. Therefore, when he hits his brother or sister, you understand there needs to be some consequence. You do not accept his behavior or make excuses, but you ask yourself, "He has ADHD. Why discipline him for being impulsive?" Consequently, you may not act with total conviction when pressed to discipline. You may look the other way, or excuse his behavior, knowing full well that society does not tolerate these kinds of behavior. Steven's mother had similar thoughts and feelings when she asked the therapist, "What is the right thing to do?"

When she shared her son's "I didn't take my pill—don't blame me!" comment, the therapist may have thought, "Why didn't the mother make sure her active and sometimes aggressive eight-year-old son took his medication?" Medication was given to help Steven be less impulsive. When he was on his medication, he was more receptive to parental directions and was less impulsive. The medication acted as a brake pedal, slowing him down. The mother told the therapist that she decided not to give her child his medication because she wanted him to have a "vacation" from medication on the weekend. Unfortunately, for mother and child, he was coasting along without the benefit of brakes when he hit his sister. She took away an important support system for her child. He may have hit his sister when on medication; however, by not giving him the pill, the mother faced a troubling dilemma: was it fair to discipline Steven for hitting his sister when he wasn't on his medication?

Steven, whether on medication or not, needs to be held accountable for hitting his sister. Hitting is not an acceptable option for settling arguments. No child can hit, steal, break property, and not be held accountable, and a parent who allows antisocial and aggressive behaviors to go undisciplined is hurting the child, not helping him. Parents need to set limits and consequences, and consequences should always be logical and benevolent. Consequences differ from punishments in that they are administered in a calm and businesslike manner.

Society will not tolerate behaviors that interfere with the safety and well-being of others. All children need to be taught ways to limit negative interactions with others and find better ways to control their impulsiveness. Your child's aggressive behaviors should not be rationalized away or minimized because he has ADHD. In the words of John F. Taylor (1994), a parent needs to stand behind the child, not protectively in front of him. Avoid running interference between your child and others. He needs to deal directly with others regarding his behavior. He needs to know that you care about how he behaves. When he begins to feel you or others don't care how he behaves, he loses "an important motivation for remaining socialized" (Taylor 1994). Sometimes a negative consequence is required, but hopefully this is not the only or last intervention to help your child. Positive consequences, such as incentives, should always be used before negative consequences, if possible. However, in cases like Steven's, the mother needed to act immediately and set negative consequences for his inappropriate behavior.

Affected children, even when on medication, need to be educated about better ways to deal with problems. Steven needs to be shown better ways to deal with angry feelings. For example, instead of Steven hitting his sister when angry, he can be told that when angry, he is not to hit or break things but go to his room until he feels less angry. Hitting is not an option, and he will be disciplined if it happens. Like Steven, these children are generally not good problem solvers. Your role is to help your child become more competent through education. Punishment tells you what *not* to do, not what *to* do.

Your child, if he's like many children with ADHD, will tend to make two errors when presented with a problem. One, he will make decisions too quickly without stopping to think about better ways to solve the problem. Like Steven, your child may know better than to hit his sister, but he reacts impulsively and doesn't stop to think about the consequences of the act, or of alternative ways to deal with his anger. Children with ADHD generally make a series of quick guesses, rather than thought-out choices. Two, your child will become sidetracked by unimportant factors and neglect the important issues needed for solving the problem (Taylor 1994). One boy in therapy would spend a large amount of his homework time making sure his sister wasn't watching the TV program he liked, rather than getting the homework done early so he could watch the program with his sister.

A child's difficulty with disinhibiting behavior makes it more difficult for him to make good decisions. The following interventions can be helpful in teaching him ways to compensate for delays in inhibiting behavior. No behavioral intervention will make any behavior disappear permanently; however, interventions can help minimize problem behaviors.

Counting to Five Silently

One way to help your child make better decisions is to model, or teach, him appropriate reactions to various situations. One method to help him slow down his reaction time and to react less intensely is to teach him to count to five silently before saying or doing something. Practice this intervention often, especially when he's not upset. Any intervention will be less successful if tried in the heat of battle, so practice when your child is not upset about something. Prepare him for this activity by saying, for example, "Steven, we're going to practice counting to five silently before opening the car door. Now, count to five, then see yourself opening the car door and shutting it gently. Let's try it." Practice sessions like this need to be repeated frequently so your child begins to internalize the process. This activity can help him to slow down so he is more open to practicing other interventions that can help him be less impulsive.

Talk to Yourself

Another step you can add to *Counting to Five* is to have your child practice self-directed talk. Children with ADHD generally do not develop age-appropriate self-directed speech (Barkley 1995). Our ability to talk to ourselves helps us better control our behavior. Your child, by practicing self-directed talk (out loud or silently to himself), will be able to delay responding and be better able to apply learned rules to current problems. You could give him an example, such as, "Okay, Kevin called me a name. I am upset. I need to stop playing with Kevin and go play with Chris." This example both teaches and reinforces appropriate ways to deal with angry feelings. Model and have your child practice self-directed talk so he feels more comfortable with the new activity.

Sometimes children will resist practicing self-directed talk and say it is boring or stupid. It is often helpful to respond that very successful people from doctors to fighter pilots commonly practice self-directed talk—boys seem especially responsive to fighter pilot examples. Share, especially with older children, that because of chemistry, certain activities require more effort and practice. Use an example that is not threatening to your child, such as practicing free throws with a basketball. Children understand that to perform well in a basketball game, they need to practice shooting baskets and dribbling. By practicing, they are developing *muscle memory,* so when in an important basketball game, their body will do what they want it to do. They don't have to think about shooting the right way—they just do it. They also know that this doesn't mean they will make every basket. Talking to yourself doesn't mean you will always make the right decisions, but it can help you learn to problem solve better by slowing down your reaction time. Your child may still not do it, but you have introduced an activity that he may later find helpful.

Remember that self-directed or self-reminding statements often will not be as powerful as biochemical treatment. The best improvement occurs when both methods are applied simultaneously.

Plan Ahead for Problem Areas

Have a plan in mind before introducing your child to difficult situations. You know where and when he acts up the most, so don't start the day without reviewing with him rewards and consequences he will receive when involved in these activities.

Russell Barkley, an authority on ADHD, presents a five-step process before entering any problem setting (Barkley 1995).

Step 1: **Stop** before entering a problem setting, such as a store, friend's home, or restaurant.

Step 2: **Review** with your child two or three rules that he often has trouble following in that situation. Store rules could be "Stay next to me, don't touch things on the shelves, and do as I say."

Step 3: **Set up a reward or incentive.** You could stop for an ice cream treat after he successfully follows the rules, or he can stay up one-half hour later if he behaves at the store.

Step 4: **Explain** the disciplinary action if he doesn't follow the rules. He could be told that he will be put in time-out in the store or taken out of the store immediately if he acts up. He will lose TV privileges that night or have to go to bed a half-hour early.

Step 5: **Follow your plan** as you enter the situation and give him immediate and frequent feedback. Most important, be consistent.

Medication

If your child is on medication, confer closely with your doctor about its effectiveness and don't alter or change the dosage without your doctor's approval. Medication is a controversial issue for many parents, but for some children, it is necessary for their healthy emotional development. ADHD is a neurodevelopmental disorder that affects the regulation of certain neurochemicals that affect behavior. Medications help normalize the levels of neurochemicals needed to make the brain function more efficiently, and affected children may need medication to help them slow down so they can learn better ways to deal with problems. Tempering behaviors will often be more difficult without the benefit of medication. It's a disservice to children not to give them the opportunity to try medication when their behavior significantly interferes with their social and educational development.

These children, in the words of one writer, need a "one-two punch" therapy: medication for dealing with the biochemical aspect, and psychotherapy to help the child readjust emotionally (Cady 1996). When the biochemical component is not supported through medication, the child will have more difficulty limiting his problem behaviors. Medications can cause side effects, but so can being sent to the principal's office, being left out of group activities, and being reprimanded by parents.

Society sets limits and will not excuse his aggressive behavior, so your child needs to understand, in the safety of his home, ways to minimize problem behavior. You can use his age and severity of the problem as a factor in deciding the kind or degree of discipline, but serious actions such as damaging property or hurting others or oneself must be addressed.

Your child will have his good days and bad days, but with patience, forgiveness, and consistency on your part, he can be successful. So if he yells, "Don't blame me! I didn't take my pill!" calmly tell him that he is responsible for his behavior and you will help him find better ways to deal with upsetting feelings.

Review and Tips

- Your child needs to be held accountable for his actions. Learning ways to control certain behaviors is not always easy, but with proper interventions and support, he can be successful.

- Provide support for your child by learning ways to minimize environmental situations that can exacerbate his behaviors. For example, don't leave the house or go into a store without a behavioral management plan in place.

- If your child is using medication, make sure he takes it. Don't change the dosage or stop without consulting the doctor. If you are uncomfortable with the medication, talk with his doctor.

He Seldom Says He's Sorry

Many children with ADHD seem to have difficulty saying, "I'm sorry." Parents, siblings, and caretakers wonder why saying, "I'm sorry" is so difficult for these children. We find that three traits can partially explain this behavior.

First, they generally don't take responsibility for their behavior. They act harmfully, then show no remorse for their behavior. They are generally not open to suggestions and seldom admit to being wrong. Since they don't see themselves as responsible, they see no need to apologize. In fact, they are quick to blame others and will argue that the other party should apologize. Unfortunately, this behavior pushes people away—people grow tired of the constant commotion and lack of remorse.

Second, they can be self-centered. Because of distractibility and under-focusing, they are often poor observers and do not read people's body language or normal social cues. They will often interrupt others' games or take a brother's CD without asking, and then be honestly puzzled that people were upset with them. Because of their self-centered nature, they tend to relate poorly, especially in group settings, and they are left out of group games and activities because of their behavior. One nine-year-old boy in therapy was upset because his classmates didn't want to play basketball with him anymore. When the therapist asked why the boys didn't want to play with him, he sincerely didn't know why. He could only say that they were mean and unfair.

His teacher shared that while the boy was playing basketball in PE, he suddenly became extremely angry when he fouled out. While stomping around the court, he yelled at the top of his voice that the game be stopped and started over. He went into a tantrum, and when this didn't work, he tried to bully his classmates and the PE teacher into submission. This *emotional hijack* left reason and good manners to the wind. The hallmark of an emotional hijack is that when the moment passes, those possessed don't have an understanding of what came over them (Goleman 1995). Driven by the moment, the boy didn't process the impact his behavior was having on his friends. Although his actions seemed willful, he was surprised and confused when he discovered that others were upset with him. When talking about his behavior, he had great difficulty taking ownership for his actions, and like a broken record, he kept returning to the PE coach and how unfair he was. Only after the therapist repeatedly walked him back through the steps leading up to his fouling out, did the boy begin to look at his own behavior.

Third, they seem to have difficulty discussing or expressing their feelings. Some would argue, *not angry feelings*! This observation may be more perception than fact, but still it seems valid for a large number of children we see in therapy.

Language development is important in helping us increase our ability over self-control. Speech becomes a substitute for actions. Young children with language delays often manifest behavioral problems because of their difficulty finding words to express their feelings. Sometimes overarousal and attention problems can become more problematic for children with coexisting speech and language delays. Children with ADHD have been found to have deficits in speech (fluency/syntax) because of motor control delays when compared to a control group of unaffected children. Both fluency and syntax are important for effective communication through speech (Barkley 1997).

These children usually lack verbal skills and tend to rely on nonverbal cues such as facial expressions and body movements. Unfortunately, they may often interpret nonverbal communications as negative. They may see neutral responses from adults and peers as negative and threatening. This suggested pattern of negative interpretation of others' behavior can cause them to react defensively.

Finally, another explanation is the possibility that the child, after years of making mistakes, disappointing loved ones, and getting into trouble, builds defenses that come across as "I don't care." He can be heard saying, "I don't care what you think." He looks around and, comparing himself to his brother or sister, sees that he is the one who seems to get into trouble the most. Like many people with histories of poor decision making, he may distance himself, putting up defenses that protect him from painful feelings, feelings that are too threatening and too hurtful. He will say he doesn't have a problem, or somebody or something else was the reason for his behavior. He can develop a low self-image that makes dealing with threatening feelings even more difficult.

Also, saying, "I'm sorry" is not always received with open arms by the parent or other caretakers. They have heard it too often, and dismiss it as dishonest or insincere, but it's not always a child's excuse. Remember, these children are driven by the moment and do not always learn from their mistakes as successfully as do other children.

Here are some suggestions that you can use to help your child better understand the importance of saying, "I'm sorry."

Acknowledging Mistakes

Encourage your child to acknowledge his mistakes. Reward him for admitting his error without being asked first. Give him examples of things to say to a friend if he does something wrong. Example: "Bobby, I'm sorry I took your basketball without asking first. I didn't think before taking it." Find time to practice examples that show ways to acknowledge mistakes. Also, give him verbal praise when this behavior is observed.

Making Amends

If your child has offended someone, talk with him about making amends. Tell him the importance of saying, "I'm sorry." People will be more forgiving if he is honest with them and makes some amends. Examples could be, "Bobby, I'm sorry I was careless and broke your bike. I will let you use my bike until your bike is fixed."

Chart "I'm Sorry" Statements

Set up a reward chart for "I'm sorry" behaviors. We have found this intervention to be effective with younger children (five to nine years old). Hang the chart where it can easily be seen, and when your child admits his mistakes, apologizes, or demonstrates regret, give him a star that goes on the chart. Show him the stars and tell him how proud you are about his new behavior. You are not bribing him, but rewarding him for learning an important skill for getting along with others. Charts and token rewards for good behavior can be quite effective with children 12 years and younger, but older children often find charts too babyish.

Time to Talk

Set time apart after your child's playmates leave to talk with him about his behavior. Point out when he showed friendship skills and coach him in better ways to handle problem areas you observed. Demonstrate the skill by acting it out. Let him perform the skill in a realistic simulated situation.

You're probably asking yourself, "When do I have time to do all of this? I work and have other children to raise." Unfortunately, your child *will* take more of your time and attention in order to learn better ways to keep and make friends. He will need to learn and practice behaviors that other children seem to learn by themselves, such as saying "I'm sorry."

Review and Tips

- Children with ADHD require more attention and time from parents to help them develop appropriate social skills, like saying, "I'm sorry." Saying "I'm sorry" is often especially difficult for affected children.

- Practice the suggested interventions when you and your child are not upset. Practice often and present the activities as a way for him to learn to keep friends, and not as a punishment. He will probably be defensive at first, but be patient and persistent. Most children need additional encouragement and patience.

He Is So Emotional—Is This Normal?

Children with ADHD are emotional, and yes, it's normal. They have difficulty regulating their emotions—if they are happy, they're really happy; if they are angry, they can be really angry. They have difficulty inhibiting their feelings or thoughts and will blurt out or share whatever is on their mind.

It's important to let people know when you're pleased or unhappy about their behavior. People like to know how you feel. Sharing with people how you feel about things is normal and should be encouraged. However, it is also important to know *when* and *how* to let people know how you feel. It wouldn't necessarily be wise to tell your boss that you think she acted like an idiot at the Christmas party. You may be right, but being right isn't necessarily being smart. Most people learn that honesty is important, but good judgment is also important if we are to get along with people.

People with ADHD don't reflect on the consequences of their actions in many situations. They seem to have great difficulty inhibiting reactions to a number of life challenges, reactions which can sometimes be embarrassing and harmful.

The time between impulse and action can be very short. A fifth-grader, when seeing his teacher in a short dress, blurted out in class, "I see your underwear!" He was sent to the principal's office, and his parents were told of his inappropriate behavior. An eighth-grader, when upset with his math teacher, yelled out in class, "You jerk!" His teacher did not appreciate this emotional outburst. Good judgment dictates we keep our feelings to ourselves in such situations. However, for this adolescent, poor impulse control led to his getting in trouble because he was controlled by his emotions.

Medication can help temper your child's reaction to events around him; however, medication cannot teach appropriate behavior, which is learned. Younger children often have not learned the skills useful in getting and keeping friends, or in controlling their temper. You need to teach your child more acceptable ways to deal with his emotions. The suggestions given below are helpful in slowing a child's reaction time—the time between a stimulus and response—which needs to be increased or strengthened.

Counting to Five Silently

Counting to five, a simple and proven technique for slowing reaction time, can be effective with both young and old children. Have your child practice this exercise with an imaginary or real situation that gets him upset. Practice this activity often, and when he is not upset.

Stop, Look, Think, and Do

Have your child practice a self-talk intervention called *Stop, Look, Think, and Do.* Before your child says or does something, help him learn to silently say to himself, *Stop, Look, Think, and Do.* An example could be practicing not getting angry when a friend misses a basket. **Stop:** Child counts to himself silently, 1, 2, 3, 4, 5; **Look:** "No one else looks upset because Jimmy missed the basket"; **Think:** "If no one else is getting upset, maybe I need to forget it"; and **Do:** "Forget it and pass the basketball to Ryan." Again, practice this technique with your child often when he's not upset, and talk with him about situations when he can use this procedure. But remember, it will work, but not all the time.

Prepare Your Child for Changes

These children have difficulty with changes, which can present unwarranted reactions such as changes in mood and emotional outbursts. Unexpected change can trigger emotional outbursts, and even simple changes such as transitioning from watching TV to going to dinner can present problems. A parent or sibling is often the victim of these outbursts. Unfortunately, not expecting the emotional outburst, the sibling or parent can often escalate the situation, so let your child know ahead of time that changes will be coming. His impatience and impulsivity make delaying his displeasure with others difficult.

Review and Tips

- Your child may be more emotional than his unaffected sister or brother. These children are emotional, and their moods can change in a heartbeat. Expect it and know that this may be part of your child's behavior.

- Practice self-talk exercises like *Stop, Look, Think, and Do* when your child is not upset, and practice often so it becomes more comfortable for him.

- Children with ADHD have a difficult time delaying their reactions to events or situations—their difficulty in inhibiting behavior is a critical component in understanding their behavior. They seem to do better when prepared for expected changes.

He Never Seems to Learn from His Mistakes

These children do not learn from their mistakes to the same degree as children with ADHD. Repeating mistakes is expected and normal; however, they seem to repeat the same mistakes more often than other children. Yet, just as there is a wide variability in types and ranges of behaviors, there are also wide differences in the degree to which these children learn from mistakes. Your daughter with ADHD may do better than her brother with the same disorder. Younger children will repeat more mistakes than older children. A younger child will need more reminders than his older brother, and a child who is not held accountable for his behaviors will tend to repeat those mistakes more often than a child with clear guidelines.

The child, knowing he can be suspended from school or have his favorite toy taken away, may still punch Johnny in the face or take his brother's CD without asking. Parents report they sound like a broken record: "Ask your brother before taking his toy," "Don't leave the faucet running," or "Knock before you enter the doctor's office"; nothing seems to work for long. He continues to take his brother's toy, run into his sister's bedroom without knocking, or repeat any number of other things he was told not to do.

Understanding this difficulty in learning from mistakes can be explained by reviewing two underlying patterns seen in children with ADHD: poor inhibition and poor acquisition of rule-governed behavior. These two concepts are covered in chapter 1 in more detail.

First, these children have great difficulty in not acting on a thought that comes to their mind. Our ability to inhibit our behavior affects many areas of our life, from interacting well with people, to performing well on a job. One writer compares the difficulty of a child with ADHD in controlling improper behavior to that of a child who stutters. A stutterer knows the disadvantages and difficulties associated with stuttering and wants to stop. People generally understand the stutterer's difficulties and are patient with the stuttering, but even with the best of intentions, the stuttering can continue. The difficulty is in the control of self-expression, not the knowledge or lack of caring (Taylor 1994). The child with ADHD usually knows what to do, he just has difficulty doing it. It's not an issue of will or caring, but a neurodevelopmental delay in his ability to inhibit behavior. He may know he shouldn't hit his younger sister, but his difficulty with inhibiting behavior makes it difficult for him to stop before getting into trouble. He acts before thinking about the consequences, which leads to repeated transgressions.

Second, the child, in addition to having delays in inhibiting behavior, seems to have great difficulty with rule-governed behavior. As covered in chapter 1, rule-governed behavior is the ability to control future behavior. When people set goals and then do things to reach those goals, they are using rule-governed behavior. These children, because of difficulty in delaying actions, are less adept than other at using rules or instructions to control themselves. They respond so quickly and do not weigh the consequences of their actions. The ability to delay responding to immediate rewards or discipline is an important process for not only controlling behavior, but also for reaching future goals. Affected children generally have a hard time keeping rules and their consequences for the future in mind.

Ideas to Help Your Child Learn Better from His Mistakes

The first step in helping your child eliminate repeated mistakes is to make sure he understands that there is a problem. This child is a poor judge of his own behavior. He is quick to point out others' shortcomings, but the last to find fault in himself. You are helping him to develop a level of self-awareness by pointing out to him how his behavior affects his ability to keep friends. He may not hear your words the first time, but eventually with support, he may make the changes necessary for success in making friends or getting good grades in school.

Second, many children do not understand or accept that they have ADHD. This can especially be true for adolescents, but elementary school-age children can also be in denial or confused about their disorder.

Be honest when talking to your child about ADHD. He has heard others' explanation of his behavior: a "bad kid," "brat," or "spoiled." It's your responsibility to help him separate myth from fact, and show him how his disorder may be influencing some of his decisions and actions. Don't mince words or try to minimize his difficulty. When your child begins to understand that he is presented unique challenges because of ADHD, he will take the first step in acceptance. Until these children become active participants in their treatment, progress can be slow and results minimal. Successful interventions, such as self-monitoring, are based on the assumption that they will be active participants, and not active or passive resisters to suggestions meant to help them.

Those traits that make school so frustrating can be used later in life to build successful careers. Point out that many successful people have ADHD: doctors, professional athletes, actors, business people, and scientists, to name but a few. Let your child know there is life after school. One activity we do with high school juniors and seniors is to take them to a local junior college or university and introduce them to the disability center on campus. They can see both young and old benefit from accepting help for their disabilities. They usually enjoy this experience and leave with a better appreciation of their choices. You may want to visit a college with your adolescent.

Be your child's expert on ADHD. Make sure your explanations are age-appropriate and do not offer more than he is able to understand or accept. A six-year-old child isn't old enough to understand detailed medical explanations, whereas a middle school or high school child can be introduced to detailed explanations and written materials on ADHD. If you have a very young child, spend time focusing on management of his behaviors, rather than trying to explain the reasons behind his difficulty with certain activities. This is not to say you can't simply say, "Bobby, I know it's hard for you to listen closely at times. You are taking this pill to help you listen better, just like your sister has glasses to see better." Especially try to minimize the medical aspects of this disorder with your young child. Children under 11 years of age often have a hard time understanding and conceptualizing medical terms and explanations. However, we encourage parents to explain to older children that this disorder is not a disease, although it can present challenges at school and in the home—challenges such as paying attention, completing tasks, and waiting turns. These challenges are more pronounced because of chemistry, and not because the child is always careless, rude, or forgetful. Keep it simple and factual. Children understand that friends and parents have difficulties and differences: Dad's quick-tempered, Mom's forgetful, a best friend is not the best speller—they may not like their difficulties, but with support they will work on them.

- Children with ADHD don't learn from their mistakes as well as those without ADHD.

- Driven by the moment, they do not slow down long enough to measure the consequences of their actions.

- Become your child's expert and provide training time to help him "put brakes" on his actions. Practice often and reward with praise and sometimes treats for doing well.

What Scares Me the Most Is
When He Gets Violent

An adolescent with ADHD grabbed his mother in a rage and pushed her against the wall, yelling, "You bitch! Leave me alone!" His mother, ashen white from fright, broke down crying as he slammed the front door after himself. Children who become violent can be frightening to parents, siblings, and other caretakers. They punch holes in walls, break windows, throw things, kick, punch, and cuss at anyone or everyone around them. One eight-year-old seen in counseling would get mad at her mother and bite and kick her, and on more than one occasion, threw garbage from one end of the kitchen to the other. This mother was scared of her daughter and lived in constant fear of her tyrannical rages. She described her as agitated, short-fused, and volatile most of the time. She felt victimized by her daughter, and would sometimes let her get away with things out of fear her daughter would turn on her.

Affected children's emotions tend to be extreme and poorly filtered. Their emotions go up and down like a yo-yo, causing those around them to walk on eggshells in fear something or someone will set them off.

They seem to have difficulty expressing their emotions verbally, so unhappy feelings will build up and sometimes present themselves in violent outbursts. When they do verbally deal with their anger, however, it is generally expressed through cussing, teasing, and name-calling, often sending the recipient running to a parent or adult for support. This behavior, unfortunately, sometimes only escalates the problem, and often leads to violent outbursts. One important role a therapist can play is helping families deal with this seemingly common pattern. You may find this pattern in your family, and it probably makes you frustrated, angry, and puzzled about what can be done to stop it.

The suggestions below are helpful to parents when dealing with an angry child.

I C.A.R.E.

One activity to help minimize violence and redirect angry feelings is Taylor's *I C.A.R.E.* method. *I C.A.R.E.* stands for *I*nterrupt, *C*ool off, *A*ffirm, *R*edirect, and *E*ducate (Taylor 1994). You must be willing to **interrupt** conflicts and aggressive interactions. When you get involved, the negative interactions come to a "screeching halt, and your child must face a new set of issues having to do with your presence and your involvement." Taylor suggests you use the code word *huddle* as you call your child aside for a quick talk. Try to keep these huddles calm. You can say, "Steven, this is the second time you have yelled at your younger brother. Maybe you need to go play by yourself until you feel less angry."

If your child is getting angry, he needs to find a place to **cool off** before talking about his angry feelings. Help him understand this is not a place of punishment, but a place where he can get himself back together. Also, Taylor notes, the parent can calm down while the child is cooling off.

Try to **affirm** your child's feelings. He may be feeling picked on, left out, or upset about any number of things. You can say something like, "If I felt the way you do, I would be angry at Bobby, too." You are not saying your child is right, only that you can empathize with his feelings from his interpretation of events.

After intervening to stop the violence, help him **redirect** his behavior to something else that will make him less focused on his angry feelings. These children can become very fixated on thoughts or feelings, and redirection can be quite a chore at times, but it's not impossible. You may want to get out your child's favorite toy and encourage him to go to his room to play alone with it until he calms down. If it's your teenager, suggest he go to his bedroom and listen to his favorite CD.

Lastly, **educate** your child about the series of events that may have led to this violence. He could be told that, "Whenever you spend too much time playing the board game 'Guess Who' with your brother, you end up getting mad and throwing the cards. Your brother gets upset and you get upset. You may only want to play one or two times and then play something else by yourself." Give him examples of choices he could have made, or elicit from him ideas he may use to help him to be less violent next time. Take a few minutes to practice the suggestions when he is calm: "Why don't you play 'Guess Who' one more time with your brother, and then I want you to go to your room and play with your favorite toy." Modeling and practicing appropriate behaviors will help him learn better ways to deal with unhappy feelings.

Green, Yellow, Red

Another successful technique is what we call the *Green, Yellow, Red* intervention. Cut strips of green, yellow, and red paper into 2x8 lengths. The paper strips should be available for you or the child to access when angry feelings are being observed or expected. The green strip indicates the child's feelings are under control and he's generally in a good mood. The yellow strip suggests he may be close to losing his temper or is beginning to get upset and angry. The red strip means he is very upset and needs time by himself to calm down. The child, if feeling angry, can pick a yellow or red strip, indicating to others around him how he is feeling. He then can leave the group activity and find a quiet spot to be by himself until he feels less angry or agitated. This technique can be helpful in teaching your child to self-monitor his feelings. You also can hand him a yellow or red strip when you observe him getting agitated. Some families find *Green, Yellow, Red* helpful with unaffected siblings, and will encourage its use during activities that are known to start fights.

Zip My Lip

Taylor's intervention, *Zip my lip, turn around, and leave,* can be effective in de-escalating aggressive interactions (Taylor 1994). This simple rhyme, practiced often, can help the child remember to stop, leave, and find something else to do until he calms down.

Know What Makes Your Child Angry

You generally know which activities cause your child the most frustration. Take a mental inventory of these activities and write them down as a reminder for him. Remind him that when he is involved in these activities, he can quickly become upset. Show him where he can go if upset, what he can say to his friends, and how to make up afterward. Reinforce the fact that violence will not be accepted and severe consequences will be implemented if he hits, throws, or damages property. If he becomes violent, he will be restrained, and if you're not present, you will administer severe consequences for violent behavior when you find out. There is no compromise or second chance. Children do respond to firm limits and can learn to find more appropriate ways to deal with unhappy feelings.

Exercise

Running, jumping-jacks, or riding are effective ways of decreasing anger. If it is winter and cold or wet outside, running in place can be just as effective as running around the block or around the backyard. If you can afford it, getting a portable rowing machine or indoor bike is helpful.

Review and Tips

- Teach your child appropriate ways to deal with angry feelings.

- Violent behavior is not to be tolerated. Your child needs to understand that hitting others, breaking property, or hurting himself will not be accepted.

- These children can be very emotional, and controlling their emotions will be harder than for unaffected children. Help your child learn to recognize when he's getting angry and give him activities to do and places to go until he feels calmer.

- Know what events generally cause him to become violent, and try to limit those events as much as possible.

- Help him find more acceptable ways to deal with angry feelings. Practice various techniques as often as possible when he is not angry.

Is My Child Noncompliant or Just Incompetent?

Does your child not understand, or is he being noncompliant? This question is important, and the answer you give yourself will determine how you respond to his actions. All children can be noncompliant *and* incompetent. If you feel your child simply does not understand, you will generally be more forgiving and supportive; however, if you feel he is being noncompliant, you will probably be more punitive and unforgiving. An important goal in counseling parents is to help them make a distinction between behavior that results from incompetence and behavior that results from noncompliance.

Sam and Michael Goldstein (1990) provide some important guidelines. They point out that a child's difficulties in settling down, getting easily frustrated, being impulsive, or not paying attention, often result from a number of generally nonpurposeful behaviors, which can be upsetting to parents and other caretakers. Parents can often find the interactions with the child to be negative: "Stop it!" "Quit it!" and "Don't do that again!" The child sees his environment as overly controlling and negative. A possible result of these negative interactions over time will be for him to take on oppositional behaviors. When a parent has a better understanding of incompetent and noncompliant behaviors, she can reduce the negative feedback and increase compliant behaviors. One way the parent can make a distinction is through a model the Goldsteins call *positive direction*. The rule is for a parent to ask what she wants the child to do instead of what he is doing at the moment. The Goldsteins suggest that through mastering *positive direction* parents can separate incompetent from noncompliant behavior.

Positive Directions

To demonstrate positive directions, the Goldsteins present a scenario of a child whose feet are on the wall. The parent directs him by saying, "Don't put your feet on the wall." This is not a positive direction, in that the parent is asking him to *not* do something, rather than telling him what *to* do. The child has too many choices—most of which the parent doesn't want, such as putting feet on a table or on the couch. The child would be complying, but the parent is likely to become angry. A positive direction would be: "Take your feet off the wall and put them on the floor." The child has 10 seconds to comply, and if he doesn't follow his parent's direction, it is not incompetence, but noncompliance. The parent must then stay in the room to make sure he complies. If the parent gives a direction and then walks out of the room and comes back a few minutes later, she will not be sure whether he was being noncompliant or incompetent. He may have complied at first, become distracted by something, and put his feet up on the wall again.

The Goldsteins use another example of a child who is asked to lower his voice, but after a short period of time, the voice becomes louder again. This is an example of incompetence, and not noncompliance. Children with ADHD often have difficulty modulating their voices. The parent would then give another positive direction asking the child to lower his voice. The parent in this situation "acts as the control system for the child." The parent may have to remind him a number of times in a play event.

Incompetence

If a parent punishes her child for impulsive behavior, there is a strong possibility that he will be remorseful and promise to behave better. Unfortunately, the next time he is in that situation, the "impulsive need for gratification will outweigh any capacity to stop, think, and plan, resulting in a reoccurrence of the problem" (Goldstein and Goldstein 1990). The child's behavior stems from incompetence. The Goldsteins point out that a parent would not expect punishment to increase the reading capacity of a five-year-old.

They also note that punishing your child for impulsive, inattentive, restless, or non-persistent behaviors is unlikely to change his behavior. These behaviors are symptoms of ADHD, and skill building and education are required to minimize them, not punishment. However, violent or destructive behavior cannot be tolerated, and all children need to be held responsible for antisocial behavior (see "I Didn't Take My Pill—Don't Blame Me!" in chapter 4, for further discussion).

Included below are some interventions you may find successful with an incompetent behavior that is often brought to our attention by parents: *remembering to remember,* or forgetting.

Reminder Sheets

Set up visual reminders to help your child *remember to remember.* Reminders can be posted on the inside of his bedroom door, on the bathroom mirror, or on the refrigerator. One reminder sheet may not be enough, so don't hesitate to put reminder sheets throughout the house. You may want to take them down when you know your child's friends are coming to visit. Older children often feel uncomfortable about visual reminders—feelings which are not always unwarranted.

One Direction at a Time and Be Specific

If your child has difficulty following directions, limit the number of tasks required or suggestions given at any one time. Don't ask him to remember three tasks to do if you know he sometimes only remembers the first request. For example, you can say, "Bobby, put your shoes in your closet now, and then come back to Mommy." Praise him when he returns, and then say, "Thank you for putting your shoes away. Now I want you to pick up your toys on the floor in the living room and put them in your toy box." Be clear with what you want him to do by giving a positive direction. If you had said, "Put your toys away," you may not have found them in the toy box. Lastly, ask your child to repeat back to you what was asked of him, and then praise him when he's correct.

If he becomes upset by being reminded, try an intervention suggested by Taylor, called the *ticket-to-talk method* (Taylor 1994). The contract is that you agree to give no more than three sentences of instructions or correction; in return, your child agrees to "really listen" and try his best to do what you asked. This intervention sometimes helps minimize negative interactions often observed in affected families; however, Taylor notes that when severe communication problems exist, outside counseling is often necessary. This method is often effective with teenagers, who respond well to contracts, so present it as a contract: "I will do this if you will do this." It doesn't work all the time, but it can be effective if presented in a positive way. If presented as a punishment, your teenager will continue to resist you, but if you show that both you and he can help each other by making changes, he may be more receptive to working with you.

Keep a Stopwatch Handy

Have a stopwatch handy to reinforce behaviors such as putting shoes away, cleaning off the kitchen table, or taking toys out of the bathtub. Say, "I started the stopwatch. Let's see if you can get the toys out of the bathtub and in the toy box in less than five minutes." The stopwatch gives your child a visual reminder that reinforces your request. Also, affected children seem to perform better if time limits are set—the timer helps the child stay focused on the task and reduces distractibility. When he successfully performs the chore, be sure to praise him.

These simple interventions can help a child minimize incompetent types of behavior such as forgetting. The parent, by reinforcing a request both verbally and visually (reminder sheets, one direction at a time, and the stopwatch), teaches her child methods for remembering.

Noncompliance

When your child is noncompliant, be firm and set consequences for his behavior. Each time a noncompliant behavior is allowed to go unaddressed, it increases the chances that behavior will be repeated.

Commonsense Rules

Rule 1: Commonsense tells you that children make honest mistakes, and saying, "I'm sorry" is enough. However, for repeated behavior that is purposeful, consequences need to be set.

Rule 2: Commonsense tells you that if you watch your child long enough, he's going to make a lot of mistakes. Set priorities, try to ignore small indiscretions, and focus on serious noncompliant behaviors, such as taking money from your purse, staying out after curfew repeatedly, or ignoring you in a store when asked to stop running around. These behaviors, if allowed to go undisciplined, will only escalate.

Rule 3: Finally, commonsense tells you that if all you do is punish, then you will hurt your relationship with your child. Give him attention when he does something good, not just when he is misbehaving. Catch him being good and praise him right away! Don't wait.

Be Firm

If you ask your child to do something, follow up and make sure it's been done. If you have to send him to time-out (discussed below) for refusing to pick up his toys, make sure he picks up his toys when he returns from time-out. Your goal is to get him to comply with your request to pick up his toys, not to punish him.

He may seem noncompliant most of the time, but with patience and consistent follow-up on your part, he can show improvement in compliant behavior. These children respond to limits and structure, but may not respond as consistently as others.

Time-Out

Time-out is an intervention where the child is asked to spend a period of time by himself. It is mainly effective with children four to 12 years of age. Time-out is an effective intervention for addressing noncompliant, not incompetent, behaviors. We recommend that parents put their child in a "time-out chair," and not send him to his room. Your child can be better monitored in a chair, and bedrooms can be entertaining. The time-out chair should be in a place such as in a hall or corner of a room, where he can be observed but not entertained.

The purpose of time-out is not to punish, but to help him make behavioral changes. Of course, he perceives the act as punishment, but parents should see it as a way to help him become more compliant. The parent tells him why he is going to time-out and what behavior is expected during that time. He should be seated (butt on seat) and told there will be no rocking, yelling, or getting out of the chair. If he screams or yells, you can have a reminder like *Zip my lip.* If your child continues to not comply by getting out of the chair, you may have to restrain him in the chair. Place your body behind the chair and wrap your arms around him as lightly as possible until he complies with your demands. A younger child often can be placed on your lap and restrained until he complies with the time-out rule. If you are upset and feel you may hurt him, walk away until you feel calm. Once you are calm, tell him he needs to return to his time-out chair. Remind him again that time-out starts only when he complies with the time-out rules.

The child should be in time-out for a short period of time (15–30 seconds for young children, and one to two minutes for older children). Our experience is that the common recommendation of one minute for each year of the child's age is often unrealistic for young children with ADHD. We recommend that parents count out loud (10—9—8—) the number of seconds left in time-out with very young children. One mother who was taught to keep her child in time-out one minute for each year of age would use an egg timer or hourglass with marks on it, because she would forget about her child being on the time-out chair. Fortunately, limiting time-out to one or two minutes should make it easier to remember. Your goal is to increase compliant behavior, not punish. Each time your child successfully complies, it reinforces that behavior and increases the positive management of him. When he complies with time-out, the parent praises him for complying and then asks him to do what he was told to do before being sent there.

Have your child think of one or two things he could have done differently so he wouldn't be in time-out. When he completes it, have him tell you his ideas. If he can't think of any ideas, give him some examples. This intervention helps your child use time-out to problem solve and also can redirect angry or upsetting feelings. It doesn't always work, but for children who are not too upset, it can be helpful.

Be firm and follow through with your demand until he complies. Be assured he will test you, and if you fail, it will make it much harder the next time you ask him to comply with a request.

Changing Habits

The parent will need to change some habits as much as the child will need to change some behaviors. One way to stop the cycle of seeing only the negative in his behavior is to recognize good things he does. We encourage parents to have a bag of beans and a jar in the house. Every time they see their child doing something good, such as closing the front door gently, he should be praised and given beans to put in his jar. At the end of the evening, the beans can be counted and for every five beans, for example, he gets a star. The parent should be generous in giving the beans at first. It doesn't matter how many beans, it's the positive gesture by the parent to the child that is important. The stars are put on a chart and posted on the refrigerator. This intervention will help your child understand that his good behavior is recognized and affects how people see and treat him. He will begin to see, along with you, that most of the time he is good, not bad! You may find that his noncompliant behaviors will decrease.

Be Preventative, Not Reactionary

The Goldsteins point out that parents generally try to reduce or eliminate a child's problem behaviors by either being *reactionary* (after the problem occurs), or *preventative* (before it occurs). The reactionary method for affected children is usually not successful and can increase noncompliant behaviors. These children often have skill deficiencies, and punishment does not improve skill competency. If a parent continues to use reactionary methods and success is not achieved, more problems can develop between the child and parent.

A preventative method such as skill building or modifying the environment is generally more effective and helps minimize noncompliant behaviors. If your child continues to go into his sister's room without permission, you could put a lock on the sister's door. Modifying the environment minimizes a noncompliant and possibly incompetent behavior.

Your child can be noncompliant *and* incompetent. The hardest job is knowing when he is being noncompliant and when he is incompetent. You will make mistakes; we all do. However, you probably know your child well enough to know the difference.

Review and Tips

- Your child can be both noncompliant *and* incompetent.

- When he is noncompliant, set limits and consequences for his behavior. When noncompliant behavior is allowed to go unpunished, it reinforces that behavior.

- Find time to praise your child often. Parents sometimes get into a pattern of punishment and criticizing, and the child is not given the praise that all children need from their parents for healthy growth.

- Review the *Reminder Sheets* and *Stopwatch* techniques and use them often. Your child will see them as a positive way to find more success in remembering to remember. It also gives you times to praise him when he's being good.

- *Beans in a Jar* is a good way of reinforcing good behavior. Keep the jar handy and, on a regular basis, have your child put beans in it when he demonstrates positive or compliant behaviors. At the end of the day, count the beans and post the numbers on a chart for everyone to see.

Summary

"Don't Blame Me—I Have ADHD!" is not the "Get out of Jail Free" card from Monopoly. Children with ADHD are expected to follow rules, and when they break them, society doesn't give out free passes. All children need to learn to follow rules that are necessary for living cooperatively with others. Society will not tolerate aggressive, disruptive, or noncompliant behavior, and neither should you. Your child has no right to abuse you or others, and he needs to know that if he hurts you or others, or takes things that do not belong to him, there will be consequences. You are doing him a disservice if you let him get away with socially unacceptable behavior. He has a disorder, but he still needs to be held responsible for his behaviors—when he grows up, he will get a ticket if he runs a stop light, or he could be put in jail if he punches someone.

Parents and schools need to be preventative, but unfortunately, both are more often reactionary. Affected children often suffer more than they probably need to because there are few preventative interventions to address their special needs. Consequently, they struggle to meet the needs of a demanding social order while trying to put brakes on their problem reactions.

Provide an environment at home that recognizes your child's weaknesses, and then put in place activities that will help teach him better ways to deal with problem behaviors. Be preventative and not reactionary, supportive and not enabling. Enabling behavior allows him to believe he is not responsible because he has ADHD.

Pay attention and become knowledgeable about separating noncompliant from incompetent behavior. Many of the interventions suggested in this book address both the noncompliant child and incompetent child. As you improve your discernment skills, you will feel more comfortable disciplining your child when necessary.

5

Our Child Takes a Lot of Our Time

Some children, such as a child with ADHD-I, cause few problems for their parents. They move along in life, not noticeably different from their friends, making normal childhood mistakes, and inflicting generally normal parental stresses. They make friends, learn to drive, and graduate from high school with little behavioral history that makes them stand out that much from their classmates. However, many do stand out from their friends and are not easy to raise.

Many seem to require more time, patience, and understanding than unaffected children. Parents share guilt, anger, and common feelings of exhaustion because of the extra time expended on their child. They go to more teachers' conferences, resolve more conflicts between siblings, and fight with neighbors and their mate more often than other parents. Everyday activities become frustrating experiences: going to the store, filling the car with gas, deciding who sits where at the dinner table, and deciding who bathes first at night. This can be a problem for any family, but not to the degree or intensity that is experienced in affected families. No family member is left untouched. A family may have more than one affected child that can make family life even more stressful. Vacations are shortened, holidays disrupted, and for some families, the policeman is called by his first name.

Parents come to our offices frustrated about failing to find some solution to raising their child. They talk about him wreaking havoc in their families and marriage. One mother, after a heated discussion with her teenage son, said, with tears rolling down her cheek, "I love you, but no matter how much I do, it's not enough. You take all my time, all my energy, but you still blame me. You say I don't love you, but I can't ignore everyone else to prove it to you."

Reminders, Reminders, All the Time

These children do require a lot of reminders, more than unaffected children. Children with ADHD have difficulty *remembering to remember.* An important component of remembering is *attending,* or paying attention. One of the three core symptoms used in making a diagnosis for ADHD is inattention, along with impulsivity and hyperactivity. Your child would not have been diagnosed with ADHD if he did not have difficulty with attention.

Children with ADHD often do not mentally attend when given directions, so they will make decisions based on partial information. They sometimes guess at what their parents or teachers have asked them to do, or ignore the problem altogether, hoping it will be forgotten or go away. One adolescent said that on more than one occasion he couldn't remember what his mother had told him to do, so he would guess or play dumb "because she forgets sometimes what she asks me to do."

Your child may be listening at first, but then becomes distracted and hears only part of what you said. Affected children are highly distracted both by internal and external events. Your child can listen and suddenly be distracted by an internal thought or external activity. You may not know his mind has left him somewhere between your saying "I" and "next door" and returns only on "Goodbye, honey. See you tonight." You leave, thinking he understands, and only later realize he understood very little of what you said. You wonder if it will ever change.

This high distractibility can affect your child's ability to stay focused long enough to complete many routine tasks that are required both at home and in school. He may head for his bedroom with the intention of cleaning up his room, but then become distracted on the way by a drippy faucet in the bathroom. You will find him playing with the faucet instead of cleaning up his room. He may start to clean his room, but after a few minutes, he'll be distracted by something else and will need another reminder to complete the job.

Children with ADHD often fail to prioritize—they'll attend to something entertaining while they're supposed to be cleaning up the bedroom before they can play in the park. You probably are saying to yourself, "Well, that's true for everyone; we all want to put off doing something we don't like to do." However, unaffected children generally learn to prioritize and self-monitor, so they complete tasks without so many reminders.

In high-interest activities, affected children usually need no more reminders than unaffected children. Children with ADHD do not need reminders to turn on their favorite TV program or pick up their Michael Jordan basketball shoes on layaway after school. They usually have no problem remembering to remember when something is of great value to them (see "Motivation," chapter 1). Where they have difficulty is remembering routine or low-interest activities like schoolwork or chores.

Now that you understand that remembering to remember is closely tied to inattention, distractibility, and interest level, how can you help your child better complete routine activities? The interventions described below have been successful for many families—some have been covered in the section "Is My Child Noncompliant or Just Incompetent?" (chapter 4).

Reminder Sheets

These children often have great difficulty with complex verbal directions. If you ask a child to do too many things at one time, chances are that only part of what was requested will be remembered, so supplement verbal requests with written reminders. Daily and regular chores can be posted around the house (front of the refrigerator, back of a bedroom door, bathroom mirror, or 5x8 card taped to the child's radio or stereo). Put the reminders where he can see them on a regular basis. If guests are coming over, you may want to put them away and bring them out after everyone leaves. Visual reminders reinforce your verbal requests and help him to be more successful in completing tasks. Use the same method for remembering to take homework to school (see chapter 6), locking the front door, or putting the dog outside when going to school. Visual reminders can teach your child a method to remember that he can use as long as necessary.

Mnemonic Reminders

"Gimmicks" such as *STOP* or *Three R's* suggested by Garber, Garber, and Spizman (1996) can be helpful in getting your child to remember to remember. *STOP* stands for **S**top **T**o **O**rganize the **P**roblem. Once he forgets an activity three or more times, use this simple mnemonic reminder. Help him problem solve ways to increase his ability to remember to remember. *Three R's* can get children to remember tasks such as taking out the garbage, brushing their teeth, and putting their homework in their backpack. *Three R's* stands for **R**emember, **R**epeat, and **R**emind. Garber, Garber, and Spizman give an example of remembering to brush your teeth, writing that time and place can trigger actions to be repeated. The routine of brushing teeth is **R**emembered after eating. Eating jogs the memory to brush the teeth. It is **R**epeated several times a day, before leaving for school and before going to bed. Lastly, something that happens once in a while will not become habitual, so a **R**eminder is something you can add to your routine of getting your child to remember.

Kitchen Timer

Children with ADHD seem to stay more focused when under time constraints. A kitchen timer can help your child stay more focused on short-term projects. Tell him what you want done and that you expect it to be done within a designated period of time. Set the timer and let him know he will be rewarded if he completes the chore on time without reminders. A timer attached to his clothing can be helpful at school in helping him to stay more focused, as well as to turn in his homework.

Oral Directions

Oral directions should be short and specific (see "Positive Directions" in chapter 4). As mentioned above, these children have great difficulty following complex verbal directions. Ask your child to do one or two things. If you ask him to do three or four things, chances are he will only remember part of what was asked. When he has completed one or two requests, compliment him for a job well done, and then wait a while before making another request.

Make Eye Contact

When giving your child oral directions, ask him to look at you. Make sure you have eye contact. When you have his attention, tell him what you want him to do, and have him repeat back to you what you said, ensuring that he understands what was requested.

Be Close to Him

Don't yell at your child from across the room to turn off the TV and come to dinner. He will probably not hear you or will choose to ignore you, so you won't know whether he's noncompliant or inattentive. Make sure you are near him when giving him directions—the closer the better. If he is young, kneel down in front of him, speak softly but firmly, and tell him what you want him to do. If he is watching TV, you may have to stand in front of the TV to get his attention; however, this may be ill-advised if your child has a history of explosive behavior.

If these interventions are followed consistently, they can help minimize problems in remembering, and you will see measurable improvement in your child's ability to complete tasks. You will use fewer reminders and he will be more successful in remembering. Understand, though, that remembering and attending will always be a challenge, and he will need more reminders than his unaffected sibling or best friend.

Review and Tips

- Your child's need to have reminders is a common trait seen in people with ADHD.

- These children can attend as well as others when involved in high-interest activities. Make sure your child has additional reminders, like notes, when asked to remember routine tasks such as turning in schoolwork or doing chores.

- Your child's need for reminders is probably not because he's defiant or oppositional. He has a neurodevelopmental disorder that makes remembering more difficult, and additional support and reminders on your part will be necessary from time to time.

- Practice the suggested interventions to help your child be more successful in remembering. You may need to change habits, so be patient and know that with time, you can be more successful with him.

Family Outings Can Be Overwhelming

All families attend weddings and family reunions, participate in neighborhood block parties, and go on vacations, yet these activities can cause additional stress for the parents of a child with ADHD. He requires more supervision, preparation, and counseling before leaving home. Some outings seem to be a better fit than others; having a picnic and playing in the park require less planning than going to a wedding. For most outings, however, having a behavior plan can make the trip or vacation less stressful and more enjoyable. The following suggestions can be helpful.

Look Before You Leap

When you parent a child with ADHD, don't walk out the door without a plan. Include realistic expectations that address your child's needs. If you need to drive out of town, plan stops on the way. Sitting in the back seat of a car for long periods of time can be difficult for any child, and stopping at regular intervals and letting older children trade places and sit up front is often helpful. Bring a travel shoe box with special toys inside for a younger child. The contents of the travel shoe box should be available *only* for car trips. Affected children can get bored quickly, and when the travel shoe box is not used for other purposes, it will be more of a special treat.

If you're going to the store, review car and store rules with your child before getting into the car. Don't expect him to settle into appropriate behavior without reminders. In your purse, keep a 3x5 card with the car and store rules listed. Review these rules with your child or have him tell you the rules, which reinforces the rules and helps him attend to their importance.

You need a plan that minimizes or addresses behaviors that can make outings difficult.

Waiting Is No Fun

Affected children have great difficulty waiting. They want to go now, not at 9 o'clock. If you have a trip planned that your child would be very excited about, you may not want to tell him too far in advance. He should have the opportunity to enjoy the thoughts and dreams and expectations that trips bring to all of us, but not for too long!

For vacations, younger children can put together a trip album with a number of blank sheets of paper. Your child can draw pictures before the trip about things he wants to do and places he would like to go, which gives him a means to deal with his excitement. Younger children can also make a calendar with the day they're leaving marked. Some children enjoy putting a star or a favorite sticker on each day as it passes. Young children often have difficulty gauging time, and this helps them visualize when they will be leaving on the trip.

If you're going to an activity where your child will have to stay seated for an extended period of time, such as a wedding, let him take a doodle pad to quietly write in if he gets fidgety. This will help him stay occupied while he waits. Affected children get bored quickly, so have a plan to keep your child entertained so you can enjoy the special event.

Teenagers can put together a traveling case with favorite magazines or CDs, which helps them practice organizational skills and allows them to feel more in charge. Remember, control and self-determination are hot buttons for teenagers. They aren't generally receptive to Mom's or Dad's advice, so let your teenager do as much as he can by himself to prepare for the trip, and talk with him about safety concerns and where he can go if he feels agitated.

Remember, being with the family is not always a comfortable feeling for teenagers; you may want to invite his best friend along as company. A friend can sometimes help minimize noncompliant behaviors as well as provide outside entertainment.

Change Is Not Easy

Children with ADHD have great difficulty with changes. As much as your child may look forward to an outing, it's a change. Transitioning from one activity to another in the classroom or at home can sometimes be hard because of his difficulty with modulating his emotions. His lack of emotional restraint can cause rapid mood changes, extreme excitability, and low frustration level, so he needs more preparation when change is required.

If he doesn't deal with change easily, understand this is a trait that will probably not change measurably. You just can't dump a request on an affected child without giving him time to deal with the change. Give him more time before walking out the door, saying, "Ryan, put your shoes on when the bell goes off on the timer, because we're leaving in 10 minutes to go to the store." Use a kitchen timer, set it for five minutes, and put it near him, especially if he's watching TV or playing with his toys. Check back in a few minutes to see if his shoes are on. If not, stop what he is doing and say, "Ryan, put your shoes on your feet now," and don't leave until he's done. Remember that oral directions need to be specific, and you must have your child's attention.

Review and Tips

- Children with ADHD do not handle change well—have a plan before an outing.

- These children have difficulty gauging time. A calendar or chart can help them visualize when the trip will take place.

- For short trips, such as going to the store, give your child a few minutes, if possible, to prepare for the change in activity.

Getting Ready for School— It's Never Enough Time

One common problem shared by parents is getting their child ready for school. Getting him up, bathed, dressed, fed, and out the door before the bus comes, or in front of the school before the bell rings can be a daily challenge. Yelling, screaming, crying, pushing, locking bedroom doors, locking car doors, and leaving homework on the counter are only some of the morning "challenges" parents deal with.

Why are these children so difficult to get ready for school, and why does it seem there is never enough time? The answer can be understood by reviewing common traits found in these children.

Sleep Time

They are not easy to get to sleep or awaken. They need greater parental monitoring than unaffected children do. When in bed, many children with ADHD have a hard time getting to sleep. They may play beyond their bedtime, toss in bed, run up and down the hall, and keep siblings and parents awake. Many children show signs of "pre-sleep agitation" (Taylor 1994). Pre-sleep agitation is a "significant lengthening of the time spent trying to get to sleep," and can involve the wearing off of medication at bedtime. An average affected child can take up to 45 minutes to get to sleep, which is twice as long as unaffected children take. Once asleep, they have shallow or short periods of sleep rather than a regular restful night of sleep, and some may rise early in the morning ready to start their day. Older children and adolescents can have trouble both settling down at night *and* arising in the morning (Quinn 1997).

The sleep patterns can be irregular, with some children sleeping so deeply that they are hard to awaken, so they often wet their beds. Others have restless nights. When you awaken your child for school, you probably find either a very sound sleeper who is hard to awaken, or a tired and cranky child who hasn't had enough deep sleep. Regular sleep deprivation, like that experienced by many children with ADHD, can affect mood as well as school performance. These children are sometimes described by teachers as tired and sluggish, and become mentally fatigued from lack of rest. Some are placed on medication to help them settle down at night so they can get to sleep.

Medication can both contribute to and help correct this problem. For children who are overaroused, methylphenidate (Ritalin) may normalize sleep patterns and allow them to settle down at night and awaken in the morning. If your child is on a stimulant like Ritalin, and his insomnia has worsened, this problem can be corrected by decreasing caffeine (cola drinks, coffee, candy), and increasing exercise during the daytime but not evenings (Quinn 1997). If his insomnia continues, talk to his doctor to evaluate whether the insomnia is an adverse effect of the drug, or is due to the recurrence of behavioral difficulties as the medication effect subsides.

Some children on stimulants can experience what's called a *rebound effect.* They are even more hyperactive and inattentive as the medication wears off than before taking the medication. A possible rebound effect can be helped by giving the child a small evening dose an hour before bedtime; however, stimulant rebound effects are dose-related, but are not generally a significant problem for the majority of children (Green 1991). Confer with your doctor if you have questions about these issues (see chapter 7 on medications for further discussion).

Bathroom Time

Bathroom time can be a parent's worst nightmare. These children need close monitoring to ensure they don't fiddle the morning away in the bathroom. They will play with the water, make faces in the mirror, and not do what needs to be done to get ready for school, while family members wait for the child to finish. Instead of this being a time for him to slowly prepare himself for the new day, it can become a battle zone for the entire family.

Affected children are easily distracted and can fixate on tasks (usually not the tasks that are important at the time). Use visual reminders and a kitchen timer to keep your child more focused. Set the kitchen timer for 15 minutes, and praise him or provide a token when the chore is completed within the allotted time. Token systems like charts are generally effective for children up to age 12.

Time-Keepers

Children with ADHD have a poor sense of time, which can affect not only their planning of school projects, but day-to-day activities like getting ready for school. This is why kitchen timers and visual reminders can help them stay more focused. Minimize distractions like watching cartoons or playing with toys until your child is dressed for school. You can say, "The TV doesn't go on until you are ready for school." It can be a wake-up call to get ready for school. Allow additional time for him in the morning—he will not usually run on the same time clock as his siblings.

Medication

Parents whose children are on a stimulant medication (Ritalin, Dexedrine, or Adderall) should confer with their child's doctor about giving the medication before the morning activities to help the child be more focused and attentive. He may need additional time in the morning for the medication to take effect (20–45 minutes). Speak with your child's doctor about ways to use medication to help your child be more successful getting ready for school.

Review and Tips

- These children often require more time in the morning to get ready for school. Get your child up 15 to 20 minutes earlier if you're running late.

- Consult with the doctor if your child has difficulty getting to sleep. Remember, "sleep agitation" is common and medication can sometimes be helpful.

- Tokens, charts, and a timer may help affected children stay more focused while getting ready for school.

Sitting Down for Breakfast Can Be World War III

Breakfast time is not always relaxing. However, a morning meal helps the child perform well throughout the day and should not be missed. Some children who go to school with an empty stomach have difficulty doing well in school.

Parents talk about breakfast being a time of ongoing negative interchanges between other family members and the affected child, and the morning atmosphere can set the mood for everyone. If the morning is difficult, your child will leave the house upset, taking his anger to school with him. Here are some time-tested ideas to help him focus at breakfast.

Table Rules

Provide structure at the breakfast table so your child is able to eat his meal. He can become distracted by toys, cartoons, or any number of other things other than what is most important—eating the morning meal. Table rules need to be established and enforced. Breakfast is not a time to play with a toy, crawl back and forth under the table, yell or fight with siblings, or talk with a friend on the telephone. Laminate table rules and put them on the table—it should not be a long list, but be clear about your expectations. The level of disruption or distraction your child causes or experiences will dictate the kinds of rules. Simple rules could be *Do not play with toys at the breakfast table, Stay in your seat until you are finished,* or *When your plate is clear, you can watch TV.* What's important is that he understands what your rules are and that they will be enforced.

Time-Keepers

As covered in the previous section, children with ADHD have great difficulty with time management, so structure and routine activities can help your child stay focused on eating his breakfast and not letting time get away from him. Use a kitchen timer to reinforce the importance of time.

Catch Him Being Good

Catch your child being good. If he is eating breakfast and following table rules, give him verbal praise such as "Bobby, thank you for sitting in your chair and finishing your breakfast." With younger children you can reinforce verbal praise with a token system (*Stars, Beans in a Jar*). Have a chart on the refrigerator, and each morning your child follows the table rules, a star is put on his chart. After getting three stars in a row, for example, he can pick something he has earned from a wish list.

Beans in a Jar is a technique some parents find helpful. The parent places near the breakfast table a jar where beans are dropped when the child is observed following table rules. That morning or later in the day, the beans are counted and the number is posted on a chart. Like *Stars*, the beans go towards special privileges or activities on the wish list. The wish list doesn't need to be material things. It can be special time with Dad, picking a favorite TV program to watch, or staying up an extra half-hour at night for the remainder of the week.

Good parenting needs to attend to both the positive and negative things a child does; unfortunately, affected children generally do more things to draw negative attention, so pay special attention to your child's good behavior.

Medication

If your child is on a stimulant such as Ritalin, administer the medication just before or during breakfast. Administration of Ritalin during mealtime does not appear to adversely affect its absorption and may alleviate problems with appetite suppression. Likewise, when at school, the afternoon dose should be given just before or during lunchtime. If your child does show decreased appetite, have him take the medication after the meal and take supplemental calories with the meal. Also provide frequent small high-calorie nutritious snacks or liquid supplements (see chapter 7, "What Side

Effects Might I Expect My Child to Have on Stimulants?" for detailed discussions regarding medication and mealtime).

Breakfast can be an enjoyable time, but you may need to put additional time into setting up a proper environment.

Review and Tips

- A morning meal is critical for your child to perform well at school, and must be your priority. Provide a balance of protein and carbohydrates (egg with toast, fruit with cereal)—studies suggest that a combination of protein with carbohydrates is best for maximizing attention and concentration in the classroom.

- Provide a routine for breakfast, and limit distractions until the child has finished his morning meal (no TV, telephone conversation, or toys on the table).

- Check with the doctor if your child's appetite changes after being placed on medication—sometimes medications can reduce appetite.

- Take time to praise your child when he follows table rules and finishes his breakfast.

- A table chart can help reinforce the rules for younger children. Use a kitchen timer to help your child manage time. A timer can help him stay focused and attend to what is most important at the time—finishing his breakfast.

Getting Ready for Bed Can Be a Nightly Battle

Bedtime can be a difficult time for both the parent and child. As mentioned previously, these children often have difficulty settling down for bed.

One parent compared getting her child ready for bed to putting an unwilling gorilla in his cage. "He never wants to go to bed, and when I insist, he throws a major tantrum. I have to chase him down and then watch over him until he finally falls asleep." This six-year-old child had a history of sleep-based problems since infancy, and his single mother, exhausted and struggling, deeply resented him. She loved him but felt drained by his behaviors. Because of his difficulties going to bed, she couldn't keep a baby-sitter for any length of time. "They will come a couple of times, but that's it."

Below are some suggestions that may help you find respite from nightly bedtime battles.

Pre-Bed Rituals

Bedtime problems can be improved by providing regular bedtime rituals or routines (brushing teeth, bathing, getting a drink, etc.). All children perform best when things are routine and there isn't much change from day to day, and younger children require more consistency and routine than older children. A five- or six-year-old can be flustered if the teacher changes her hairdo.

These children don't deal well with change. When your child is asked to turn off the TV, put away his toy, and get ready for bed, he is being asked to make a change. He needs preparation time if possible. If you suddenly ask him to stop what he's doing and do something else with little warning, he'll probably rebel. Anticipate when he needs to take his bath and provide some time for him to mentally prepare for the activity. Provide verbal reminders 15 minutes before he needs to stop what he's doing and get ready for bed. Support verbal reminders by using a kitchen timer or reward system to help him use more self-control when asked to get ready for bed.

Infants and toddlers with ADHD often present unique challenges when addressing sleeping difficulties. Some infants are *regulatory-disordered* and have difficulty not only with sleep, but with self-consoling, feeding, arousal, mood regulation, and transitions (Quinn 1997). Sleeping problems may be a prominent feature with these infants. They may never sleep through the night and will frequently awake during the night. A toddler can also have bedtime difficulties. He is often hard to get to bed because he is overaroused, sometimes aggressive and oppositional, and has a low frustration level. Those areas that seem most problematic are elevated in toddlers, e.g., hyperactivity and impulsivity, so even with the best of plans, a parent will find settling down her toddler at bedtime troublesome. Even so, it can still be helpful to establish routines at an early age that the child can follow throughout childhood.

Bedtime rituals for older children (five to 11 years) should include a quiet activity before the child retires for bed, such as a warm bath, cuddling up with a favorite stuffed animal, or a storybook. A warm bath can help facilitate a natural sleeping agent, melatonin, which helps prepare the body for sleep. One parent put a timer on the child's bed lamp that went off after 20 minutes. The light going off was a reminder to the child that it was time to go to sleep. Check later to see if your child is in his bed with the lights turned off, and if he is, reward him for complying with bedtime rules.

We discourage changing the bedtime hour on weekends while school is in session, except for special occasions. If your child insists on staying up late, do it Friday night, not Saturday. Even children who are good sleepers may be unable to fall asleep at their usual time on Sunday night if their sleeping schedule is changed. This can be especially true for children with sleep difficulties. Because they have stayed up later on Saturday night and slept in on Sunday, they are not ready for sleep Sunday night. They may awake Monday morning and go to school, but do their schoolwork feeling a little tired.

Teenagers often have difficulty going to sleep. Just like adults, they need a transition period before getting into bed and falling asleep. An adolescent's day is often filled with school, work, and social activities and, like a busy adult, needs to block off the hour before bedtime to slow down. Homework should be done early so he doesn't work right up to bedtime. He shouldn't do activities that arouse the body: no exercising, watching TV, playing on the computer, or eating a large meal an hour before bedtime (small snacks are generally not a problem). Encourage him to deal with worrisome thoughts earlier in the evening and not near bedtime. One teenager shared that the only time he had for worrying was when he went to bed, which, unfortunately, kept him awake. He was assigned a time of the day shortly after dinner for worrying, and was encouraged to limit his structured "worry time" to 45 minutes. This particular teenager found this artificial time helpful, but others think it stupid and will not participate. This intervention can be helpful for teenagers who become very anxious and obsess over thoughts or feelings.

The unaffected teenager can have difficulty going to sleep at a normal time, but affected teenagers can have more chronic problems. Frequent difficulty falling asleep at night and waking in the morning can cause fatigue during the day or yawning when concentration is required, such as during school tasks. The adolescent will often sleep in after an unsatisfactory night's sleep, and take naps each day, all in an attempt to get needed hours of rest. Unfortunately, this usually disrupts the sleep-wake cycle and has the opposite effect of causing more sleeping problems. Find ways to help your teenager get a good night's sleep. Medication can often be helpful in addressing arousal behavior, and he will often sleep better. He should be encouraged to take a warm shower and read a pleasurable book before going to bed (turn off the TV and no computer time!). Books on sleeping disorders often suggest that one should not read in bed; this is difficult to control with teenagers. If the reading material is not stimulating, it can help an adolescent go to sleep. Teenagers seem to spend a lot of time in their bedroom, and reading and doing schoolwork on the bed, whether stimulating or not, is a common behavior that is difficult to change.

You may be less successful with your teenager than with his younger brother, but you are fighting both normal developmental sleep patterns as well as ADHD arousal difficulties.

Insomnia

Factors other than ADHD can cause sleep disorders, including anxiety, depression, drugs (CNS depressants, stimulants, hypnotics), and chronic alcoholism. Some sleep-disturbing drugs are prescribed for legitimate medical problems like asthma, seizures, cancer, and thyroid dysfunction. If your child is being medicated for a medical condition, talk with his doctor about possible side effects. The reader is encouraged to review "My Child with ADHD Doesn't Sleep Well—What Should I Do About It?" in chapter 7 for a detailed discussion of medications helpful in addressing this concern.

Review and Tips

- All children do best when there are routine rituals at bedtime. Try to keep a regular bedtime hour and structure activities such as brushing teeth, taking a bath, etc.

- Recognize that these children generally require more preparation time when making changes. Transitioning from watching TV to getting ready for bed is a change. Remind your child that bedtime is coming up, which gives him time to mentally prepare for the change.

- Establish a reward system to reinforce positive bedtime behaviors. Let your child know what behavior is expected and then reward him when he follows the bedtime rules.

- Speak with your child's doctor about the appropriateness of medication if your child is experiencing serious and long-term problems settling down for bed.

His Sister and Brother Want to Live Next Door

Siblings are often put on the back burner while their parents deal with the affected child. A brother or sister, feeling second fiddle to their "bratty brother," may resent their sibling "who gets away with murder." Many siblings in counseling will express anger, jealousy, and generalized unhappiness because of the home situation. These conflicts can be more of a problem when the child with ADHD is young; however, affected adolescents can continue to have great difficulty with their younger siblings. A contributing factor to sibling conflicts is that affected children are often developmentally younger than their chronological age, so they will have more conflicts with younger siblings than unaffected children would. One mother shared that her 15-year-old child with ADHD acted the same age as his 11-year-old brother.

Siblings tend to grow tired and become impatient with their difficult brother or sister. One 14-year-old boy talked about his eight-year-old brother with ADHD, saying he "makes me want to kill him." This boy saw his affected brother getting away with things that he got punished for, and worst of all, "Mom makes excuses for him because he has ADHD." Siblings can hold onto anger and sometimes get physical with an affected brother or sister. An affected child can also be abusive with siblings. One brother and sister shared in counseling that their teenage brother would threaten them with violence, yell and scream at their mother, and make them "want to live next door."

If you have other children who live at home, pay attention to their concerns and frustrations. You are probably thinking, "I do care, but they don't believe me!" At times, family counseling will be needed to address ongoing conflictual patterns that have developed in the family. You may not be able to solve this problem by yourself, and it can become serious if it's not addressed.

Try the following techniques to deal with troublesome sibling issues.

Find Special Time

Your other children need your attention. They may not need as much day-to-day attention, but they require your time. All children, to grow up healthy, need their parents' support. They may not have significant problems with attention or difficulties regulating impulses and their moods, but they can't raise themselves. You are the most important person in their lives, and no one else can replace you. You say, "I want to be there for them, but how can I when my child with ADHD takes so much of my energy and attention?"

Put special time on your calendar for the siblings. It doesn't have to be a lot of time, but it needs to be on a regular basis. Lie on the bed together and talk alone with your unaffected child, and do it regularly, or provide a procedure to assure this time is available if needed. Let the affected child and other siblings know that this is a special time and you two are not to be disturbed. Your affected child may want to ruin this special time for his sibling, so make sure he understands that being disturbed will not be tolerated. These children often have greater difficulty entertaining themselves alone, so you may tell him that if he entertains himself without disturbing you, you will put a star on his chart or add additional beans to his jar (refer to previous sections on *Star Chart* and *Beans in a Jar*).

Remember that affected children are poor time managers. Help your child deal with this time alone by setting a kitchen timer for 15 minutes or whatever time you've allotted (initially limit the private talk with the sibling to 10 to 15 minutes, and slowly build up the time if needed). Let your child with ADHD know he can't knock on the bedroom door or ask a question until the bell on the timer rings. If he disturbs you before the bell rings, he should be given one warning. The next time it happens, put him in time-out or take away a privilege. Follow through on your consequences because he will continue to disturb you until he knows you mean business.

This process can also help him learn to deal with delayed gratification: you are not always at his beck and call. These children have a hard time delaying thoughts or actions, which often leads to conflicts with peers and adults. It's important for them to learn to wait their turn, share time, and to entertain themselves.

No One Wants to Be Abused

Siblings often feel their time is not protected and that their affected brother or sister runs the house and "nothing happens." Children with ADHD can be intrusive, interrupting a sister's time on the phone with a girlfriend or dominate a birthday party for a younger brother.

No one wants to feel abused. Siblings need to know that the parent will be the gatekeeper and will not allow the affected child to come and go when or where he pleases. If you don't put limits on your child, his siblings will find their own way to take care of the problem. Unfortunately, their solutions often involve some level of hostility or violence.

Your child needs to understand, and it needs to be reinforced by you, that his brothers and sisters have a right to private time, and their property needs to be respected. He must respect a closed bedroom or bathroom door and not open it without knocking, and not interrupt when his sister is on the phone, or take things without asking. You may need to set up a reward system or punishment to help address disrespectful behaviors towards siblings. These children can learn ways to be less impulsive and more respectful of their sibling's space. It just will take more time and effort.

Brothers and Sisters Need a Vacation, Too

Brothers and sisters need a vacation from their sibling from time to time. Unlike you, they didn't sign on for life. They probably don't have the patience or motivation to try to understand their sibling's disability. They generally do well, but after a while, a vacation away from home is good for everyone involved—we don't necessarily mean a real vacation, but an overnight visit with a friend, an afternoon at the park without the sibling, or a ride to the show with a friend. Brainstorm with your children. They can be creative in coming up with activities that give them a vacation from their sibling. One wanted to have an hour a day in his bedroom without being disturbed by his brother.

Lastly, if possible, do not use an older sibling too often to baby-sit the affected child. This is not fair for him or the older sibling. Children with ADHD can be very demanding of a caretaker's time, and the older brother or sister often doesn't have the patience to deal alone with the "bratty" sibling. Also, the affected child will "push more buttons" with a sibling than with an outsider.

Review and Tips

- Attend to the feelings of siblings. They can sometimes feel they are ignored or not listened to by parents.

- Provide separate time alone for siblings. Set up times on the calendar or during the day that is their time. It doesn't have to be for long periods; however, the special time should be regular, and the sibling should feel this is a priority for you.

- Allow time for siblings to have "away" time from their affected brother or sister. It can be time in their room that is off-limits to the affected sibling, or time away from home with a friend. Take the sibling to the store alone or on a special errand by him- or herself. You can use this time to talk about his day or his concerns.

He Minds His Dad Better Than Me

Mothers and fathers are often puzzled as to why their child minds Dad better than Mom. Sometimes this puzzlement will present itself as anger. A mother will feel angry because the father thinks it's her fault the child doesn't mind. The wife, at the end of her rope, will drag Dad into our offices hoping we will convince her husband that she's not a weak or ineffective parent. Dad, on the other hand, will often say that, "I have no problem getting Steven to do what I want him to do. He pays attention to me, but not his mother," or "He does the things he does because his mother is unable to discipline him." This difference in perception can create serious marital problems, which is discussed in more detail under "Our Marriage Needs Some Attention" in this chapter. Generally, however, most parents recognize their child has a disability but want information to better understand why he minds Dad better than Mom.

Why is hard to explain. Russell Barkley writes that in most families the mother is the primary caretaker and carries most of the responsibility for raising the child. The parent who needs to tackle the behavior deficits of the child will have the most conflicts with that child (Barkley 1995). Consequently, he will challenge the mother in most cases. Barkley also suggests that mothers are more likely to use reasoning or affection to try to change or gain their child's compliance. However, because these children have difficulty with instructions and are not as sensitive to praise as others, it is generally not a good motivator. Fathers, on the other hand, talk less and impose swifter discipline for inappropriate behaviors. The father's size, deeper voice, and physical presence may be intimidating to the child, leading to more compliance and attentive behavior when given instructions. Barkley goes on to conclude that fathers and male professionals need to recognize that affected children *do* respond differently to Mom and Dad.

The end result can often be that the father blames the mother for her problems with the child, and does not see that a great many problems stem from their child's disorder. In fact, because of this difference in perception, some fathers will deny and question his diagnosis. In counseling, a good amount of time is devoted to getting the parents to see the problem the same way. These children are hard enough to raise without having the parents fight and question each other's motives and judgment.

Any child will take advantage of parents bickering and fighting over them. It's important that you and your partner are in agreement when dealing with your child. Recognize that there are differences in parenting styles between many mothers and fathers, but you have a common interest in working together. If you are in serious disagreement with your mate, counseling may help resolve these differences. Your child needs not only your support, but you need each other's support.

An overwhelmed mother can ask the father to take over more responsibilities. The father can take over activities that cause conflicts between the mother and child, such as homework, getting ready for bed, or cleaning off the kitchen table after dinner. If the father lives outside of the home, but in the same neighborhood, the parents may want to consider dividing the week with their child. He can be with Dad, for example, Thursday through Sunday every other week, so Mom can have time to recuperate and have time to herself. This intervention can be successful when there are serious conflicts between a child and one of the parents. It also can help the other parent take on a larger parental role. The non-custodial parent will see that the child does do those things the custodial parent complains about, and it's not just the parent's fault.

Review and Tips

- If there are significant differences in opinion over parenting, seek professional counseling to help you deal with your differences. All children can be masters at manipulating parents to their advantage.

- A father's size, voice, and general presence, when compared to the mother's, are many times more intimidating. Reasoning and persuasion, often used by mothers, are generally less effective with affected children.

- The mother is often the primary caretaker, so she is the parent who "taxes the behavioral deficits" of the affected child the most (Barkley 1995). Consequently, she will be challenged more and tested more.

- All parents need a short vacation from their children. Try to divide parental responsibilities and trade back and forth with activities that are especially problematic for your child.

Homework Is a Family Mission

This subject comes up frequently in family discussions when parents talk about problems in school. The child is asked to be attentive, not impulsive, and focused on his homework. Getting him to pay attention in the classroom can be a challenge, but asking him to attend after school is especially difficult.

Struggles over homework can become more intense as he advances in grades. More written work and projects such as book reports, long-term projects, and daily assignments are required. Homework is generally the norm in upper grades, necessitating not only efficient use of time, but also understanding and comprehension of the assignment. These children are not good managers of time and they don't always attend or understand directions or concepts given in the classroom. They will come home without a good understanding of what is asked of them, or they will have only part or none of the material required to finish the assignment. Parents often find themselves running to the school after the teacher has left and begging the custodian to let their child into his classroom to get the books and material needed to complete his homework assignments.

Here are suggestions that can be helpful in helping your child with homework.

Don't Jeopardize Your Relationship with Your Child

Your relationship with him is the most important thing, and it must take priority over his completing his homework. This is not to say that homework is not important, too. It can help him by reinforcing material learned at school as well as in developing skills that make him a more independent learner. However, it shouldn't cause so much stress in your family that it damages the long-term trust needed for you to successfully raise your child.

Homework is not easy for affected children. Your child needs to know that you understand this difficulty by your providing support and guidance to help him be more successful. Provide support by establishing a balance between furthering his education and maintaining a relationship that doesn't involve nightly battles about homework.

You May Not Be Able to Be His Teacher

Parents may make poor teachers of their own children, especially if they are dealing with the overwhelming stressors of parenting a child with ADHD. As one homeschooling parent shared, "My son was going to have a near-death experience at my hands if I continued teaching him." If you find it difficult to patiently teach your child, then provide support for him and don't do his teacher's job.

Parents sometimes say they feel pressured or obligated to make sure Bobby finishes his math so his teacher will not be upset with Bobby and think that they are irresponsible parents. They get into the role of being the teacher at home. This can sometimes lead to serious conflicts, with the child feeling angry and betrayed. One seventh-grader said that his "father is not his teacher, and he shouldn't act like he is!" This child wasn't just upset with his father because he made him do the homework, but because "all Dad does is ask about my homework." The relationship had become one-dimensional. He was no longer playing catch with his dad at night, going to the card shop to find new baseball cards, or riding bikes with his dad after work. The majority of conversations centered around homework. In one session, a dad said, "I make sure Don gets his homework done, no matter what happens." Unfortunately, this obligation had created serious conflicts between the father and his son. Like many parents who become the teacher at home, he spent much of their evening policing his child, and begging, pleading, or threatening him over the homework.

Parental Responsibility

What is your responsibility when it comes to homework? Sandra Rief, in her book *How to Reach and Teach ADD/ADHD Children,* offers some excellent guidelines (Rief 1993). Ms. Rief shares eight guidelines:

1. Provide a quiet place for your child to work, away from the TV.

2. Have appropriate materials, supplies, and lighting for homework.

3. Provide a place and system for checking the assignment calendar or homework sheet with the child. This list of things to check would also include school notices, permission slips, and other school communications.

4. Help the child prioritize activities and things to do in the evening.

5. Try to enforce as consistent a routine as possible (dinner, home-work, and bedtime).

6. Make sure books, completed homework, and binders are in the child's backpack for the next day.

7. Help the child write lists, schedules, and reminder notes.

8. Reward good organizational skills at home.

Nowhere does Ms. Rief suggest that the parent do the homework. Doing the homework is your child's responsibility. Your responsibility is to check to see that he is working in an environment that will minimize his problem behaviors and increase his productivity.

An important responsibility for the parent is to communicate with the teacher on a regular basis. Communicate with your child's teacher if your child is overloaded with homework. Sometimes the homework is too long or complicated, and as he advances in grade levels, the material can be too advanced for the parent to help. This is very important, because affected children, even though they want to be successful, can become overanxious. Because these children are not good problem solvers, this anxiety can lead to serious problems. Many children will show avoidance behaviors such as lying about what homework was assigned or leaving books at school. Attend to such behaviors, because they usually are early signs that the material is too difficult or the homework is too much.

These children will say they don't have homework. Let your child know that you will talk with his teacher if this pattern seems out of the ordinary. Sometimes he will honestly think no homework is required, and this may be true. At other times, however, he may be confused or simply doesn't want to be bothered.

The Homework May Be Too Hard or Long

Sometimes teachers give assignments without considering the special needs presented by some children, and they need some guidance in under-standing the unique difficulties of ADHD face with homework. You may need to talk to your child's teacher about accommodations for your child's special needs. Accommodations are made daily in the classroom, and you are not out of line requesting a meeting to discuss your homework concerns. Most of the time, the teacher will listen and make accommodations. However, as the child moves up in grades, this understanding is less common.

First take your concerns to the teacher if she does not understand your child's learning challenges; if you are still not being listened to, speak with the principal or the principal's supervisor at the district office. Your child has an identified disability and the school is obligated to make educational accommodations if his disorder is significantly or measurably interfering with his learning. You can request that your child be brought up for an educational review by a *student study team* or its equivalent in your school district.

The student study team meeting is often called when a child is having difficulty with his education. Generally the child's parent, teacher, principal, special education representative, and a school psychologist will be present at this meeting. Your child's progress will be covered and recommendations will be discussed to better help him in school. Your input is important, and a report from your child's doctor can help identify some of your child's medical needs.

However, he can't use ADHD as a crutch for not doing the schoolwork. An accommodation for homework, except on very special occasions, does not mean no homework at all. Affected children, like all children, need to learn ways to be more successful with homework.

Your role in relation to your child is as a loving coach, a person who gives guidance and provides structure for him to do his homework, not the person who plays on the field. You don't do his homework, he does. Provide support at home and be his advocate to ensure that accommodations, if warranted, are made at the school site.

Review and Tips

- Homework can be difficult for your child, and it can put a great amount of stress on the whole family. An assignment that would generally take a half-hour may end up taking more than an hour for an affected child because of difficulties with focused and sustained attention, as well as distractibility.

- Provide an environment in the home that can minimize ADHD behaviors. Set up a learning environment with few distractions. Put your child in a quiet area and break up the study period into small blocks of time.

- Remember, homework is your child's responsibility, not yours. You can provide guidance, but don't do the work for him. If the material is too difficult, ask for a conference with the teacher.

- Communicate regularly with your child's teacher. Let your child know that communication with his teacher will take place on a regular basis.

- Don't jeopardize your relationship with your child over homework. If need be, and you can afford it, hire a tutor after school to work with him.

Let's Not Talk about Going to the Store!

Taking an affected child to the store can be stressful, to say the least! Some children are less of a problem than others. In fact, a child with ADHD-I who is neither hyperactive, impulsive, or noncompliant generally does not stand out from the unaffected child during a shopping excursion. However, you probably turned to this section because your child is a problem in the store and causes you much frustration.

Going to the store will bring out many ADHD characteristics in your child. First, he can be impulsive and stubborn. He acts before thinking and doesn't like "no" for an answer. He will pull things off the shelf, run away and hide, or pester you until he gets what he wants. Second, affected children don't learn from their mistakes to the same degree as unaffected children. Knowing what the rules are, they may still make the same mistake over and over again. A child who is very impulsive may continue to touch items on a shelf, even after repeated warnings, and the parent may need to remind him a few minutes later not to touch the items. Third, they are highly distractible. Stores have a lot of items to keep the child's mind hopping, especially where toys or treats are available. Treats and toys are often placed at the height of six- to 10-year-olds so they will be sure to see them. An unaffected child will be attracted to an item but, given a warning by the parent, will move along. He may show some displeasure, but normally he is more easily manageable and remains little-noticed by customers or store employees. Fourth, a child with ADHD can be noncompliant. After being given a warning by the parent, he will often not leave the item alone and ignore or fight with the parent. Interactions between him and parent can escalate and attract attention. Fifth, he can have difficulty managing his emotions. When asked to stop or when reprimanded, he can suddenly go into a rage, falling on the floor or running around the store until physically restrained by the parent who, red-faced, swears never to take him to a store again, yet most parents will, praying and hoping the child behaves.

Experience suggests that he will continue to act up unless the parent makes changes. The suggestions given below may be helpful to parents when taking their child to the store.

Have a Plan

Never leave the house without a plan, especially for children with ADHD. They do best when there is structure and routine. Discuss what the store rules are with your child before leaving the house: "No running through the aisles, walk next to me, don't touch items on the shelf without my permission." You know which behaviors seem to be most difficult for your child, so set up a plan to address these concerns.

Rules on a Card

Put the store rules on a 3x5 card and keep it in your purse or pocket. When you are ready to leave the house, review the rules with your child and have him repeat them to you. When you do this, you are reinforcing the rules and your expectations for his behavior. You can review the rules again if necessary before getting out of the car to go into the store. We suggest the card be laminated—it makes the card more resistant to rain, slows down normal wear and tear, and discourages an upset child from trying to tear it up.

Take a Photo of the "Time-Out" Chair

Take a photo of the "time-out chair" and have it in your purse (turn to "Is My Child Noncompliant or Just Incompetent?" for discussion of time-out). You can discreetly show your child the photo by holding it in the palm of your hand. Don't escalate the situation by embarrassing him. Tell him ahead of time that when you show him the photo, it is a warning, and that the next time he misbehaves, there will be a consequence. He can be given consequences when he gets home or put in time-out at the store. We recommend immediate time-out over waiting until you get home. Phelan, an expert on ADHD, recommends some places for time-out: the grocery cart (for small children), a corner of the store, the store bathroom (not by self), right where you stand (holding your child's hand), in the car for a few minutes, or at the front of the store (Phelan, 1996). If you put your child in time-out, have him face you or stand in a corner of the store for 15 to 30 seconds with his hands folded and mouth closed. Your goal is to redirect his behavior, not to punish. When he complies by following the time-out rules, praise him and ask him what behavior he is to stop in the store; if he answers correctly, praise him again and finish shopping. By intervening immediately, you redirect your child's attention from the problem behavior to paying attention to you. If he doesn't behave, he again goes to time-out until he complies. You may need to provide more consequences at home if the situation seems unmanageable in the store. Unfortunately, there may be times when you need to forcefully take him out of the store before you finish shopping. If the other parent is present, he or she can sit with him in the car until you have finished shopping. If not, you may need to take your child home and finish shopping at another time.

If you would rather wait until you get home to administer the consequences, you might say something like, "When you get home you will have time-out. Stop running ahead and put your hand on the shopping cart and walk with me or there will be additional consequences" or "When you get home, you take five beans out of your jar." Again, if your child's behavior escalates, you may need to take him out of the store.

1–2–3 Magic

Phelan has developed an intervention that is one of our favorites with children two to 12 years of age (Phelan 1995). His intervention can be very effective with getting your child to *start* a behavior or *stop* a behavior. *Start* behaviors include things like cleaning the room, homework, eating, and going to bed. *Stop* behaviors include temper tantrums, whining, fighting, yelling, or running through store aisles.

When addressing *stop* behaviors, you use the counting procedure, "1–2–3." For *start* behaviors such as eating or going to bed, use a combination of tactics, such as a kitchen timer, charts, *Beans in a Jar*, etc., to monitor and reward compliant behavior.

How does *1–2–3 Magic* work? Let's say your five-year-old is having a tantrum on the store floor because you said no when asked to buy a toy. With *1–2–3 Magic* you hold up one finger, look at him and say, "That's 1." He doesn't care and keeps up his tantrum full force. So you let a few seconds pass, put up two fingers, and say, "That's 2." Perhaps he still continues his tantrum. After a few more seconds you hold up three fingers and say, "That's 3." He's had two chances to shape up, so a consequence is administered. Pick him up off the floor and firmly tell him he is going to have time-out. Put him in immediate time-out in the store or when you get home—we recommend immediate time-out. When you get home, you will have another fight when putting him in time-out. Immediate consequences are generally more powerful and effective than delayed consequences. Do not get emotional and don't talk. Simply use the counting method. No lecturing, no pleading, no yelling during this period!

This intervention can be quite effective with children with ADHD. They tend to misbehave more in public places than at home. Practice time-out at home so your child becomes familiar with the procedure. Also, practicing at home can help you learn to deal more effectively with his testing behaviors.

Reward Him for Being Good

Rewarding your child when he is good is very important. Unfortunately, parents don't always do this. When a child is following store rules, many times the parent fails to reward this good behavior through either verbal praise or a token. Even though praise and tokens seem not to be as effective with affected children as unaffected children, they can still work if used immediately. Rewarding good behavior can serve two purposes. One, the child is recognized for making good choices. Two, the process helps the parent move beyond just having negative interactions with him. He can make a lot of mistakes, and it is easy for a parent to pay attention only to her child's mistakes and not his successes.

Review and Tips

- Never go into a store without a plan! Children with ADHD need coaching more often than other children. Review the store rules with your child before getting out of the car.

- Have consequences for good and bad behavior. Children up to the age of 12 respond well to token systems. Your child earns special privilege or a treat for following the store rules. When he misbehaves, set up consequences on the spot or when you go home.

- *Photo of time-out chair* and *1–2–3 Magic* should be practiced at home so your child will understand the program when going into a store.

- Whatever program you choose for your child, follow through and don't make idle threats!

- Don't get emotional, just do it!

Our Marriage Needs Some Attention

Marital conflicts are common in families with children with ADHD. These children can put extreme stress on a marriage at times. How a couple handles their differences in raising their child is critical for his successful development. How couples resolve differences, make up, show affection or lack of affection between each other are important lessons their child learns from them.

John F. Taylor (1994), an authority on ADHD, suggests four patterns of marital reactions to problems presented by affected children. These four patterns are *denial, abuse, overinvolvement,* and *one-upsmanship.* It is not that uncommon to find one parent in *denial* about the child's disorder, even though both parents can be equally in denial. These children are at risk for *abuse* because of their behavior, and both parents can be abusive, depriving the child of a protector. When one parent is abusive, the nonabusive parent can become overly involved in the child's life or become self-righteous. *Overinvolvement* by one or both parents is a common reaction found in families. One parent may be so involved in the child's life that other family members are neglected. The less-involved parent will often try to compensate by being too uninvolved. The child will be ignored or blamed for the fights between the parents. *One-upsmanship* is a pattern where one parent criticizes the other and acts self-righteous and superior, so the other parent feels misunderstood and picked on.

When there are divisions between parents, Taylor notes, the child will often capitalize on this division by pitting one parent against the other. Knowing one parent is easier to convince than the other, he will ask that parent to do things he knows the other parent will say no to. He will be a "bulldozer," pushing everything out of the way until he gets what he wants. When he feels he has conquered, he can become tyrannical, making the parent feel abused and defeated.

These parental reactions can add stress to a marriage, leading sometimes to separation or divorce. If you find some of these patterns in your marriage, seek outside professional help—you may need help in identifying stressful areas of your marriage. However, if your partner will not go, go by yourself.

Here are some suggestions for strengthening your marriage while you parent your child with ADHD.

Taking Care of You Is Important

Take care of yourself, both emotionally and physically. As expressed throughout this book, affected children can be very demanding of a parent's time. Set time apart from your child to deal with your needs. If you don't take care of yourself, you can't take care of him.

On a calendar mark off times weekly when you will take care of yourself. Put an *X*, for example, one half-hour each day to exercise or take a quiet bath by yourself when the children are at school or have gone to bed. Pamper yourself. Block off time for lunch with a friend, a trip to the mall to shop, or a tennis game after work. This time doesn't have to be long or expensive, but it needs to be on a regular basis. If you don't mark off time for yourself, someone or something else will mark it off for you. You probably have appointments all month (doctor, teacher, Little League). Even working moms with little support can find some time for themselves—it's difficult, but the effort is critical for you and your child. Some of the suggestions above can still work for you. Try to get up a few minutes earlier in the morning and take a warm bath or participate in a morning TV exercise program. One working mom would practice yoga a few minutes each morning before the children woke up. She said it energized her and made her feel more in control of her body. Another mom was into photography and would quickly take pictures of still-life objects in the house three times a week. She kept an album of her pictures and would share them with friends. These kinds of activities help you connect with that part of you that is not *Mom*.

Do not lose your sense of self. Raising children and taking care of a family can often leave you with little time to think about your own needs. When your needs are not being met, you can become resentful, which is not good for those you love.

It's Okay to Say No

It's okay to say no to your child, husband, wife, or child's teacher. It may be difficult and you may look to others to give you permission. We joked about having a bumper sticker stating, *I'll be assertive, if you don't mind.* Accept the idea that you are not someone's doorbell that can be pushed whenever it pleases them. You have rights, and when you feel harassed by others requesting your time, saying no sometimes keeps your emotional and physical tank from going empty. There is no way you can be all things to all people all the time. Give yourself permission to say no and then feel okay about doing it. Try with small and unimportant things, such as with getting the dishes put away before a certain time, or making the youngest child's bed before leaving for work. Say no to these chores or others until you feel it's a *want* and not a *should*. You probably have a list of things that you could start with.

Stop Trying to Control Things

If there's one thing that aging teaches us, it's that there is little that we can really control. As much as we want to control events or people's actions, all we can really control are our own reactions and behaviors. There are things in your marriage and actions by your child that you may not be able to change. Your child and spouse will do upsetting things despite all your hard work and good intentions. Your affected child will often be forgetful, impulsive, and disorganized, and you may be able to minimize these traits, but you can't erase them. These traits are part of who he is; when you accept this fact, you can love him for himself. Your spouse may never be as understanding or knowledgeable about ADHD as you. He may be more volatile, impulsive, and less sensitive to your child's challenges than you. You can try to involve him in your readings and education on ADHD, but in the end, it's his decision to learn or not learn. We deal with many couples where one partner invests most of the time in reading, going to seminars on ADHD, and attending support groups. They try to change their partner by example and sometimes shame, but the partner will change only when he sees a need for himself. Remember the old saying, *You can't push a string.* You can try to lead by example, but you can't control whether your partner wants to follow.

Often marital stress is created when one spouse tries to change the other. That's not to say people can't make changes, but rather, don't put additional stress on yourself by trying to make your partner into someone else. Everyone comes with his or her own temperament and personality, and it doesn't change much. Change is ultimately the partner's decision.

Don't Neglect Your Partner

In addition to not neglecting yourself, don't neglect your partner. Your child is one member in your family—an important member—but not the only one. Put time into your marriage. Block off time to do special and private things with your partner, such as taking walks, driving out of town, or having quiet moments together after the children go to bed. A marriage needs attention and if ignored or put on the back burner, it will slowly cool down. You can find many books in the self-help section of the local bookstore to find ways to keep your marriage alive.

Try to Share Parenting

Sharing responsibility for raising your child can take a lot of stress off of a marriage. By checking with each other over decisions related to the child, taking responsibility for him when the other parent is burned out, or recognizing the other parent may have some good points, parents can create a more harmonious marriage.

When a couple makes a decision to raise their child, they must recognize that they will not always see a problem the same way. Reasons for differences in opinion or perception can be numerous: temperament, upbringing, knowledge of ADHD, or level of involvement of a parent in a child's day-to-day life. How a couple resolves these differences is important not only for the quality of their marriage, but for the healthy development of their child.

Some marriages make co-parenting difficult. A parent whose job puts him out of town a lot or late coming home at night may not have the energy or time to be involved in day-to-day decisions. In such relationships, we recommend that one parent be the primary decision-maker and the other parent support that parent's decisions.

Review and Tips

- Your marriage, like your child, needs attention, so don't neglect it.

- Children with ADHD can add great stress to a marriage. If your marriage is at risk, seek out marriage counseling with a professional familiar with ADHD.

- Part of taking care of your marriage is taking care of you. Learn to say no and understand that you didn't marry yourself, so don't expect a mirror image in your partner. You will have differences in opinion. This is to be expected.

I Am a Single Parent—Help!

No job is more demanding than being a single parent. Our hat is off to you! Each and every time we counsel single mothers and fathers, we try to close with a compliment on a job well-done. No matter how many mistakes they may make, they have found the time and the energy to seek outside advice to be a better parent.

An affected child can be demanding on a single parent's time and energy. The single parent often has a limited income and is tired from holding down an eight- to 12-hour job. The mother will often drag herself and the child into our offices, disheveled from juggling multiple tasks, including picking up the child at daycare, driving to the office, and grabbing a snack to pacify him until dinnertime. The mother plops herself down on the office couch, looks up with pleading and sometimes questioning eyes, and hopes this hour is worth her time and energy. She performs daily activities with little support. She must put her trust in others for the care of her child, and she may not have a family member nearby or an older child to help with the responsibility.

Listed below are the primary concerns and challenges shared by single parents who come for counseling.

I Can't Find a Baby-sitter

Finding a baby-sitter to care for a child with ADHD can be a real challenge for single parents. Frankly, couples even have a difficult time finding a baby-sitter to return more than once. However, for the single parent this problem can be serious and very stressful. Unlike the intact family, a single parent doesn't have someone to watch the child for a variety of needs, such as going to the doctor, going out on a date, interviewing for a job, or having the freedom to take a walk and be by herself.

These children are not easy to take care of, and neighbors and baby-sitters are not running to the parent's door to help. In many cases, the grandparents are out of town or may not have the health or energy to watch their grandchild for any length of time. Sometimes transportation and time make it difficult even if the grandparents are willing. You are probably saying to yourself, "Okay, I know this, what can I do?"

Contact a national support organization for families affected by ADHD in your area, like CHADD (Children and Adults with Attention-Deficit/Hyperactivity Disorder), or contact your child's school to possibly find names of adults or teenagers experienced with baby-sitting children with ADHD. Your child is not the only one who has ADHD at his school, and his teacher, school administrator, or school secretary may know other parents whose children have ADHD and can get you in touch with them. These parents may know of a good baby-sitter or be willing to trade baby-sitting times with you. One of these parents, like you, may be a single parent, and you can help each other out.

Set up a reward system for your child concerning expected rules when a baby-sitter is watching him. Discuss these rules with your child ahead of time and when the baby-sitter is present, and let him know that there will be rewards for good behavior and punishment if the rules are not followed.

Don't act guilty or pitiful when you leave your child with a baby-sitter. Your child will pick up these feelings and capitalize on them before you leave or when you get home. If you look nervous or apprehensive when leaving him with a baby-sitter, he will know, and your apprehension can elevate his anxiety, causing him to be more hyperactive or agitated than usual. Sometimes he will play the guilt card, dividing your decision to go out. Affected children can be experts at creating horror stories about how unfair the baby-sitter was and how you are so mean for leaving him. Use good judgment and question suspected behaviors by a baby-sitter that seem legitimate, but consider that the real problem may be that your child doesn't want you to leave.

He needs to learn to take directions from others and know that your needs are also important. He would be given the wrong message if he felt that you had no life outside of him, and you don't want to raise a selfish and self-centered child. What message are you sending your child if he feels that only *you* are capable of taking care of him? He can be taught ways to deal with your absence and take directions from others. He is at school a great deal of the day and seems to survive without you, so don't feel that after-school hours or weekends are any different. There will be times when you need to do things without your child, so finding someone to take care of him is important.

Dating? Say That Word Again!

It's hard to date when you're a single parent—child with ADHD or no ADHD. After working long hours and raising a very demanding child, you may have little energy or desire to date. However, when the opportunity does present itself, it's difficult to find and hold onto baby-sitters who will watch a difficult child, let alone explaining your child's behavior to your date, and leaving the house without major disruptions.

A frustrated single parent pleaded, "I'm single, but I'm not dead. I need companionship!" There are steps you can take that will help. One, don't feel guilty for wanting adult companionship. This is normal human behavior, and without it, you could be less effective as a parent. Two, let your child know earlier in the week, if he is school age, that you will be doing something special with a friend one day on the weekend. Children with ADHD have difficulty with changes, so give your child time to deal with your absence. Third, provide a special movie, privilege, or "dating toy" to keep him entertained while you're gone. The "dating toy" is a special toy that only is played with when you are out on a date, so it's special and the child doesn't get bored with it. These children get bored easily, so use it sparingly. Fourth, tell your child when you're going to be home and be home by that time. Don't break your promise or he will find it more difficult to believe you—trust is very important. Fifth, develop a routine around dating. Try to have the same baby-sitter, special privilege, or special meal. Sixth, minimize negative behavior by giving it minimal attention, and reinforce positive behavior. Set up a dating chart that goes towards a special treat or privilege. Tokens are very effective with children up to the age of 12.

Where Do I Go When I Want to Explode?

Establish ahead of time a lifeline for times when you feel you're going to explode. Make contacts either through your child's school, CHADD, close neighbor, or relative. Call these folks when you feel you must get away, especially when you are afraid you might hurt your child.

All parents need time alone. Don't wait until a crisis comes up before you set up your lifeline. You may want to trade baby-sitting with a friend or support person from CHADD. You baby-sit their child, for example, two evenings a month if they will reciprocate. Even the thought that *Next Wednesday evening, I can have coffee with Sally* can relieve stress.

If you feel your child is at immediate risk and you cannot contact a support person, call 911 and share your problem with them. An officer can be sent to your home to give you support. Obviously, this is a rare intervention, but sometimes it's necessary.

My Partner Isn't Patient or Understanding

"He thinks I spoil Brian," said a mother of a 10-year-old boy, "and my partner thinks the only reason Brian acts out is because I don't make him mind." This mother had been in a nine-month relationship with this man. They recently moved in together and she didn't feel supported or understood by him.

This pattern is similar to that of other mothers and fathers seen in counseling. The parent feels misunderstood and asks for the therapist's help in convincing the partner that the child has ADHD, and is not just spoiled. Part of the problem stems from blended family issues, e.g., the new member trying to establish authority in the family unit, the partner not being familiar with age-appropriate behaviors, and the parent trying to balance time between the new love relationship and the child. The new partner may not be knowledgeable about ADHD and see the child's behaviors as purposeful and noncompliant, rather than understanding that these children forget and do things impulsively.

If the relationship is to be healthy for the child, both the parent and partner should attend an ADHD support group or seek counseling to address their differences in perception (refer to "Our Marriage Needs Some Attention" for suggested ideas). Don't stay in a relationship where the partner is verbally, physically, or emotionally abusive to you or your child. If he or she is unwilling to go to a support group or read material on ADHD, then make it very clear what behaviors you will accept with your child. You are your child's advocate. There are national support groups for women, such as *Women Escaping A Violent Environment (WEAVE)*, that can refer you to local support groups in your area for counseling and advice. Often hospitals have referral lists of counselors or support groups. Don't hesitate to call if violence or verbal abuse is a common pattern in your home. Violence and/or verbal abuse can have long-term negative effects both on you and your child's emotional development.

Try to Be Supportive, Not Enabling

Your partner may see things that you have not noticed that can be a positive contribution to the care of your child. A loving and supportive partner can sometimes point out problems the parent may not recognize because of the parent's enmeshment with her child.

I Feel Alone and Nobody Cares

Being a single parent can be a lonely job. You may have no one to talk to about your frustrations and important decisions. You may feel lonely for adult companionship but are unsure how to find it. You can feel victimized by your child, loving him but at the same time feeling limited in your choices by his behavior. You get calls from school, comments by co-workers, and criticism from relatives about the way you raise your child. You feel guilty, not listened to, and convinced that no one cares.

Seek support if you find yourself feeling down a lot of the time. Depression doesn't suddenly show its ugly face but creeps up when you least expect it. It has a way of distorting reality, making you overgeneralize and selectively recall only negative events. Like shaded glasses, it distorts reality, but you are convinced you are seeing it correctly.

If you feel you could be depressed, talk with your doctor. If you have no primary physician, call your local county mental health service and ask for a referral. Counties usually have mental health services ranging from inpatient psychiatric care to outpatient counseling. Private therapy is often costly; however, most mental health services have a sliding scale or no cost at all.

Review and Tips

- Being a single parent is a demanding responsibility.

- Finding a baby-sitter for an affected child can be challenging, so utilize your child's school or daycare agencies to find childcare.

- Leave your child with other caretakers. Children need to learn how to take directions from other adults besides their parent.

- Take care of yourself so you can better attend to your child's needs. Part of taking care of yourself is doing things apart from your child, like special time with adult friends or dating.

Summary

Children with ADHD do take more time than other children do, and you will usually spend more time and energy on your affected child than will parents of unaffected children.

Your child will need more supervision and direction, so don't go anywhere without a plan. Affected children are not self-starters and have difficulty with daily routines such as getting ready for school, going to the store, and finishing homework. You will need to have a plan for your child longer than for an unaffected child.

These children also need reminders, both visual and auditory, to help them *remember to remember.* Visual reminders such as written rules are simple and can be posted in the house. Verbal reminders can reinforce and help the child to remember. Affected children seem to perform best when there are time limits, so build within the reminders time limits. This is especially important with homework, chore completion, and transitioning from one activity to another. Use a kitchen timer or stopwatch to help set time limits and reinforce task completion.

Children with ADHD need to be told when they are being good. Catch your child being good—it's not always easy, but make sure you do compliment him—he needs parental praise like any child.

Be consistent with your child. All children respond to structure and consistency, especially with regard to consequences for incomplete work, anger outbursts, or any number of problem behaviors presented. Have positive consequences as well for completed work and when he makes positive choices.

This chapter has encouraged you to take care of yourself. Unless you practice self-care, you will be less effective in raising your child. The first step in being an effective and loving parent is to "heal thyself." Take care of those stresses in your life that are limiting your effectiveness as a parent.

6

My Child's in School—
Can I Tell You Some Stories!

Parents often feel sad, frustrated, and angry about their child's experience in school. They want it to be positive and rewarding; unfortunately, for many children with ADHD, it can be an unhappy experience.

Children who need to move around and get bored easily with routine activities are not good candidates for success in the average American classroom. Many of them are bright and energetic, but are failing and not reaching their potential in school. Because of difficulty with sustained attention, organization, time management, and impulsivity, these children can get in trouble at school and fall behind in their education.

The cognitive style of the affected child is qualitatively different from that of most people. His tendency to move from one thought to another and from one project to another without completion creates challenges in the school setting. He can be inattentive one moment, and be overly focused on an activity and thought the next (Hallowell and Ratey 1994). However, he is generally not focused on what is most important to focus on at the time. This pattern of over- or underfocusing leads to many incomplete assignments, missed lecture material, and poor test taking skills.

He often leaves the classroom having no idea what is due the next day or what materials he needs to finish the assignment, so doesn't take the books or papers needed to complete his homework. When questioned by his parents, he'll say he doesn't have homework. As he advances in grades, these problems can become very serious.

Parents, in trying to explain or understand their child's inconsistent performance and disruptive behaviors in the classroom, will go to more conferences with school staff than parents of unaffected children. Unrelenting frustration led one mother to therapy. She said, "My child's in school—can I tell you some stories!" The youngest of three siblings, this child was diagnosed with ADHD, as was his middle brother. His affected brother, three years older, had set the scene at school. Like many parents of children with ADHD, the mother felt misunderstood by her child's teachers and principal. She had met resistance from the school with the older sibling, and came to the therapist hoping to find better ways to communicate with the school.

Your child will spend a large percentage of his waking day in school. How you interact with his school and understand the educational challenges presented by children with ADHD can make an important difference in your child's school experience. The ideas presented in this chapter are intended to help you find solutions to make his school experience positive.

Should I Tell His Teacher He Has ADHD?

We recommend that you tell your child's teacher he has ADHD. Why? Affected children often present problem behaviors throughout their education to one degree or another. Research shows that they generally don't outgrow the disorder, but they present symptoms differently or to different degrees as they move through school. If your child's teachers know he has ADHD, they will be better prepared for some of the disruptive and educational challenges he presents. He may have difficulty with paper-and-pencil tasks, copying from the blackboard, listening and taking notes at the same time, remembering to turn in assignments, and following directions. Most teachers are caring and sensitive people, and when informed about the special needs of your child, will try to make accommodations. This seems to be especially true in primary grades where the "independent" learner is not the holy mantra of educators, and teachers seem more amenable to modifying a child's curriculum. Additionally, many children take medication, and a teacher's feedback is important so that the doctor can evaluate the appropriateness of the child's medication and change the dosage as needed.

Some parents want to give their child medication and not tell the teacher. We generally discourage this for two reasons. First, some medications have side effects, and the teacher can report to the parent or doctor any negative changes in the child's behavior. Secondly, teachers must be team members in the child's treatment. Most teachers feel more positive about the administration of the medication when they are informed and feel they have the confidence of the doctor and parent. Teachers who dispense medication may feel anxious and unsure about their role; however, when they understand the importance of their participation, they are generally less resistant. A child's teacher is the primary person who will need to remind him to take his medication, because younger children on stimulant medication may have difficulty remembering to take their afternoon dose.

Sometimes a parent may want to keep the medication a secret from school staff out of personal embarrassment. Embarrassment is not that uncommon, especially when the child is first placed on medication. One child's mother, a pediatrician, would meet her child at lunch to give him his pill. He was told by his mother not to tell the teacher he was taking Ritalin. Fortunately, with counseling, the mother accepted the importance of being honest with her child's teacher. Even this mother, who administers medication daily to patients, was embarrassed that others would know her child was taking Ritalin. All parents have similar feelings at one time or another. However, it's important to work through these feelings because a child's comfort in taking medication is often dependent on a parent's comfort with it.

A parent will sometimes hold off telling a teacher about the medication to test its effectiveness. The parent thinks the teacher will see improvement in the child just because he's on his pill, and not because the pill is doing what it was meant to do: stimulate underactive areas of the brain. It is true that a child will sometimes show improved behavior when given positive attention by his teacher, but this improvement generally lasts for only a short period of time. Over time, his inattentive and impulsive behaviors will again present themselves. Not telling his teacher he is on medication is usually a waste of time. Medications, such as stimulants, are fast-acting and the effects are usually noted quickly by the teacher. Frankly, teachers will guess a child is on medication when they observe a sudden change in his behavior.

Communication with your child's teacher is imperative. The majority of teachers will work with you if properly informed about your child's disorder.

Review and Tips

- Be honest with the teacher, and let her know your child has ADHD. Honesty is the first step towards positive communication.

- Your child's disorder will often manifest itself throughout his education. ADHD does not generally go away, but more often presents itself differently at different stages in a child's life.

- Your child's teacher can be an important player in your child's treatment. If he is taking medication, the teacher can monitor for possible side effects and/or the effectiveness of the medication.

I Think I Should Get a Diploma, Too!

Most parents of affected children deserve a diploma along with their child. It is not easy to get most children with ADHD to graduation. In fact, statistics suggest they are at risk for a number of academic problems. Parental attention and hard work are necessary components to an affected child's academic success. You will spend time in school conferences, monitoring homework, outlining school projects, and being a coach for him long after you think it should be necessary. If you find yourself spending more time on his education than your other children's education, you are not alone.

Your diploma is the personal satisfaction that comes from knowing you have been a significant player in your child's educational success. You have tempered the negative comments and looks. You have been the loving and supportive shadow that has followed him throughout his education. Your shadow, like a calming breeze, has provided respite when needed and given him the essential support necessary for success. Reward yourself for a job well done!

I Feel Like Hiring a Tutor

If you can afford it, hire a tutor. You are your child's parent, not his teacher. All parents need to monitor and check their child's progress in school; that's normal and goes with being a parent. Younger children require closer monitoring than older children. The daily checkups and interactions regarding schoolwork, however, can deteriorate quickly into negative interactions between child and parents.

These children are not easy to work with even under the best of circumstances. They're not self-starters, are bored quickly, and are unfocused. Close monitoring by the parent is often required to get the child through his homework and into bed. He has difficulty modulating his emotions, and he is quick to lose his temper, yell, cry, and give up quickly if he doesn't understand or feels criticized. Consequently, parents spend an unwarranted amount of time trying to get him refocused so he can complete his homework. Some nights, homework is not completed and both parents and child go to bed upset. He will leave important materials at school or forget what is due the next day. The child, if older, can sometimes call a classmate or have the parent drive him to his friend's house to get that math book needed to complete the homework assignment. However, night after night of reminders, trips to classmates' homes, telephone calls to the teacher, and threats to "Never forget your math book again!" can make parents and child frustrated and angry.

Some children simply present mild organizational difficulties and need guidance in finding ways to keep their schoolwork together so they can find materials easily. A training tool to help your child develop organizational skills is a program called "Skills for Success," by Dr. Anita Archer and Mary Gleason (Rief 1993). The program's key components are a monthly calendar on which students are taught to record assignment due dates, and a standard three-ring binder with subject dividers and side pockets to separate *take home/leave home* from *take home/return* papers. A tutor can be your child's coach and help him learn to use such programs.

One school district uses "Binder Reminder," a program similar to "Skills for Success." A child writes his assignments in a binder daily and takes it home each night, and the parents monitor his homework and projects. This program must be modified for children with ADHD to ensure the assignments are correctly copied and recorded. These children often forget to or only partially copy the assignments and do not take home the material needed to complete the schoolwork. The teacher can put the child on a weekly checklist from Thursday to Thursday. She records any missing assignments and the student has the weekend to make them up without penalty if he turns them in the following Monday. This program can be a good motivator; if he completes all the work, he doesn't have additional homework over the weekend.

We recommend that a good note-taker in class write the daily assignments on NCR paper (copying paper) and give a copy to the teacher. The child's teacher gives the copied notes from the NCR paper to the affected child, who is still required to take notes, but uses the NCR copy to supplement his own notes.

Many schools have peer or cross-age tutors who can help with projects, write down answers, and copy items off the blackboard. Cross-age tutoring can benefit both the affected child and the tutor. The tutor learns that being a helper can be rewarding, and the child makes a new friend. One upper-grade teacher allowed a student in her classroom to accompany an affected child to recess two times a week. This was helpful both in modeling appropriate play behaviors and in making the child feel special.

Additional sources of support are parent volunteers, senior citizens, and civic groups. A school in a district close to our town was fortunate to have young airmen from a local air force base volunteer their time and resources at a school with low-income families. Two of the airmen were assigned to two children with ADHD with significant behavior and learning needs.

If your child has special academic needs, find a specialist who is trained to work with children with ADHD. Children with ADHD *and* learning disabilities can have significant delays in reading comprehension, decoding, written language, math skills; they will need a specialist who understands how to teach to those areas. Children with learning disabilities can have problems with difficulty controlling and organizing their thoughts when activities have to be done either simultaneously or in close succession; failing to use self-regulatory strategies such as planning, checking and revising; and having limited knowledge of strategies that might be used on various tasks presented in schoolwork (Lyon 1994).

If your child has some of these characteristics and needs a specialist trained in learning strategies, go through your child's school for recommended tutors or find learning specialists in your local phone book. If you are fortunate enough to live near a university, you will sometimes find students training for advanced degrees in special education who would be willing to tutor your child. You may find credentialed teachers tutoring after school hours to supplement their income. They can be very helpful in that they understand classroom expectations and many have had experiences with affected children.

A positive relationship with your child is very important. If you are having daily and nightly battles about schoolwork, find someone to help you. You are not failing as a parent if you find it necessary to get outside support. You show strength in recognizing that you cannot be all things to your child. You have a right to take his schoolwork off your calendar—you don't have to be his teacher. Parents may be too emotionally connected to their children, and as the child advances in grades, the subject matter often becomes too advanced for the parent to help.

If you cannot afford a tutor, you can sometimes find high school students working for community service credits volunteering to tutor other children. You may also want to check with your county library. The librarian may know of community tutoring programs, either at their site or through civic organizations such as the PTA.

- You may be doing both you and your child a favor by hiring a tutor. Parents can sometimes make the worst teachers, because they are often too emotionally involved with their children.

- These children often have special learning needs, and it sometimes takes a specialist to help your child be successful.

- Talk with your child's teacher or school to get tutor recommendations. Children with moderate needs can benefit from peer or cross-age tutoring.

- Affected children often need weekly reminders regarding organization and homework completion from another person besides Mom or Dad.

How Much Does the Teacher Know about ADHD?

It all depends on the teacher and the level of training provided by her school district. Some districts provide more training than others, and some teachers are more open to acceptance of ADHD. If your child is lucky enough to have a teacher knowledgeable and accepting of ADHD, count your blessings. No one person is more important in your child's day-to-day progress in school than the teacher. She can and does make a big difference in your child's attitude towards school. When your child feels understood and cared for by someone, he will generally be more willing to work with that person.

The number of seminars or workshops a teacher has attended on ADHD cannot measure acceptance of ADHD. Acceptance comes first when the teacher willingly accepts ADHD as a real disorder, and uses this new awareness to change how she deals with the child in her classroom. Unfortunately, some teachers and school administrators do not accept ADHD. They go to a training workshop skeptical and are resistant to any new information that challenges their biases. One reason it is difficult to convince teachers and administrators that ADHD is real is that they are looking at the disorder conceptually, rather than experientially. Unless the teacher lives with a child or adult with ADHD, or knows one closely through a relative or friend, the teacher is often unable to relate to the child in the classroom.

Even though some educators seem to be skeptical and under their breath say, "It's baloney," the majority of teachers understand ADHD is a real disorder and not the fabrication of a few zealots. However, most teachers have limited understanding of the learning difficulties often associated with ADHD. These children can be very disorganized, inattentive, forgetful, anxious, compulsive, and emotional. They often will not learn their multiplication tables—especially with higher numbers, are often poor spellers, and cannot comprehend what they read. Teachers often don't understand that the characteristics above are often the norm for affected children, and this lack of understanding leads to many misunderstandings of their behavior in the classroom, which is seen as purposeful and not a manifestation of ADHD.

Teachers sometimes judge a child's forgetting to turn in homework as laziness. They see affected students not remembering what they read as poor memory, and their exploding in class as being undisciplined. Children with ADHD can be lazy at times (like all children), lie about doing their homework, and get angry in class and yell out inappropriately. However, for these children, not turning in homework, not finishing classwork, and yelling out in class are often the result of high distractibility and poor impulse control, not always purposeful behavior.

Even a teacher diagnosed with ADHD can be resistant to more positive ways to work with children with the same disorder. A teacher's personal history of the disorder will sometimes create such painful experiences and memories that she will be the most resistant and loudest objector to modifying a child's school day. His behaviors bring back the years of trying to avoid the pain, suffering, and disappointments ADHD has brought to the teacher's own life. The disorder can leave deep emotional scars, and many affected adults seen in therapy share the pain, anger, and loss they have experienced because of it. Similar to a smoker who has stopped smoking, an affected adult can become the most intolerant and loudest spokesman against accommodations.

A child with ADHD is a teacher's enigma—a puzzlement, a child who is difficult to teach and disrupts the learning of other children in the classroom. As a parent of such a child, you probably know more about ADHD than the vast majority of educators. Don't sell yourself short. Raising your child is not easy, and to have survived with some level of emotional well-being, you learned ways to work with him. You are reading this book, which demonstrates your commitment to finding better ways to work with him.

You have collected information that can be helpful to the teacher. If you are like most parents dealing with this disorder, you have set a goal to become an expert on it. Many families seen in counseling have a library comparable to most therapists' on ADHD. The self-help section in the local library or bookstore becomes as familiar as the produce section in the neighborhood grocery store. The question asked by, and often the major problem presented to, parents is how to best share this vast knowledge with the teacher without offending anyone. This is an important question.

You won't be successful with all teachers. Some are more open and accepting of parental help than others. Like all people, they come into the classroom with their own temperament and history. Frankly, some of them will never be open to your suggestions or ours. They see change as threatening and something that requires effort on their part. However, teachers don't have a monopoly on this attitude. Many people simply don't appreciate someone questioning their behavior, and when encouraged to look at other approaches, they can be close-minded. If your child has a teacher who is close-minded, you may need to put him in another classroom or ask the school principal to provide accommodations for him.

You can give important information about your child to those teachers who are open to suggestions. Share interventions that work and do not work. Some children are more anxious and moody than others, and this information is important to a teacher. At Back-To-School Night or before school starts in the fall, ask for a conference with your child's teacher to share information about your child. Tell her at this time that he has ADHD and you have found certain interventions that work better than others.

Please, don't present a box with ADHD information you have gathered over the years and ask the teacher to look at it. It won't happen. Slowly, and we emphasize slowly, introduce her to ideas that you have gathered that can help in the classroom. Let her know you understand your child can be difficult to work with and you appreciate the teacher's challenge. A child with ADHD in a classroom with 36 other children is not a good mix, and even the best of teachers can have a difficult time with an affected child in this kind of environment. Remember your child is not the only one in the classroom. Parents can sometimes be insensitive to the teacher's difficulty in dealing with their child while still meeting the needs of other children in the classroom. To you, your child is the most important child in that classroom; however, that doesn't negate that the teacher is also responsible for educating other children who are equally important to their parents.

Put together a small booklet on ADHD for your child's teacher. The booklet should be no more than five pages and should contain a one-page summary of the behavior interventions your child responds to best and interventions that can escalate his behaviors. Pages two and three can include recommended teaching methods reported to work with affected children in general. Page four should include information on your child's medication and any possible side effects. Page five can list reading materials you have found helpful. You can find great suggestions from a number of sources that are often available in bookstores, libraries, or at CHADD (Children and Adults with Attention-Deficit/Hyperactivity Disorder) support group meetings. You may also want to ask the teacher if her school has reading material on ADHD.

Review and Tips

- Understanding of ADHD can vary from one teacher to another, even within the same school. Don't expect your child's teacher to know as much as you do about the disorder—*you* have a driving need to understand. She may care and is willing to listen, but may not be self-directed to find alternative ways to work with your child.

- Be a support to your child's teacher, not a pest! Some parents can be overbearing, demanding, and not recognize the difficulties and stresses their child causes the teacher. Most are caring people and they are not out to hurt you or your child. Stand behind them and don't be too quick to judge harshly.

- Meet with your child's teachers regularly to brainstorm ways to deal with your child. Ask his teacher how you can support her.

- Provide supporting literature and readings on ADHD for the teacher. You might be more successful if you put your ideas in short book form (one to five pages). Understand that you can provide helpful information, but you can't guarantee that it will be used.

I Hate to Hear from My Child's School

The telephone rings. Mr. Smith, the school principal, is on the other end of the line. Your heart misses a beat and, taking a deep breath, you answer, "Yes, Mr. Smith, how can I help you?" Mr. Smith is calling about Bobby, your eight-year-old child son who has hit a child on the playground. He needed to be restrained and taken to the office and he will not calm down, so you are called to pick him up. Calls from school generally come not to tell the parent what a great day their child had, but to report an altercation with a teacher or child. Parents usually hate to hear from their child's school.

School is not always a good fit for a child with ADHD. Unfortunately, you may hear more bad news than good news from your child's school. As mentioned in previous sections, he may find many aspects of school challenging, including sitting still, standing in line, following directions, completing schoolwork, and holding back angry feelings and words. Schools, often limited both by ideas and staff in dealing with them, look to you to help solve the problem. Somehow you are expected to provide some kind of consequence to help Bobby be less impulsive or more compliant in the classroom. Unfortunately, the solution is not that easy or quick.

Some parents avoid answering the phone or screen calls during school hours. They know this is wrong and potentially dangerous, but after an unending series of calls from their child's school, they shout, "Enough! Enough!" Frankly, they run out of ideas on how to stop Johnny from being disruptive or aggressive, and simply stop answering the phone until they find the emotional strength to deal with the school.

When your child disrupts the education of other children or damages property or hits other children purposely, the school will call you. Schools are responsible for the education and safety of children under their care, and they cannot let any child hurt or disrupt a classroom to the extent that other children are being denied their education. In most cases, the school is not out to get your child or take revenge on you because Johnny's misbehaviors continue. Rather, they're attempting to balance his needs with the needs of other children under the school's care. Sometimes the behaviors are so disruptive and aggressive that he cannot stay at school; however, most of the time he is disciplined at school. Sending him home or calling you is the last resort used by most principals. Most teachers and principals will talk with the child, take away a recess, or try any number of other consequences before you are called, so when you get that phone call, try to understand that you were probably at the end of a list of attempted interventions.

Very seldom do schools call parents immediately, although they may call right away if there has been an earlier conference. Sometimes it is arranged that when the child hits another, or runs out of the room again in anger, the parent will be called. Usually, however, this kind of arrangement is the exception rather than the rule.

Communicate closely with your child's school. Yes, even answer the phone when you don't want to. Share with his teacher and the school principal interventions that you are trying at home. If need be, ask his doctor to write a short letter outlining medical interventions being used with your child. Let people know you are not ignoring his problems, but have taken an active role in trying to minimize some of his disruptive and aggressive behaviors. School personnel are often more accommodating and understanding if they see that the parents are not making excuses but are actively trying to help the school deal with their child. By presenting a helping role, rather than an adversarial one, you can often defuse and significantly change the dynamics between your child and the school. A teacher who was seen as rigid may begin to make subtle changes and become more accepting of new ideas.

Little change can take place that will benefit your child if you and the school are not talking. The school needs your support. The staff needs you to take him home when his behavior is unacceptable. View your role as a team member in your child's education. Sometimes part of his education will be to learn that when he hits others or is disrespectful of his classmates' right to learn, he will be held responsible for his behavior. Affected children do have more difficulty controlling their emotions and can be impulsive; however, they still need to be held responsible for their inappropriate behaviors.

The school's responsibility is to provide environmental changes that can minimize problematic behaviors. Schools have a legal obligation to make accommodations for affected children when their disability substantially limits learning (which is covered under IDEA) and major life activities (Section 504 of the Rehabilitation Act of 1973), and state laws may provide even broader coverage of educational needs than federal laws require. For many years, the Rehabilitation Act's main thrust had been in the area of employment; however, within the last several years, the federal Office for Civil Rights (OCR), charged with enforcement of Section 504, has become proactive in the field of education for disabled individuals. However, not all children with ADHD qualify for Section 504. What's important to emphasize here is that schools have a legal responsibility to make accommodations for your child if his disorder is substantially limiting his ability to learn in school (see "My Neighbor Says Schools Have a Legal Obligation to

Accommodate My Son's ADHD. Is This True?" later in this chapter), but the school district may resist providing services and accommodations, or its special education department may not be knowledgeable about the various interventions that are effective with this population.

Accommodations do not necessarily guarantee success. A school can have the best of intentions and plans, but for one reason or another, a child's behavior still can be disruptive. Many factors determine and influence behavior; school is important, but it is just one of many influences in his life. Children can have anger and feelings of loss from a divorce or death in a family, or deal with any number of other stressors, which affect their behavior in class and at home. If your child continues to misbehave, don't necessarily blame the school.

Your child and his teacher need your support. As painful as some of the calls from the school can be, they are not meant to hurt you or your child. Most teachers are advocates for children, but when presented with a child with ADHD, they often have limited training and support. Your child is probably difficult to handle at home, so understand the school can find equal difficulty dealing with an active and sometimes noncompliant child at school.

Review and Tips

- See your role as a team member in the education of your child. He needs your support and to know you will back him when he is treated unfairly, but that you will not accept aggressive or disruptive behavior at school.

- Your child's school needs your support. Schools have an obligation to set up a fair and reasonable program to deal with your child's inappropriate behaviors, but equally, you need to support them when he misbehaves.

- You will often hear from your child's school more than parents of unaffected children. Affected children present behaviors that get them into trouble at school, and when this behavior is so disruptive or aggressive that other children are denied their safety and education, you will be called.

- Teachers may overreact and lose their patience just like you do. Try not to hold grudges, and don't keep score.

His School Says It's My Child's Responsibility to Remember to Take His Medication

It is the school's responsibility to ensure your child's medication is properly administered as outlined by the doctor. As mentioned in an earlier section, teachers are sometimes uncomfortable acting as a "drug dispenser"; however, even after recognizing a teacher's apprehension, schools are still obligated to administer medication. In our home state, California, schools are required to provide a safe place for the storage of medication considered necessary for students who have potentially life-threatening medical conditions and for students who need medication during the school day to address medical disorders, such as ADHD. Check with your state's department of education for education codes regarding medication administration. This is a legal obligation and schools cannot ignore this responsibility.

States may vary in terms of how this obligation is met. In California the basic legal provision states that during the school day medication can be administered by the school nurse or other designated school personnel if the district receives (1) a written statement from the physician detailing the method, amount, and times the medication is to be taken, and (2) a written statement from the parent or guardian of the child giving permission for the school district to assist the physician. In addition to these guidelines, all medication stored and dispensed by the school must be in the original prescription or over-the-counter container, clearly labeled with the child's name, doctor's name, pharmacy, dose, frequency and duration of administration, and expiration date, if any (California Ed. Code, Section 49423, [1976]).

A school district near our home requires that the medication be stored in a safe place under lock and key, and only dispensed by school personnel designated by the principal. In large districts the medication is usually stored in the main school office where a secretary, nurse, or administrator can access it. In small districts, the teacher may store it in a locked file cabinet or desk in her room. Schools are not asked to force a child to take his medication—if he refuses to take his medication, the parent should be called. Schools are required to keep a log of the time and dates the medication was administered, and the log should be kept in a private and safe place for review by the parent or the child's doctor. This is especially important for purposes of documenting the appropriateness of dosage and evaluating its effectiveness. Again, check with your child's school for details and guidelines concerning administering medication. The bottom line is that schools are legally required to administer medication to your child if all procedures have been adhered to.

Lastly, administering medication is a private, as well as a medical, matter, and only with the consent of the parent may a school nurse communicate with school staff regarding the possible effects of the drug on the child's physical, intellectual, and social behavior. Most parents will list the child's medications on a school emergency card, but this is optional. Schools have a legal and ethical responsibility to maintain confidentiality about student educational and medical histories. As an example, with educational records, only a person with a legal right, such as a student's teacher, principal, school psychologist, or parent, may look through a student's educational folder.

We encourage parents to give permission for the nurse or doctor to discuss issues such as side effects and what symptoms the medication will or will not correct with the child's teacher. For example, medication can make a child with ADHD more focused and less impulsive, but it doesn't help him necessarily be more organized, become a better speller, or correct a learning disability. Also, the teacher can give you and your child's doctor important information.

Review and Tips

- Schools have a legal obligation to monitor and administer medication for children under the care of a licensed physician. Check with your child's school about necessary paperwork and procedures.

- Discuss the role of medication in treating your child's disorder with his teacher. Your child's doctor can provide literature and/or write a short letter outlining what the medication will and will not do, and possible side effects to be monitored by your child's teacher.

Homework Takes Forever

Homework can be a long, bitter, and unhappy task. Homework that would take an unaffected child an hour to complete will often take a child with ADHD two to three hours to finish. As mentioned in an earlier chapter (see "Homework Is a Family Mission" in chapter 5), struggles over homework can become more intense as the child advances in grades. Normally, middle and high school demand more written work, such as book reports, daily assignments, and long-term projects. Homework is generally the norm in secondary education, requiring not only efficient use of time, but also comprehension of the assignment.

These children don't always understand directions or concepts given in the classroom, so they may spend an unwarranted amount of time calling classmates, looking for misplaced assignment sheets, or praying the parent is too busy or distracted to ask about the homework.

The following ADHD traits make homework especially difficult.

Distractibility

These children tend to be highly distractible—distracted internally as well as externally. Your young child will read a passage from his storybook about the snow and then start daydreaming or remembering the last time he played in the snow with his sister. Only after a parent or older sibling notices is he brought back to his studies. He will often spend a good deal of time at the kitchen table over a math or reading book thinking or daydreaming about everything but what's at hand. His mind jumps from one thought to another. External sounds or movements are distracting—a police siren, TV noises in the next room, or a fly landing on the work area. He may pick up his pencil, start to write, and then make unending circles on the kitchen table. Unaffected children can also be distracted by daydreaming and noises, but they generally catch themselves and quickly return to their schoolwork.

These suggestions are helpful in limiting distractibility during homework.

- Provide a quiet place away from the TV for your child to work.

- Work in an area that is plain and simple, e.g, face a white wall or close the curtains and use a reading light.

- Purchase a portable tape or CD player that your child can wear while doing homework. It drowns out outside noises. The tape played should be instrumental. Environmental noise tapes such as nature sounds can be effective in focusing the child. Keep the volume low. In the summer, a running fan near the work area also can help drown out outside noises.

- Provide a stopwatch for your child to use while doing his homework. This can be quite effective for older children (fourth grade and up).

The child sets the stopwatch when he starts his homework. If he looks up or gets a drink, he stops the watch. If he fiddles with the stopwatch, he is told to put it on stop. You may need to monitor closely at first. This intervention can help him self-monitor distractions as well as be more focused. Children with ADHD are often more focused when working under time restrictions.

- Break tasks into smaller parts. Estimate how long each part should take, use a timer, and set it for your checkpoint times. This method helps you monitor your child's progress on his homework.

- Give him regular breaks, and change the subject area after short intervals. For example, he can work on his math for 15 minutes, and then after 15 minutes, switch back to math. Remember, these children get bored easily. By varying the subjects you can help your child stay more focused.

- Provide time for exercise. Children need time to run, jump, and burn off excess energy. Don't make your child do homework right after getting home from school. He needs time to unwind and run around. In the winter when the weather makes going outside difficult, provide an inside game that lets him move about. Also, if possible, enroll him in after-school sports activities (gymnastics, basketball, karate). If he is in daycare, make sure the program provides exercise activities and not simply board games and TV.

- If your child takes an afternoon dose of medication at 4 p.m., for example, consider starting his homework after a 30- to 45-minute play period. Most non-timed released stimulants have a half-life of two and a half hours, so medication taken at 4 p.m. would begin to lose its effectiveness after 6:30 p.m. or 7 p.m. This loss is often quite abrupt as it is broken down, or *metabolized*, by the body and eliminated. Most children start their homework after dinner; even though there may be some residual benefits from the 4 p.m. dose, they are asked to do their schoolwork without the full benefit of the medication. If your child is in daycare or with a baby-sitter, give instructions to start homework after 30 to 45 minutes of play so he has the maximum benefit from the medication.

- Praise and give rewards when your child completes his homework and turns it in on time.

Disorganization

Children with ADHD can be very disorganized. Parents must be creative to get their child to complete and organize his homework to turn in the next day. Unaffected children are often self-starters and better managers of time. Affected children are poor in both areas needed for on-time completion of homework. They lose things, leave things, and generally require more time to complete homework because of their disorganization. One child in counseling would put all his homework in his backpack, and that is where it usually stayed until the winter snow melted! Affected children often spend hours doing their homework but fail to find it or turn it in. It is crumpled up and shoved in a jeans pocket or covered up at the bottom of a desk or backpack. "Out of sight, out of mind" is the controlling factor. If they can't see it easily, they won't remember to turn it in.

Try these interventions to help with organizational skills. Remember, practice makes better, not perfect.

- Make sure your child does his homework in the same place each night, preferably where there is little distraction and/or where he can be monitored.

- Keep all papers and books off the work area except the subject at hand. The less to look at and fiddle with, the better.

- Place an in-box near your child's work area for work that stays home (long-term projects) and an out-box for material that needs to go back to school the next day. When he says he is done with homework, review the paperwork in the boxes with him for accuracy and completion. Have him put his out-box work in his school binder.

- Purchase a three-ring binder that can be divided into subject areas. At the beginning of each subject area, put in a pocket where homework due the next day can be placed. Also on the following night, you can review the pockets to make sure material has been turned in during class time. These children do not do well trying to keep two or three binders organized—often one will be lost or misplaced. For elementary-age children, put the homework in one manila envelope that is turned in or collected by the teacher the next day. All the homework done that evening is put in the envelope (math, science, etc.).

- Purchase a hole-punch for three-ring binders. The hole-punch can be attached to the binder and when papers are passed out without holes, the child can immediately punch the paper and put it in his binder. This helps keep papers from being lost.

- Ask your child's teacher to send home a weekly homework sheet for your records. Review the weekly assignments and any long-term projects with your child. Help him plan as to when and how he is going to complete the homework assignments for the week. One parent provided a homework calendar that was tacked above the child's work area for him to reference and cross off when finished. Younger children respond to concrete reminders. They can draw a favorite animal or car, and like a puzzle, divide the drawing into the number of days or weeks that are needed to complete the project. As he completes a part of the project, he cuts out that piece of the puzzle and pastes it on blank white paper. As he completes each section, he rebuilds his animal or car. He can see how much he has done and how much he needs to do to complete his project. With older children, who will often resist nightly monitoring, you can contract to monitor two nights a week; the other school days you don't review the homework. However, he understands that if he doesn't keep up his homework, you will start monitoring him nightly until he again shows more responsibility.

- Set up a reward system at home for completion of homework. Remember, a reward is recognizing a child for a job well-done, whereas a bribe is given before anything is done. It's okay to reward children for working hard and doing a good job.

Review and Tips

- Homework for affected children can be stressful and difficult. You will need to more closely monitor your child's homework than his unaffected sibling.

- Provide for regular breaks during the homework period. Use a timer to help monitor the time away from the work area. Your child should be told ahead of time how long his break will be.

- Provide incentives for work completed. Use your child's interests to determine which incentives are most effective.

Homework May Be Too Hard or Long

Children will sometimes receive homework that is too difficult for them, and parents should be aware of this possibility. Teachers sometimes unknowingly give homework assignments without considering a child's special needs.

These children can find homework difficult, and it can create considerable stress not just for the child but for the parent as well. The child may have difficulty with homework for a number of reasons, e.g., he can be highly distractible, the material is too difficult, they are often poor managers and poor self-starters, and they get bored quickly. As mentioned earlier, schools are required to make accommodations for children when their disorder substantially limits their learning. Accommodations can be made for the length of assignment, the penalty for late assignments if returned in a reasonable time, and for a classmate/teacher to remind the child to turn in his homework. All three accommodations are recommended from time to time for these children because of chronic problems with forgetfulness and distractibility.

Review and Tips

- Homework can be a stressful and frustrating experience.

- Communicate closely with your child's teacher to ensure the homework is being turned in to her. Affected children often spend hours working on a homework assignment and then forget to turn it in during class time.

- If your child is on medication, speak with his doctor about ways to use medication to help minimize behaviors during homework time.

- Provide play or exercise times for your child after school. All children need time to run off excess energy and relax.

- Provide a home environment that can help minimize behaviors. All children function best with routine and structure.

Help your child choose an established time to do homework and a place to do it. These children work best in an environment with as few distractions as possible.

- You are your child's coach—give him support, but he does the homework.

He Does His Homework and Then Forgets to Turn It In!

This is a common complaint both from parents and teachers who deal with children with ADHD. This pattern of not turning in homework may be an issue throughout your child's education. Unfortunately, the teacher will suspect purposeful behavior or that he is not trying hard enough to remember—why not? If Johnny can remember before lunch to turn in his math homework, why not his social studies report in the afternoon? What makes this behavior so puzzling is that Johnny does not always forget, and sometimes he will be attentive and pass in his homework.

Affected children, when asked to pass in homework, can be distracted by something or be daydreaming. Other children in the classroom have turned in their homework, but your child, often oblivious to what is happening around him, walks out of the room with the homework still in his desk or tucked away in his jeans pocket or backpack. He will forget to turn in assignments even after threats, apologies, and promises to "never forget again!"

This pattern is so common that we recommend that the parent meet with the school counselor, teacher, or principal to set up accommodations so the child is not penalized for general non-purposeful behavior. Educators and parents often view failure to turn in homework as purposeful, rather than forgetfulness stemming from both poor organizational skills and high distractibility—facets of the disorder. The challenge is determining when the child is truly forgetting to turn in homework because of distractibility, and when, like other children, he's making excuses. Implementing the suggestions given below can make it easier to meet this challenge.

Monitor Your Child's Homework

Unlike other children, affected children will often continue to need close monitoring into middle school and beyond. One mother amusingly shared with a therapist that her son, who was about to go off to college, still needed her watchful eye over his shoulder to make sure that the last project was turned in before high school graduation.

Younger children are easier to monitor than older children. They want to please, and the homework assignments are still understandable for the average parent. What seems to work best at school is to have a classmate serve as a *study buddy* to remind the child to turn in his homework. The teacher can also place the child up front, so when the homework is passed down the aisle, the teacher can quietly check to see if his papers are in the pile.

At home, the parents will need to devote more time with the younger child, but the benefits are worth the effort. They'll need to check over his homework and make sure it is in its proper place before he leaves for school. When properly monitored at home, the younger child will not be confronted, as often happens, with complaints about missed assignments or critical looks from teachers. Most important, he is learning successful ways to deal with his challenges, rather than negative behavior patterns that can cause pain and frustration in school.

Adolescents are more difficult to monitor, and checking up on them can often be an unpleasant experience. They would rather do it themselves and have you stay out of their room, but no matter how much they may plead, you still can't let the average affected adolescent go solo. Teachers may say to parents, "Let Johnny fail. He will learn." Unfortunately, if Johnny is like most adolescents with ADHD, he won't learn and will continue to forget his homework. As mentioned in an earlier section, you don't stop a child from stuttering by punishing him.

One successful method with adolescents is to contract with them. A parent can contract that their adolescent will be monitored, but only on certain days, like Tuesday and Thursday. If the homework is going well, the parent can ask the teacher for a semimonthly report on their child's progress. If she reports a pattern of missing assignments, the parent can go back to weekly progress reports from the teacher. In high school, a school counselor or vice principal will often facilitate weekly progress reports with the adolescent's teacher.

They can learn coping skills. One teen who was starting to drive would put all his completed homework under his car keys, because he knew he wouldn't leave without his keys. A teenage girl in counseling discovered a fail-safe way of remembering to turn in her homework. She would put her favorite lipstick in the pocket of her binder where she placed the homework due that day. Another teenager had his digital watch set to ring at certain times during the day as a reminder to turn in his homework. If he forgot to turn in homework during second period, he found his teacher before going home.

Organizational skills are taught, and an important role the parent plays is positively reinforcing these skills of organization and "remembering" when practiced by the child.

Communicate Regularly with the Teacher

These children are not necessarily good judges of their progress. They may think they are doing well in school, only to find out later that they have many missing assignments. This lack of awareness is not always purposeful, but often stems from their tendency to not check with the teacher regularly. They are generally not self-directed, and you seldom find them up at the teacher's desk asking if any homework is missing, so weekly or semimonthly progress reports from the teacher can be helpful. These progress reports let you and your child know how he is doing in his classes. If missing homework is a problem, you can monitor more closely. One method is to have the progress report go from Thursday to Thursday. The teacher documents missing homework assignments on the progress sheet that is sent home on Thursday. The parent signs the progress sheet, which is returned to school the next day with the child. An arrangement is made with the teacher to turn in late work the following Monday without penalty. Any material needed to complete missing assignments or homework can be collected on Friday. Request that the teacher monitor to ensure that proper books and materials are in the child's hands when he leaves at the end of the day. This way he is not penalized for behavior that is a symptom of his disorder.

Review and Tips

- Children with ADHD often need close monitoring of their homework—you will need to be your child's coach. Be there for support and guidance, but do not complete the homework. An important component to coaching will be helping him find ways to remember to turn in his homework.

- Have your child's teachers sign off on a weekly or semimonthly check sheet in order to monitor whether or not he is turning in his homework. Communicate closely with his teachers.

- Check for long-term projects that have been assigned, as well as weekly assignments.

He Doesn't Seem Motivated to Get Good Grades

All children at times find schoolwork boring and not a high priority in their lives, but staying motivated to keep up with schoolwork seems especially difficult for children with ADHD. However, most children understand and learn that keeping up their grades can benefit them, whether with parental praise, monetary rewards, or the personal satisfaction from knowing they do well at something. Why doesn't the knowledge that good grades can bring personal rewards seem to motivate the affected child? The answer lies in a number of traits associated with ADHD.

1.) There may be neurodevelopmental factors that contribute to low motivation for reaching such goals as good grades. Research, such as discussed in chapter 1, suggests that the prefrontal lobes, the least-understood and most-complicated part of the brain, not only affect functions related to paying attention, planning, and execution of thoughtful behavior, but also to motivation (Comings 1990). Though it is difficult to prove or to measure the degree to which this motivation deficit contributes to low interest in getting good grades, it may be a factor and should not be dismissed.

While these children quickly lose interest in routine tasks, such as schoolwork, they can become highly motivated when involved in high-interest activities, which seem to elevate attention and focus. The more focused the child is on an activity, the more successful he is and the more motivated he is to stay with the activity. In fact, in high-interest activities, he can be hyperfocused. Try, for example, to get his attention if he's playing a game like Nintendo.

These children are often drawn towards high-risk behaviors because they are more focused when involved in challenging activities. The body, when confronted by danger or excessive stress, releases adrenaline, the chemical that mobilizes us for emergencies. Adrenaline is one of the body's natural stimulants; the mind is most alert and the body most sensitive when adrenaline is running through our system. Under the influence of adrenaline, we are constantly monitoring our environment and are quick to notice changes in it. People with ADHD often seek dangerous activities to experience this sense of mastering attention over distraction. The adrenaline high makes them more focused and goal-directed than they are at other times. This is a concept that is hard for adults without ADHD to understand. Never having a problem with staying focused long enough to reach most goals, they see no need to put themselves at risk.

2.) These children are often not motivated to work hard for good grades because they lack confidence and optimism about school. Because they have great difficulty with routines such as those required in school, they feel a sense of failure rather than the positive enthusiasm and confidence needed for success. They don't seem to develop the attitude that things will turn out all right in life, despite setbacks and frustrations. In the words of Daniel Goleman (1995), "Optimism is an attitude that buffers people against falling into apathy, hopelessness, or depression in the face of tough going." Academic success, he says, "is the combination of reasonable talent and the ability to keep going in the face of defeat that leads to success." Optimism makes people more likely to make the best use of their talents and to do what it takes to develop them. Affected children, lacking a sense of optimism, will simply give up, and giving up does not result in good grades.

3.) Inconsistent work habits interfere with academic success. Affected children will turn in their schoolwork one day, and the next day walk out of the classroom with little to show for their time at school. It is not that they cannot be productive, it is that they cannot maintain that level of productivity the way other children do. Consistent work habits require the ability to resist momentary thoughts or distractions, an ability that children with ADHD lack (refer to "Inconsistent Performance," chapter 1, for more detailed discussion). Inconsistent work performance contributes to low grades and over time, low motivation regarding schoolwork.

4.) Because of poor organizational skills, children often spend a great deal of time trying to find lost assignments, spellings lists, or any number of things that they're responsible for on a daily basis. It is very demoralizing for these children to deal with ongoing parental and teacher comments concerning poor organizational skills. Motivation for schoolwork can be destroyed, and a child will just give up. If he hasn't given up, his inconsistent performance often leads parents and teachers to think he has.

5.) Affected children are often poor self-managers. Being successful in school requires doing well on tests and finishing long-term projects. To achieve that, the child must pay attention and manage himself so he does not get too far behind. He may be working on a test or project when something else catches his attention, and his mind quickly jumps to the new distraction without considering the consequences of not finishing what he started. He may play with an eraser when he should be working on a test, and before he knows it, class time has run out, and he can't finish the test.

6.) Children with ADHD can be the world's best procrastinators, leaving everything to the last moment. Why do it today when there is always tomorrow? They will wait until the night before a science project is due to start it, even though they have had the assignment for three weeks. It is not that they don't want good grades, it is that their poor sense of time and poor organizational skills leave them little time to do a good job.

7.) These children have a distorted sense of time, according to Thom Hartmann (1993). They can have an "exaggerated sense of urgency when they're on a task, and an exaggerated sense of boredom when they feel they have nothing to do." The child's sense of time speeding by when he is working on a project can lead to chronic impatience. This elastic sense of time can lead to emotional ups and downs, which often make it more difficult to complete assignments.

8.) They often have learning disorders as well that can affect their school performance. A child frustrated daily with schoolwork and doing poorly in school is often turned off to school.

Because of these interacting factors, the child is often perceived as poorly motivated, when in fact the basic problem is inconsistent productivity and poor grades, which lead to personal discouragement, and over time, eventual low motivation towards schoolwork. Any child whose day is filled with challenges that make hard work less rewarding for him than for other children might not be motivated to get good grades. However, most children do want good grades, but have great difficulty in reaching this goal.

The following interventions can help your child become more motivated to work for good grades.

- If your child's grades are not satisfactory, make sure the material is not too hard for him. He will quickly stop doing schoolwork if the material is beyond his ability.

- Monitor your child's progress on a regular basis for both accuracy and completion. Refer to section "Homework Takes Forever" in this chapter.

- Alternate subjects. Remember that affected children get bored quickly. They will stay motivated longer if they can alternate back and forth among subject areas (15 minutes on math, 15 minutes on social studies, etc.).

- Praise your child when you find him keeping up on his studies. We all like praise when we do well.

- Add interest to the schoolwork by taking your child to places or events that bring his schoolwork alive, such as a trip to the fire station, a local play, or a weekend trip to an historical event or place.

- Review "Homework Is a Family Mission," in chapter 5, and "Homework Takes Forever" in this chapter for ideas about keeping the work manageable.

- Motivation to get good grades often comes with maturation. Younger children find little intrinsic value in getting good grades, and only when they're older do they see the benefit.

Review and Tips

- Affected children do have more difficulty staying motivated about schoolwork. Those traits associated with ADHD often make consistent performance and optimism more difficult.

- Closely monitor your child's progress. Even in high school, he will require closer supervision than his peers. A school counselor or vice principal can provide a program to help your child be more successful, and therefore, more motivated to keep up with his schoolwork.

- Remind yourself that any child will go through periods when he is less motivated about schoolwork than at other times. Middle school children often show a drop in academic performance; as peer relationships become more important, the affected child's lack of maturity makes balancing social life with academic performance difficult. Maturation often is a great healer for high school problems, from keeping and making friends to getting good grades.

My Neighbor Has a Child with ADHD, and He Is Doing Fine in School—Why's That?

There can be many explanations why children with ADHD vary in their successes at school.

Some children are not significantly affected by their disorder. One child may be less hyperactive, have better social skills, and be more compliant than another. The more impulsive, hyperactive, and oppositional child will have more conflict with school staff and peers. It is a strong possibility that the more problematic of the two children has a learning disability.

All children have different temperaments, intelligence, strengths, and weaknesses. A child who demonstrates good athletic skills can often emotionally compensate for his poor performance in academic areas. A bright child can often mask problem behaviors until reaching upper grades where more independent work is required. Remember that your child is more than his disorder. School success comes from a combination of factors and failure cannot be blamed on any one problem or disorder.

Review and Tips

- Your child might have ADHD, but he is more than his disorder. All of us are better at some tasks than others; this is no different for affected children.

- Your child may have a different temperament than your next-door neighbor's child. Your child may have more difficulty relating to his peers, listening in class, and getting along with adults, and may have a learning disability. It does little good to compare your child with others.

He Did So Much Better in the Third Grade Than He's Doing in the Seventh Grade

These children may do better in lower grades than in upper grades. Often school personnel do not refer a child for evaluation until the upper grades. This is especially true if the child is not hyperactive or impulsive, is of average intelligence, and has no learning disability. Both the behavior and academic performance expected from a third-grade student differ both qualitatively and quantitatively from those for the seventh-grader.

Behavioral Expectations

Behavioral challenges stem from poor impulse control and hyperkinetic behavior. The hyperactive child with poor impulse control is the one school personnel most often identify as a problem. He creates the most challenges in the school environment. He has difficulty following directions, controlling his temper, not talking back to teachers, and gets into conflicts during recess. Generally, in the early grades, educators more readily tolerate these kinds of behaviors. They recognize that younger children have more problems with impulsivity and anger control. Also, there is often no observable difference between the third-grade affected child and other active children in his classroom. He has "ruffians" like himself to play with at recess, and he often gets along with his classmates. He is not the only third-grader who runs in the hall, pushes other children in line, and doesn't line up. However, gaps in social development increase as these children get older, and teachers will often describe affected students as more immature than their classmates.

When entering the seventh grade, classmates often find the behavior and antics of the affected child funny, but they quickly get bored with his ongoing classroom pranks and temper tantrums. He is no longer regarded as fun to be with, but as someone who acts like a fourth-grader and can get others into trouble. Some seventh-graders will view him as a buffoon and not a friend to invite to parties or have over to visit. Many seventh-graders with ADHD, sadly, are left out of class activities or after-school get-togethers because of their behavior. More often than not, their few friends either behave as they do or are younger children in the neighborhood. One adolescent in counseling found most of his playmates among his younger brother's friends.

Teachers in upper grades expect appropriate behavior and have little tolerance for disruptive or immature behavior. An affected child will get in trouble, sometimes daily, with school staff and peers. He will have great difficulty learning to adjust to teachers' different personalities and teaching styles. Unlike the unaffected child, who seems to find ways to accommodate to different teaching styles, the affected child is especially challenged by this important task.

The emotional toll on the child can be significant. The happy and entertaining third-grader is now seen as the troublesome and immature seventh-grader. Low self-esteem and mood swings are not uncommon in adolescents with ADHD. They are at risk for a number of problems, such as alcohol and drug use, depression, and antisocial behaviors that can lead to poor school performance.

Academic Expectations

Academic requirements of third-graders are measurably different than those for a seventh-grader, who is not only asked to be a more independent learner, but to have mastered skills that a child with ADHD can find difficult, e.g., copying and taking notes in class, putting thoughts down on paper, remembering to take home materials for homework, turning in homework, attending to oral directions, and utilizing class time wisely.

In the third grade, the child does some writing and is asked to do homework, but not to the same level as found in the seventh grade. A younger child has more supervision and monitoring of schoolwork, which is important for success with these children. Oral directions are supported by written work in the third grade, whereas by the seventh grade, the teacher lectures more and the student is required to follow and take notes. He often has great difficulty taking notes and listening at the same time. In the seventh grade, unlike the third grade, much of a child's grade is measured by written work, from test-taking to homework. Poor grades and school suspensions will often reflect his secondary school experience, unfortunately, unless the school provides accommodations.

In summary, the affected child will often be more successful in the third grade than in the upper grades, because his educational environment is generally more amenable to his learning style in the lower grades.

Review and Tips

- Children with ADHD often have more difficulty in school as they advance in grade levels. Expectations and skills necessary for success in higher grades are greater than those required in lower grades.

- Your child may need an academic accommodation or the support of a tutor. If he is having significant problems in school, ask for a meeting to discuss the possibility of accommodations.

- Review the sections on legal rights provided to children with ADHD in relation to their education. The parent may need to bring these rights to the teacher's attention.

Writing Assignments Are
Especially Difficult for My Child

It is writing, according to Sandra Rief (1993), that these children seem to struggle with the most. Children with ADHD, she says, are poor spellers and typically have difficulty organizing their thoughts in written expression. They may be poor spellers because they are inattentive and don't pay attention to detail. They are also not visually aware of patterns in words and are careless with their spelling and writing. They can have deficits in visual-sequential memory, causing difficulty in recalling the letters and putting them down correctly on paper. They have poor handwriting and are weak in mechanics and written organization (e.g., spacing on the page) and have tremendous difficulty with speed of written output. Their written work often has numerous erasures and is difficult to read (Rief 1993).

The child without hyperactivity (ADHD-I) may be slower than the average child in doing paper-and-pencil tasks. This is supported by findings showing children with ADHD-I do worse on tests involving motor speed and eye-hand coordination (Barkley 1995). Children with ADHD, unlike children with ADHD-I, generally have trouble synchronizing motor movements with their fast-moving thoughts. They can produce interesting ideas at a rapid rate, but their poor motor ability prevents them from keeping pace with their thoughts. Consequently, their writing is disorganized and does not represent their knowledge of the subject (Levine 1987). Some children present these difficulties because of their impatience, so they need further evaluation to determine whether the problem is impatience or a visual-motor coordination problem.

They often find cursive writing so difficult that they prefer to print in class. Because they find neatness and speed difficult, they should be given the opportunity to learn proper computer keyboarding. This important skill can help compensate for their delays in speed and neatness. Learning the keyboard is especially important in upper grades. The computer or word processor can be an important tool for minimizing writing frustrations. A computer allows a child both the luxury of spell-check and a faster way to document ideas. Teachers should let children who do not have access to a computer or word processor dictate written homework to a parent rather than become overly frustrated and discouraged. One compromise is to ask the child to write one paragraph and allow the parent write a paragraph. He can also record his answers on a tape recorder. This accommodation allows him to share his knowledge without being penalized for writing delays.

Writing assignments can also be difficult because of organizational deficits. These children often forget to include headings or margins, and their cross-outs and erasures are not neat. They turn in papers that are not legible and must be returned, and they may forget what is required, or complete only part of the job. They are often poor editors, spending little if any time reviewing their written work. An important intervention to help minimize careless errors is to provide extra time for editing and rewards for doing this before handing in written work.

They often need additional time to complete written work. The difficulty they have with writing assignments has been well-documented, and accommodation often has to be provided in the classroom to address this concern. A local university near our home provides paid note-takers in classes for students with ADHD. You can request accommodations to help your child be more successful with written language assignments. As will be discussed in a later section, these children are provided legal protections under IDEA and Section 504 (refer to "Could My Child Have a Learning Disability?").

Review and Tips

- Children with ADHD often have great difficulty with written language assignments.

- Schools are required to make accommodations for writing delays if they significantly affect a child's academic performance.

- Research demonstrates that writing tasks can be especially difficult. Provide additional time at home for written tasks when your child uses paper and pencil, and help him learn keyboarding.

- Because of difficulty with academic motivation, these children often put minimum effort or time into written assignments. Check your child's work closely at home, and encourage him to spend a certain amount of time for review and editing of his written work. The school can support your efforts and reward him for his efforts.

- Adolescents are more resistant to parental monitoring, so you may want to hire a tutor or have your child's teachers reinforce self-editing of written work.

Could My Child Have a Learning Disability?

In addition to ADHD, your child may have an associated learning disability, which interferes with his learning basic academic skills. Depending on whom you read, 10% to 50% of children with ADHD will have a learning disability depending on the learning disorder and how it is defined.

Having your child identified as *learning disabled (LD)* is not a simple process—it requires a thorough multidisciplinary evaluation. The federal special education law, *Individuals with Disabilities Education Act (IDEA),* specifies that the student must be achieving at a level significantly lower than what is expected according to intelligence results. There must be a large gap, the size of which is usually determined by individual states. This means that your child's attention problem, or other associated disabilities, must have kept him from learning basic skills measured by standardized tests. Poor study habits or goofing off in class are not considered to be learning disabilities.

The model used to determine a learning disability is the *discrepancy model.* A learning disability is said to exist when professionals find a significant discrepancy between a child's cognitive ability (intelligence quotient, or IQ) and his achievement scores when compared to other children his age. The IQ test tells us what can reasonably be expected from a child and to what extent he is underachieving. The IQ is a necessary component in identifying a learning disability. Some would argue, however, that the discrepancy model overidentifies children as having learning disabilities (LD) with high IQs, and children with low IQs are underidentified as having LD. Consequently, achievement manuals such as for the Wechsler Individual Achievement Test (WIAT) recommend using the regression-based predicted-achievement method to eliminate potential bias in the identification of learning disabled children (Mayes et al. 2000, 417). Achievement tests measure a child's mastery of core subject areas taught in school: mathematics, reading, and written language.

A child with ADHD will often struggle in class, but when tested for a learning disability, will do well both on the IQ and achievement tests. Consequently, he will not show a discrepancy between his IQ and achievement test scores, and the learning disability (LD) criteria for special education will be ruled out by definition. One explanation, we would suggest, is that neither IQ nor achievement testing is an accurate representation of the day-to-day classroom tasks that challenge affected children. These children do well with one-on-one tasks with adults, with novel situations, and with tasks of short duration. The IQ and achievement testing experiences generally fulfill all three conditions. Your child may be highly distractible and impulsive in the classroom, but these behaviors may not necessarily occur in the test setting, allowing him to do well on an intelligence or achievement test. Additionally, he may know his math facts and be able to write down thoughts in an abbreviated time; however, the primary problem is often consistency in performance, rather than knowledge of subject area. Neither test behavior nor measured knowledge may accurately reflect the problems presented in the classroom.

After testing is completed, a parent is notified of a meeting date to review the results and develop an *individualized education program (IEP)*. The IEP team (a regular education teacher, a special education teacher, the school psychologist, an appointed school administration representative, any other school personnel who have administered testing, any person the parent wants to have present at the meeting—including an advocate or a friend for moral support—and, most importantly, *the parent*) determines whether a child is eligible for special education services. Standardized tests usually weigh heavily in making this decision.

If there is no discrepancy, i.e., no gap between intelligence and achievement test results, your child most likely will be found not eligible for special education. If you want to pursue special education eligibility for your child, there are two ways to go. One would be to appeal this decision. Your local school district can provide you with literature concerning your appeal rights. Another way is to seek special education through a category called *Other Health Impairment (OHI)*, which does not require the achievement-intelligence discrepancy.

My Neighbor Says Schools Have a Legal Obligation to Accommodate My Son's ADHD. Is This True?

Because affected children often perform poorly in school because of disorder-based behaviors, they have been provided legal protections in public schools when their disorder substantially limits their learning or affects major life activities. These legal protections fall under three federal laws:

- Individuals with Disabilities Education Act (IDEA, or Public Law 105.17)

- Section 504 of the Rehabilitation Act of 1973

- Americans with Disabilities Act of 1990 (ADA)

IDEA

On June 4, 1997, President Clinton signed into law the new Individuals with Disabilities Education Act (IDEA), and the final regulations took effect on May 11, 1999. Under Part B, IDEA recognizes ADHD as one of a number of health conditions that can qualify a child for special education services under the category of *Other Health Impairment (OHI)* or *Specific Learning Disability (SLD)*.

Children with ADHD are considered eligible for special education services under the OHI category when their disorder is considered to be a chronic or an acute health problem that results in limited alertness that adversely affects their educational performance. However, this impairment must be substantiated by a child's school performance and not just be an opinion of the parent. These children are a very diverse group, and not all children who are diagnosed with ADHD should be classified as eligible for services under the OHI or SLD category. No child is eligible for services under the act simply because he is identified as being in a particular disability category. A child getting satisfactory grades would not necessarily demonstrate that his disorder is adversely affecting his educational performance. He is eligible for services only if he or she meets identified criteria. He must demonstrate that the disability is chronic and results in limited alertness, and that the disorder adversely affects his educational performance. The testing and the IEP team must establish that the child, because of the impairment, needs special education services.

If your child qualifies under the OHI or SLD category, the school must provide an appropriate educational program designed to meet his individual needs. This is termed an *individualized education program (IEP)*.

Section 504

Children with ADHD also have protection under *Section 504 of the Rehabilitation Act of 1973*. Section 504 prohibits discrimination against any person with a disability in any program in school districts receiving federal financial assistance. Under the act, an individual with a disability is anyone who has a mental or physical impairment that substantially limits one or more major life activities. Learning is considered one such life activity. Section 504, like IDEA, requires that schools receiving federal funds address the special needs of children with handicapping conditions, such as ADHD, that substantially limit their learning. Included in the U.S. department of education regulations for Section 504 is the requirement that handicapped students be provided a *Free Appropriate Public Education (FAPE)*. These regulations require identification, evaluation, provision for appropriate services, and procedural safeguards in every public school in the United States. However there is a difference between IDEA and Section 504. IDEA requires that the child meet the criteria for special education services; Section 504 requires only that he have a disability that substantially limits a major life activity, like learning. A child with ADHD may not qualify under IDEA, but can be provided accommodations in the classroom under Section 504. Additionally, he may qualify for accommodations under both IDEA *and* Section 504.

Schools are required to draw up a Section 504 plan at the local school site. In our town's school district, the *student study team* is generally the educational team that implements Section 504; your child's school district may call it by a different name (for example, *Student Solutions Committee*). The intervention team will normally include a teacher, the parent, the principal, and a Section 504 coordinator. If the limiting condition is a child on medication, for example, a school nurse may be involved. The team goal is to write up an accommodation plan to meet the child's needs. Sometimes a special education teacher or other representative will be included, but it is important to understand that Section 504 is not a special education program. It is enforced by the federal Office of Civil Rights (OCR) and is a general public education responsibility, meaning regular, not special education.

Under Section 504 procedures, the parent or guardian must be provided with notice of actions affecting the identification, evaluation, or placement of the student, and she is entitled to an impartial hearing if she disagrees with the school district's decisions in these areas.

Many affected children are legally entitled to accommodations through Section 504. They may be challenged by their disorder in school, and often need accommodations to help address their disorder. They often know what to do, but because of their disorder, they have great difficulty doing it.

In summary, yes, your child may have a learning disability and you can find support and accommodations through federal law if his disorder is found to substantially limit his learning. Check with his school to see if he can get additional support so he feels better about school and you can sleep better at night. If you get resistance, check with local advocacy groups or call the department of education or Office of Civil Rights about information on ADHD, IDEA, and Section 504.

Review and Tips

- An child can qualify for special education services under *Specific Learning Disability* or *Other Health Impairment (OHI)*.

- Parents should become familiar with both IDEA and Section 504—both educational protections can be important for your child's success in school.

- A child may qualify for Section 504 services, but not necessarily meet the criteria for IDEA. Most children with ADHD are provided with support through Section 504 rather than IDEA.

My Child Has a Hard Time at Recess

Children with ADHD often have difficulty at recess. They get into trouble more than other children. They have conflicts with classmates and school staff and end up losing more recess time than their classmates. The characteristics below can help explain their difficulty at recess.

Impulsive Behavior

As discussed in chapter 1 ("I Am Confused—So What Is ADHD?"), these children have great difficulty inhibiting their behavior. This impairment affects their ability to learn from their mistakes. The time between thought and action can be short—sometimes nonexistent. Driven by the moment, they often act before thinking, leading to negative interactions with peers and school staff. Their difficulty in inhibiting their behavior creates problems with free time.

Difficulty Modulating Emotions

They often have difficulty modulating their emotions. They can be emotionally volatile, and their moods can go up and down in a heartbeat. They show little restraint and do not restrain their emotions, which overwhelm and sometimes frighten those around them. They have low frustration tolerance and can be irritable, easily upset, and sometimes react viciously to others who irritate them.

When you consider this profile and put an affected child in an unstructured environment like school recess, he will often get in trouble. Running, jumping, playing tag, or participating in team sports at recess can sometimes take the high-energy edge off; however, it also changes the physiological state of the body, putting the child in a high-arousal state. Physically and emotionally aroused, he can have negative interactions with staff and peers on the playground. Because of his limited self-control, he will strike out at other children or bark back at teachers who try to intervene.

Noncompliant and Oppositional Behavior

Children with strong hyperactive and impulsive traits are at risk for noncompliant and oppositional behavior. The noncompliant and oppositional child with ADHD is commonly argumentative with adults, frequently loses his temper, swears, and is often angry, resentful, and easily annoyed by others. On top of this, he normally will not take ownership for his own behavior and blames others for his actions.

Impatience

These children can also have little patience for others' space, feelings, or wishes. Their impatience, combined with impulsivity, leads to poor respect for others' boundaries. They will jump into a game without being invited, take a ball without asking, or run off the playground without checking with the teacher.

Ideas to Help at Recess

When an affected child is put on a behavior management program that attempts to minimize these problematic traits, his behavior at recess can improve significantly. Recess will be more positive, and you will get fewer calls from his teacher and principal. We have recommended to school staffs the following interventions that can make recess positive for affected children.

Don't Leave the Classroom without a Plan

A child who has a hard time at recess should not leave the classroom without a plan for what to do when he gets upset. He will do better at recess if he is given a plan for how to deal with possible conflicts. As discussed above, affected children are poor at regulating their emotions, and when they are aroused, any noncompliant trait will be more of a problem. We recommend that teachers talk with the child for a few seconds before dismissing the class for recess or after the class has lined up for recess. The huddle can be brief, but it should include an overview about where he can go when he feels angry and to whom he can talk about his unhappy feelings. The teacher can say, "Tell me where you will go if you get upset with someone on the playground, and who can you talk to about your feelings?" The child should be able to answer both questions before leaving the class-room or recess line. Normally he is asked to talk with the recess monitor, who should be told about the plan before it is implemented. Often, different monitors may monitor recess during a week, so the school principal can pri-vately brief all of them about the child's plan.

There should be an identified time-out place somewhere on the recess grounds (next to building, on bench by office, standing next to the monitor) where the child knows he can go before getting too upset. This should not be seen as a place of punishment, but a place where he is to be left alone until he feels less agitated. However, if he hits another child, he will be removed from the playground area and held responsible for his aggressive behavior.

Green Card

The *Green Card* intervention can be very effective. It is a procedure to help the child better monitor his own behavior and a way the teacher and parent can reward him for good behavior. The teacher gives the child a green card (2x8) with the numbers 1, 2, 3, written on it (*1* represents poor behavior; *2,* fair behavior; and *3,* good behavior). He is to give the green card to the recess monitor at recess before going out to play. He is told that she will monitor his behavior by circling one of the numbers. At the end of recess, the child is to pick up the green card and give it to his teacher.

Affected children often find it difficult at first to remember, or if they have had a bad recess, they don't want their teacher to know, so when this happens, the recess monitor will return the card or have another child not at the student's grade level return it to the teacher. If the affected child gets a *1,* he loses the next recess time. The teacher collects the green cards at the end of the day and sends them home with the child for the parent's review. The parent is asked to set up a reward system for good behavior and a con-sequence for a bad day at recess. This intervention serves two purposes: one, it provides a monitoring system that is simple to score; two, it gives the child a reminder to work on his behavior.

Time-Out Areas

Time-out areas should be in a place where the child has minimum con-tact with other children on the playground, not in a place where there is high traffic, such as in the principal's office or on the basketball court. The purpose of time-out is not to punish, but to allow the child time to calm down. A child who has difficulty modulating his or her emotions will often strike out at other children, even those he doesn't know. Keep other children away as much as possible.

Your child may need special support at school to help him stay out of trouble at recess. He will need a school program to help him better deal with his impulsivity.

Review and Tips

- Recess is not always a safe or positive experience for children with ADHD. Because of traits discussed above, they will often get in trouble.

- An affected child should not go to recess without a plan. He needs reminders and a place to go when upset.

- Because of difficulty modulating their emotions, these children are quick to get angry and often yell at peers and school staff. Some children do best when recess is an earned privilege, rather than an expected one. Talk with your child's teacher about setting up a program so your child is more successful at recess.

- Support him by providing rewards at home for good behavior at recess. Children under the age of 12 respond well to token systems. You may be successful in improving your child's behavior at recess when you are consistent in giving both verbal praise and concrete rewards for good behavior.

- Share some ideas presented in this section with your child's teacher, but do it diplomatically.

My Child's School Asked for a Student Study Team—What's That?

A *student study team* can be called by different names. Parents are often called to attend a student study team meeting when their child is having academic or behavioral problems in the classroom. Participants in the student study team include the parent, school principal, possibly a special education representative, and other educators who work with your child. The child's strengths and academic concerns are listed, along with recommended interventions to address these concerns. Sometimes the child will be referred for special education evaluation, but not always. You may also request a special education evaluation without the intervention of a student study team.

If your child is referred to a student study team, try to view it as a helping tool. The student study team is not a legal or binding committee, but a vehicle wherein all interested parties can brainstorm and find more effective ways to address a child's educational needs. Don't feel threatened or intimidated by this committee. If you perceive unreasonable demands or threats, the committee has not met its educational goal. The goal for the student study team is to work with the parent in finding more effective ways to help the child. You are one of the most important members of the team, and your input is critical.

The student study team can be an effective tool for finding more positive ways to address an affected child's needs. Often it is through the student study team that a child is offered Section 504 services (refer to "My Neighbor Says Schools Have a Legal Obligation to Accommodate My Son's ADHD. Is This True?" in this chapter for discussion of Section 504).

Review and Tips

- A *student study team* can be a positive and effective tool to discuss your child's educational needs.

- Recommendations coming from the student study team are not legally binding, but simply a committee's recommendation that you can accept and that leads to a better educational environment for your child.

- The tone of the student study team should not be one of blame, but of support for the parent and teacher dealing with a sometimes-difficult child.

I Worry My Child Will Be a School Dropout

Your worry is not unfounded. Children with ADHD generally have great difficulty in school. As mentioned in earlier sections, roughly one-third of affected children will be held back one grade in school and about one-third will not complete high school. Unfortunately, retention is a negative educational intervention for all children. Studies find that a child retained one year has a 30% chance of not graduating from high school, and a child retained two years has an even greater chance of not graduating from high school. More than half of affected children have an oppositional component that gets them into serious trouble with school staff and up to 15% to 20% will be suspended or expelled from school because of their behavior. (Barkley 1995).

However, recognize that the majority of children with ADHD, even though they find school difficult, do graduate from high school. One success story is that of a challenging and bright child with ADHD who had great difficulty in high school, but upon graduating, attended a junior college for two years. He came back a few years later and told a staff member that he had been accepted to the University of California, Los Angeles. He was successful because he was given support and guidance by a special teacher in his high school and was provided educational accommodations for his disorder.

Your child may not have a high IQ and may have a learning disability; however, there are things you can do to minimize the chances your child will be a school dropout.

- Monitor your child's schooling closely. Children with ADHD are not self-starters or good managers of their schoolwork. They often need to be monitored long past the age of other children.

- Be your child's coach. He needs help in finding ways to be better organized, remember to turn in schoolwork, and keep friends. Even an adolescent will need your ongoing coaching. Being your child's coach does not mean you do his work—he does the schoolwork. Your job is to provide an environment at home that provides support for good work habits.

- Ask your child's school to provide weekly or bimonthly progress reports. These children are poor time managers and are often poor judges of their academic progress. They will think they are getting a passing grade, and are later surprised when they receive a failing grade.

- Maintain a positive and constructive relationship with your child's teachers. Blame is no friend to a child with ADHD. Blaming the school or a teacher often does your child no good and can often create more problems than solutions.

- A positive relationship with your child is the most important contribution you can make in ensuring he is not a school dropout. He needs your unqualified love, understanding, patience, and yes, forgiveness. There are other people in his life who can counsel him on his academic choices and decisions, if necessary.

- You are an important factor in your child's development, but not the only one. Many factors contribute to his success or lack of success in school: temperament, choice of friends, teachers, cognitive ability, emotional status, physical attributes, and social skills. If he has dropped out of school, try to forgive yourself. Also recognize that a decision your child makes at 16 or 17 is not irreversible. Many affected adolescents have dropped out of high school, but have later received their high school equivalence diploma and have gone on to become successful adults.

- These suggestions, coupled with ideas shared in other sections, can provide positive interventions to minimize the chances your child will be a school dropout.

Review and Tips

- Children with ADHD are at risk for dropping out of school. Your fears are not unfounded or unreasonable; however, the majority of affected children do graduate.

- Be your child's parent, not his teacher. There are other people who can counsel him on his academic choices and decisions.

- Affected children often require parental support long after other children their age. Consequently, you may need to monitor your child more closely than is required of his friends to help him graduate from high school.

Summary

School can be difficult for children with ADHD; however, the majority do graduate from high school. Your involvement in your child's education will be more intense and will require more of your time and energy than you will need for your unaffected child. You will need to keep close contact and provide coaching for him and his teachers. Become the expert on ADHD, because you cannot depend on his teacher knowing about his disorder. The rewards for good parenting are found in your child's academic success. You may not get a diploma, but you can smile and say to yourself, "I did it!"

7

Even My Pharmacist's Wife Says She Wouldn't Put Her Child on Ritalin

One mother, after being confronted by a pharmacist's wife, came to the therapist's office angry, embarrassed, and hurt. When she had picked up her child's medication at the pharmacy, the pharmacist's wife told her, "I wouldn't put my child on Ritalin, and you should think twice about giving your child Ritalin." The mother left feeling attacked and guilt-ridden.

Medicating children for ADHD continues to be controversial, especially in light of the dramatic increase in the number of prescriptions being written across the United States for stimulant medications in the past few years. An outspoken physician and writer, Peter Breggin, advocates stopping the current trend in medicating children for ADHD, arguing that not only is Ritalin uncalled-for on many occasions, but that it can have serious side effects that are not brought to parents' attention. He writes, "The debate about Ritalin and ADHD has been lopsided" (Breggin 1998). He suggests that teachers, much like parents, feel pressured to find shortcuts for dealing with the disruptive and fidgety child, and they are being misled by support groups and drug companies for both political and financial reasons. The consequence is that more and more American children are now being medicated for ADHD.

Opposition groups, who are strongly against medicating children for ADHD, have filed lawsuits in Texas, California, and New Jersey, claiming that Novartis Pharmaceuticals Corporation and its Ciba-Geigy division (the manufacturer of Ritalin) "conspired with the American Psychiatric Association to create and promote the diagnosis of ADHD, thereby enhancing the profits of the pharmaceutical company." Also named in the suit is the nonprofit support group CHADD (Children and Adults with Deficit/Hyperactivity Disorder), which has received financial support from Novartis (Wagner 2001, 25). The American Medical Association (AMA), however, in a recent news release, pointed to a study by Larry Goldman, MD, and colleagues from the Council of Scientific Affairs of the American Medical Association showing "little evidence that ADHD is overdiagnosed or that Ritalin is overprescribed" (Goldman 1998). Many experts feel that the rise in the number of prescriptions written for stimulants merely represents a much greater recognition of the disorder itself in both children and adults, as well as an appreciation for the important role that medication plays in the treatment of ADHD symptoms.

Parents may wonder how they can possibly decide whether to medicate their children when doctors themselves can't seem to agree. Unfortunately, this dilemma is often worsened by the media war between those who overstate the dangers of medication and those who overstate the benefits of medication.

This chapter is not intended to promote or to dispute the claims of others about the role of medication in the treatment of ADHD. Professional disagreement and continuing dialogue is important and helpful to clinicians working with affected families. Our belief is that medication has an important role to play in treatment, and our intent is to provide information that can help you better understand the role of medication, and to educate you regarding the specific medications that are currently used in the treatment of ADHD.

You may be thinking about putting your child on or taking him off of medication. The following questions and answers should give guidance and answer many of your concerns.

1) My child's teacher says that my child needs to be put on medication.

As just noted, the decision about whether or not to put a child on medication is a very difficult one for many parents. For some, this difficulty centers around guilt. You may be falsely concluding that your child's diagnosis is somehow your fault as a parent, either because you gave him bad genes or because you did something wrong in raising him. This guilt tends to increase when you are then asked to approve of subjecting him to what in your mind might be a potentially dangerous medication.

It doesn't help matters when your child, who may already be upset about getting the message that he is somehow flawed, is vigorously opposed to being on a strict medication regimen. Or, it may be that you are already concerned about the stigma associated with a mental diagnosis, now compounded by the idea that, as several parents have put it, "It must really be bad if they think my child needs medication."

Despite these concerns, the most common medications used to treat ADHD, while not necessarily completely benign, are often very well-tolerated with a minimum of side effects in the majority of children. Additionally, studies support the idea that for most affected children, using medication is the single most important intervention that you can make in managing core ADHD symptoms. Studies that have compared stimulants with psychosocial treatment have consistently found greater efficacy with stimulants, but this in no way negates the importance of all of the other behavioral and environmental intervention strategies suggested in this book. A combined approach may offer the best results.

Despite concerns about stigma and medication side effects, a decision to *not* treat ADHD may have significant negative consequences for your child, not just in terms of ongoing problems with school performance, but with the multiple social and secondary psychological problems that can occur if impulsivity and socially inappropriate behaviors are left unchecked. For example, studies show that untreated children with ADHD experience greater peer rejection, have higher injury rates, and experience higher rates of substance abuse and antisocial behavior. Their families experience high rates of marital discord, parental frustration, and divorce. The whole question of whether or not to use medication is more easily answered when considering the following advice.

Try to keep in mind that the benefits of using any particular medication must always clearly outweigh any potential risks or annoying side effects associated with the use of that medication. Otherwise, there is simply little reason to continue to medicate. Observe and compare your child's behavior on and off of medication on an ongoing basis to be certain that the medication continues to be helpful. At the same time assess his tolerance to the medication in terms of both the presence of any annoying side effects as well as his willingness to comply with taking the medications regularly.

For example, if your son is on Ritalin and the medication seems to be extraordinarily effective at improving attention and focusing, yet he is complaining of annoying headaches, insomnia, and lack of appetite which are making him feel miserable, then obviously you will need to reconsider either the dosage or the specific medication.

2) What medications are most commonly used to treat ADHD?

While there are a number of potentially useful medications for treating ADHD, the vast majority of children will be tried first on either Ritalin (methylphenidate) or Dexedrine (dextroamphetamine). This is primarily because these two medications have been available for many years and have a long, relatively safe track record when used appropriately. There are few potentially serious side effects associated with Ritalin and Dexedrine, and these medications are relatively easy to use. They have consistently been demonstrated to improve attention, hyperactivity, and impulsivity significantly better than placebos in numerous studies. Generally, about 75 % of all children with ADHD will respond well to Ritalin, and of those who don't, about 75 % of these children will then respond to Dexedrine. The converse is also true if Dexedrine is the first drug tried.

There are short-acting and long-acting forms of both Ritalin and Dexedrine. Short-acting forms generally take 20 to 30 minutes to be absorbed and begin working. They continue to help with symptoms for the next three to five hours and then lose their effectiveness, often quite abruptly, as they are broken down, or *metabolized*, by the body and eliminated. The longer-acting preparations of Ritalin (Ritalin-SR) and Dexedrine (Dexedrine Spansules) take longer to exert their effectiveness—generally 45 minutes to one hour. They usually work well for six to eight hours, followed by a more gradual decrease in their effectiveness and subsequent elimination. Short-acting Ritalin is generally used in the dosage range of 5 to 20 milligrams (mg) per dose and is usually given two to three times daily, depending on need. Dexedrine is twice as potent as Ritalin on a milligram basis and is therefore used in the dosage range of 2.5 to 10 mg for most individuals.

The long-acting preparations of these two medications usually need to be used at double the milligram dosage of the short-acting forms to have comparable effectiveness, since these long-acting forms are made to be released more slowly into the bloodstream. For example, 20 mg of long-acting, or *sustained-release,* Ritalin (Ritalin-SR) will really only be achieving a concentration in the bloodstream of around 8 to 10 mg at any given time. Since it will last twice as long as short-acting Ritalin, the total daily dosage will end up being the same regardless of whether one is using short-acting versus sustained-release formulations. The main problem with Ritalin-SR compared to the Dexedrine Spansules has been that it is only manufactured in a 20 mg sustained-release preparation, thus making its use somewhat impractical for anyone needing, for example, 10 or 30 mg of a sustained-release Ritalin preparation. The 20 mg pill cannot simply be broken in half, since doing so will interfere with the sustained-release properties of the pill.

To remedy this situation, pharmaceutical companies have recently come up with two new methylphenidate preparations. The first, and less-expensive, of the two products is called Metadate-ER. This is made in both 10 and 20 mg sustained-release tablets. Most of Dr. Rosenthal's patients thus far have reported that they see little difference between the 20 mg Metadate-ER tablet and the older 20 mg Ritalin-SR tablet. The main advantage of Metadate-ER over Ritalin-SR appears to be the availability of the 10 mg Metadate-ER tablet, which allows for more flexible dosing of sustained-release methylphenidate. The second new methylphenidate product is called Concerta, which is available in 18, 36, or 54 mg capsules. These unique capsules cost more than other methylphenidate preparations, but they feature a patented new delivery system that allows for dosing only once daily. This is because these capsules are designed to release the medication in a slow and consistent fashion over several hours. The medication starts working within the first hour after it is swallowed, and its duration of effect is generally around 12 hours. This means that Concerta should eliminate the need for either a noon dose of methylphenidate or an after-school dose to help with homework. The "ideal" candidate for Concerta would be the child with ADHD who really needs 12 hours' worth of methylphenidate in his system consistently, but who doesn't comply well with taking medication more than once daily. The main disadvantage of Concerta's 12-hour duration would be its potential for 12 hours of appetite suppression (see question #7—"What side effects might I expect my child to have from stimulants?").

Two other available prescription stimulant medications are Adderall (a combination of dextroamphetamine and amphetamine) and Cylert (pemoline). Both of these are long-acting medications. Adderall sometimes seems effective when neither Ritalin nor Dexedrine are. Adderall is being prescribed increasingly as a first-choice, or first-line, medication for ADHD, but Dr. Rosenthal's preference is to use it primarily for those children who tolerate Ritalin and Dexedrine well but fail to get an adequate response. Adderall is often effective within 30 minutes after administration and typically lasts six to eight hours but may last as long as 12 hours if the dosage is fairly high. A new, longer-acting form of Adderall, which is designed to routinely last for up to 12 hours at any dosage, is called Adderall-XR (for extended release) and became available around the beginning of 2002.

Pemoline (Cylert) is a unique stimulant that is often well-tolerated, but it has recently been downgraded to perhaps a last choice among the stimulants due to its potential for toxicity to the liver. While Cylert's potential to cause liver toxicity has actually been known for years, the manufacturer has recently advised that anyone taking Cylert will need to have blood tests every other week to assess for any potential liver toxicity. This is a dramatic departure from the past in which a blood test every six months was considered adequate. Consequently, few practitioners are willing to continue prescribing Cylert, and few patients are willing to follow such rigorous requirements despite the extreme rarity of liver toxicity from Cylert.

In summary, stimulants such as Ritalin and Dexedrine have historically been the primary medications used to treat ADHD, and Adderall and Cylert are other effective stimulants. Several nonstimulant medication choices have their place in the treatment of ADHD, but few of these other medications (which will be discussed later in this chapter) are able to directly improve attention and focusing to the same degree as the stimulants for most individuals.

3) What changes can I expect to see in my child after giving Ritalin or Dexedrine?

While stimulants appear to have some potential to help with the full range of core symptoms, their greatest strength seems to lie with their ability to improve focus and staying on task. Studies have also noted overall improvement with stimulants in social situations, in that the medication tends to reduce the intensity and improve the quality of peer interactions. Impulse control, fine motor coordination, restlessness, reaction time, and even short-term memory have been shown to improve as well. Aggressive behavior is often reduced with stimulants, but frequently the addition of secondary medications (see question #22—"Are there medications used to treat ADHD other than the stimulants?") and additional behavior management techniques are necessary to control problematic aggressive behavior or severe emotional outbursts.

4) Do stimulants cure ADHD? How do these medications work?

Unfortunately, no known medication actually cures ADHD, but medication may help control many of the symptoms and behaviors. There are various theories about exactly how certain medications exert their effects, but one of the prevailing theories is that stimulants work by stimulating areas of the brain that are underactive in those with ADHD. There are brain scans capable of measuring activity in various regions of the brain. When these scans look at areas of the brain that are responsible for inhibiting behavior and for maintaining attention, the scans usually show notably less brain activity in affected children. These same areas often begin to appear normal when scans are repeated following stimulant administration. Some researchers have drawn the conclusion that for many children with ADHD, the constant fidgeting itself may actually represent a child's unconscious attempt to self-stimulate these underactive brain areas. In such cases, stimulant administration might actually eliminate the need to be in constant motion as a means of trying, usually in vain, to stay alert and attentive.

5) How long do I need to try stimulants to know if they work?

As noted earlier, most stimulants exert their effects within the first hour of administration and are only in the system for the next several hours. Consequently, on a given dosage one should theoretically know if the medication is effective after the first dose. These medications don't generally need repeated administration for one to know if they are going to be helpful. In reality, however, it isn't always easy to assess effectiveness after one dose, and it may take a few days to know for certain just how helpful the medication is. Perhaps the most common reason for uncertainty is that there are any number of daily events or stressors in a child's life that potentially influence behavior. If, for example, your child is upset because he has just been grounded for failing to do his household chores for the past six days in a row, then it is unlikely that he will suddenly be cooperative and focused on his homework the day you give him 5 mg of Ritalin. In other words, you need to establish a pattern of responsiveness or failure to respond to medication and rule out the possibility that he just had an unusually good or bad day when assessing medication effectiveness.

In your assessment, it is also helpful to try to have something relatively objective to measure, such as a teacher's daily behavior report or the time it takes to complete a particular monotonous task (assuming you already have some idea how long it will take to complete the task without medication). If you find that the lowest dosage of medication, such as 5 mg of Ritalin, has no positive effects and no significant side effects, then the next step would be to try 10 mg of Ritalin and 15 mg later if needed.

Find the exact dosage of Ritalin that works best, and without significant side effects, before adding a second or a third dose of medication that same day. If, for instance, you give Ritalin in the morning for only three days in a row and are told by the teacher that your child had three excellent mornings followed by three typical afternoons in which he had his usual degree of distractibility, then you could probably safely assume that the medication is helping a great deal, since you would only expect it to be effective for the morning hours. At this point it would make sense to try adding a lunchtime dose equal to the morning dose and to watch for improvement in afternoon behavior.

As noted in question #2, the usual Ritalin dosage is between 5 and 20 mg per dose. There is tremendous variability, however, from individual to individual in terms of the dosage required, so despite the attempt by many doctors to guess at the correct dosage based on weight and age, I suggest always starting at lower doses and working upward slowly if there are no significant side effects noted and the lower dosages seem to be ineffective. This will avoid overshooting the correct dosage and causing unpleasant side effects.

6) How do I know when I am giving my child enough, versus too much, of a stimulant medication?

As implied in question #5, enough medication is when you and/or the teacher note significant improvement in ADHD symptoms without significant side effects. The most common sign that too much medication is being given is either your child looks wired (i.e., he looks more hyperactive, seems jittery or shaky, and is more anxious and uncomfortable—all symptoms which may manifest themselves in the form of worsening symptoms or behaviors), or he looks lethargic or withdrawn and without any of his usual spunk. In both cases you should consider either lowering the dosage slightly, e.g., 7.5 mg of Ritalin when 5 mg wasn't enough to be effective and 10 mg was too much, or changing to a different medication if this doesn't work. In Dr. Rosenthal's experience, if your child looks lethargic, this nearly always suggests that the medication will work well on a lower dosage.

7) If the medication works, does that confirm that the diagnosis is correct?

Unfortunately, not necessarily. Stimulants, including caffeine, tend to improve attention in most people at some dosage. For example, if 5 or 10 mg of Ritalin were given to 100 children or adults, measurable improvement in attention and freedom from distractibility in the majority of these individuals would be noted. Those few who don't respond are usually either individuals who are unusually sensitive to annoying or adverse side effects of stimulants, or those who have coexisting problems with their ADHD, such as severe anxiety, depression, or bipolar disorder. The crucial point, however, is that in those individuals identified as having the greatest problem with attention, i.e., those with ADHD, one would likely see very dramatic pre- versus post-stimulant differences in these individuals' ability to attend to a particular task. Those individuals with no notable problem focusing in the first place, however, would likely only see minor improvements in their ability to focus after taking the low-dose Ritalin. In summary, then, while a positive response to stimulants won't confirm a diagnosis, in most cases, those who do have ADHD will respond significantly.

8) What side effects might I expect my child to have from stimulants?

Although the extreme abuse of stimulants in adults has been known to cause central nervous system damage, vascular damage, and hypertension, virtually none of these problems are known to occur with the standard dosages used to treat symptoms. The vast majority of healthy children prescribed routine doses of stimulants have either no significant side effects, or mild, tolerable side effects. Most side effects are dosage-related, so the higher the dosage used, the greater the likelihood that some annoying side effect will emerge. At routine dosages it is extraordinarily rare to see any medically dangerous side effect in a healthy child. It is, consequently, important to be certain that your child is medically healthy to begin with; every child considered for medication should have at least a basic physical examination by his primary care doctor before starting treatment. Stimulants can mildly elevate heart rate or blood pressure, for example, and although this appears to be of little to no medical consequence in the average healthy child, it could be of significance in a child with certain kinds of pre-existing heart abnormalities.

The most common side effect from stimulants encountered in children is appetite suppression. Stimulants tend to decrease appetite for the three to four hours in which short-acting stimulants are actively working, or for the six to eight hours that long-acting stimulants are active. With Concerta, appetite suppression could even occur for up to 12 hours (see question #2— "What medications are most commonly used to treat ADHD?"). The appetite then tends to rapidly return to normal or to increase to even above normal until the next dose is administered. In most cases this side effect is easily managed by simply administering the stimulant with or following meals. While this approach generally works well with short-acting stimulants, a long-acting stimulant, if given at 8 a.m., may still be suppressing your child's appetite if lunch is at noon. This could even be a problem with short-acting stimulants if he takes medication at 3 or 4 p.m. and dinner is eaten at 6 p.m. In this case, to minimize the problem, either eat dinner later, use a lower dose of medication at 3 or 4 p.m. to minimize the appetite suppression (since, as previously noted, most side effects are dose-related), or switch to an alternate stimulant in the hope that a different medication will cause less appetite suppression. Another alternative is to do nothing and to see if the appetite suppression, if mild, will simply resolve in the next few weeks on its own with continued use of the stimulant, as is frequently the case. In the earlier case of the 8 a.m. long-acting stimulant causing appetite suppression at lunchtime, the options are similar: dosage reduction, changing medications to either a short-acting form of the same medication or to an alternate medication entirely, or again doing nothing to see if the side effect will resolve on its own. If all else fails, the doctor can add medication to stimulate appetite. One such medication is Periactin, a relatively safe antihistamine that can be given in 2 mg doses twice daily to reverse this annoying side effect from stimulants.

Another common but easily managed side effect is insomnia. As most of us who use caffeine know, taking a stimulant too close to bedtime can cause insomnia. Simply adjusting the timing of the dosing so that the stimulant is out of the system by bedtime will solve the problem in most cases. If for some reason this isn't possible, then using a lower dosage for the final dose of the day, and making sure that the last dose is a short- and not a long-acting stimulant, will usually remedy the situation. For children whose ADHD itself is the primary reason they have trouble falling asleep, sometimes an evening dose of a stimulant actually improves insomnia by decreasing the hyperactive behavior and the difficulty gearing down for bed that is so often seen. If all else fails, low doses of other medications such as Benadryl (diphenhydramine), or Catapres (clonidine), given at bedtime, can be used to help your child get to sleep whether the stimulant is contributing to the problem or not.

Mild headaches or stomach upset are occasionally noted with a particular stimulant. Usually these two side effects rapidly resolve on their own with continued use of the stimulant, but if not, a dosage decrease or a change in the kind of stimulant used, or even a change in the drug manufacturer (if generic stimulants are prescribed), will most often help.

The *rebound effect* is another common but generally manageable phenomenon that can occur when stimulant medication rapidly wears off. It is characterized by irritability and an exacerbation of those baseline symptoms that are noted without medication, such as impulsivity and hyperactivity. Sometimes the child's mood is depressed, but in any event, it is an unpleasant experience if your child has to deal with this each time the stimulant wears off. Fortunately, these symptoms, when present, will tend to only last for 30 to 60 minutes, followed by a return to the child's baseline. The likelihood of seeing a rebound effect is not only related to how rapidly the stimulant wears off, but to the dosage of medication used, i.e., lowering the dosage of medication will generally eliminate the problem. Unfortunately, this isn't always an option if the lower dosage isn't effective. Another way to eliminate this problem is to try a long-acting stimulant in place of a short-acting one, as the long-acting preparations will leave the system more slowly and so have a lower likelihood of causing this problem.

One can also try overlapping doses by always giving the second stimulant dose (when using a short-acting stimulant) at least 20 to 30 minutes before the rebound effect occurs because of the first dose wearing off. For example, if your child is on 15 mg of regular (short-acting) Ritalin every morning at 8 a.m. and has rebound symptoms daily at noon, then giving a second dose of Ritalin daily at 11:30 a.m. will eliminate the rebound effect, because the second dose of Ritalin will start to take effect by the time the usual noon rebound symptoms occur. In other words, the rebound effect is now eliminated because the blood level of stimulant is never allowed to rapidly fall from a high level to zero. Continuing with this example, if the 11:30 a.m. dose also needs to be 15 mg (because 10 mg was not an effective afternoon dose for him), then there will likely be rebound symptoms at 3:30 p.m. (Remember again that it is the precipitous drop from a high blood level of medication to zero that causes this phenomenon.) In order to prevent this, he could be given 5 or 10 mg of Ritalin at 3 p.m. This would, hopefully, be a high enough dosage to get homework done and prevent rebound symptoms but not so much as to cause appetite suppression at dinnertime or insomnia at bedtime. Of course, if all else fails and for some reason your child has rebound effects from Ritalin at any dosage with long- or short-acting preparations, then a change to another stimulant would probably be warranted. Using Concerta may be a good option if rebound is a major issue and concerns about appetite suppression are minimal (for a description of Concerta, please again refer to question #2—"What medications are commonly used to treat ADHD?").

9) Can stimulants cause problems with growth?

Generally speaking, the answer is no. For many years there was speculation that stimulants could cause growth deficits in children, and some early studies seemed to lend support to this idea. However, more recent studies seem to have resolved that growth deficits do not occur from stimulant use. Instead, studies suggest that small but significant differences in height previously attributed to stimulants are in fact statistically associated with having an ADHD diagnosis and are not related to the treatment of

ADHD (Spencer et al. 1996; Kramer et al. 2000). There may be temporary deficits in growth in some children that are present in early or middle adolescence, but in most cases the shorter stature tends to resolve by later adolescence. Despite these more reassuring findings with respect to stimulant use, I would recommend that your child's weight and height be followed on a growth chart over time by his pediatrician and that stimulant use be re-evaluated if for some reason there is an abrupt falling off on the growth curve while on medication (e.g., if he has consistently been in the 60th percentile for height and weight, and for whatever reason there is an abrupt and persistent drop to the 10th percentile, then, as a parent, I would want to have this evaluated and not ignored).

10) I've heard that stimulants can cause twitches or Tourette syndrome.

Tourette syndrome (TS) is a neurological disorder characterized by vocal and motor tics or twitches which tend to change in severity and in form over time (e.g., a repetitive grunt may diminish over time and then be replaced by an equally repetitive snort). Anxiety, stress, and fatigue tend to exacerbate the severity of the tics, yet these problems do not actually *cause* TS. The disorder has a genetic basis, and perhaps as many as 70 % of children with TS have ADHD symptoms as well. Fewer children with ADHD also have co-morbid TS, in part, simply because TS is less common than ADHD. While the child with ADHD symptoms may be in grammar school before actually receiving an accurate ADHD diagnosis, most of these children will have had significant symptoms early in life. In the case of TS, however, it is common for the tics not to appear until the child is seven or eight years old, so many children who are genetically at risk for TS will already be getting treatment with stimulants for their ADHD before it becomes apparent that they have the tics associated with TS. In the past there was much speculation that stimulant use caused TS, in view of the observation that tics didn't always appear until stimulants were started, and that in children who already had tics, the twitches, at times, seemed to worsen with the addition of the stimulant. The presence of tics was for many years considered a contraindication to stimulant use in a child with ADHD.

Several studies have assessed what role stimulants may play in TS, and they consistently suggest that stimulants, in the majority of children with ADHD, are no more likely to exacerbate the tics than a placebo. Nonetheless, there may be rare exceptions in which the stimulant seems to either exacerbate pre-existing tics or to bring out tics in those children with a genetic or neurological predisposition for tics. Studies, however, do not support the notion that TS is ever caused by the use of stimulants, and in most cases, the discontinuation of the stimulant will result in improvement in tics if the stimulant had a tendency to exacerbate the tics in the first place. A well-known study of six sets of identical twins, all of whom eventually developed TS, found that in each set one of the two had been on a stimulant, and the medicated twin developed tics earlier than the untreated twin. However, the untreated twin also developed TS, indicating that it was the genetic predisposition and not the stimulant that caused the TS. Most clinicians will now, consequently, consider a cautious trial of a stimulant even in children with ADHD and known TS, due to the often dramatic improvement in ADHD symptoms noted with the use of low-dosage stimulants in these children. In the vast majority of children with TS in Dr. Rosenthal's practice, the tics themselves are rarely functionally or socially disabling and, hence, there is little need to medicate the tics in these cases. In most of these children, however, the ADHD symptoms, when present, are a significant problem, requiring intervention. In these cases, the risk of a stimulant trial seems quite small when compared to the risk associated with untreated ADHD, even if the stimulant use should result in a slight exacerbation of tics.

There are cases in which discontinuation of the stimulant, especially if used well beyond the emergence of new tics, does not result in complete resolution of all tics that seemed to emerge with its use. This persistence of tics is most likely due to the fact that these children had inherited the genes for TS, and permanent tics would have eventually developed even without stimulant treatment.

In any event, when tics are present and are of sufficient severity to require medication management, then clonidine (Catapres) or guanfacine (Tenex) are generally the medications of first choice. Clonazepam (Klonopin) is generally used if clonidine and/or guanfacine is ineffective. Third choices for treating tics are the drugs known as *neuroleptics*. Examples of commonly used medications in this class are risperidone (Risperdal), olanzapine (Zyprexa), and now ziprasidone (Geodon). Haloperidol (Haldol) and pimozide (Orap) are not used as often as in the past because of Haldol's greater possibility of permanent side effects (tardive dyskinesia) and Orap's potential for heart rhythm disturbances. If treatment for ADHD is still required, but a particular stimulant always seems to cause or to exacerbate tics, then a different stimulant can be tried, or other medications such as bupropion (Wellbutrin) or the tricyclic antidepressants can be tried (see question #23 for a discussion of these other medications).

11) Are stimulants addictive?

Although prescription stimulants like Ritalin, Dexedrine, and Adderall all carry strong warnings regarding their "addictive potential," in practice actual drug addiction (or *drug dependence*, as is now the preferred and more precise term) is quite rare when these medications are used as prescribed. Two of the most important components of drug dependence are tolerance and withdrawal. Tolerance refers to either a need to take progressively higher dosages of a medication to achieve the desired effect, or a diminished effect with continued use of the same amount of the substance. As most of us are aware, drugs such as nicotine, alcohol, Valium, and even the stimulant caffeine are associated with the development of significant tolerance. Most readers of this book who drink several cups of coffee daily can readily attest to this phenomenon. These same drugs also have significant withdrawal syndromes associated with their abrupt discontinuation. Again, many who have abruptly tried withholding coffee for a few days after drinking several cups daily are well aware of the severe fatigue and withdrawal headaches often experienced.

Ritalin and Dexedrine, by contrast, have no withdrawal syndrome associated with their discontinuation, with the exception of the rebound effect previously discussed in question #8. With respect to the issue of tolerance, stimulants prescribed for ADHD in standard dosages rarely result in the development of tolerance (caffeine, as previously mentioned, is the notable exception among the stimulants and is therefore not a particularly good drug for treating ADHD). If tolerance does develop, the medication can be discontinued for several days and then restarted at the previous dosage or changed to a different stimulant, since there is rarely any significant cross-tolerance from one stimulant to the next. Thus, the stimulants do not need to be used on a daily basis to be effective and can be discontinued abruptly at any time if desired without any adverse medical consequences. Obviously, the underlying symptoms will rapidly return with medication discontinuation, since stimulants do not cure ADHD but merely treat symptoms while the medication is in the bloodstream.

12) Can stimulants lead to problems with abuse of other drugs?

Children with untreated ADHD are already at higher-than-average risk for substance abuse for several possible reasons. Poor impulse control, low self-esteem, defiant behavior, and impairment in social skills are all commonly seen in affected children, and any of these factors would tend to increase one's risk of experimenting with or abusing illicit drugs as a teenager or adult.

There would be justifiable concern if such risk were to somehow be further increased by the treatment of ADHD with powerful stimulant drugs. Many parents worry that giving their child a pill might give them the message that pills are an easy way to solve life's problems or, that the addictiveness of stimulants might multiply the risk of abusing other drugs (see question #11 above: "Are stimulants addictive?").

Current studies on this issue suggest that stimulant use for treatment of ADHD does *not* lead to later abuse of other drugs, and that aggressive treatment may actually decrease the likelihood of abusing other drugs, perhaps because treatment may directly or indirectly reduce many of the risk factors noted above.

This is not to say that the use of stimulants is risk-free. Treatment with stimulants needs to be considered only with great caution, for instance, in teens who are already identified to be abusing other drugs. If stimulants are used in these teens because it is felt that the risk of abusing the stimulant itself is small compared to the risk associated with inadequately treating ADHD, then it may be justifiable to try a stimulant, but only if the substance abuse is also addressed and only if medication use is very closely monitored by either the parent or school. These are children who should rarely, if ever, be allowed to self-administer their medication. An interesting finding in Dr. Rosenthal's clinical practice in this regard is that even in substance-abusing children with ADHD it appears to be surprisingly rare to discover that they are abusing their Ritalin or Dexedrine. What is common, however, is to find that some of them are not swallowing their medication and are instead giving it to their friends who are abusing the stimulants!

With respect to the relevant concern that giving a pill to a child sends a negative message, it is always important to teach children the difference between taking a pill to treat a legitimate medical problem versus the indiscriminate use and abuse of mood-altering drugs in order to either get high or escape reality.

13) Are there particular children who would be expected to do poorly on stimulants?

While there are few absolute contraindications to the use of stimulants, there are certain groups for whom stimulants are generally either not recommended or for whom they should be used with greater caution. The first of these would include those with psychotic disorders such as schizophrenia, in whom stimulants have the potential to exacerbate psychotic symptoms such as paranoia or auditory hallucinations. The routine use of stimulants would not normally be expected to cause any of these symptoms in children with a diagnosis of ADHD alone, but might in psychotic children with schizophrenia or bipolar disorder when their inattentiveness is mistaken for ADHD.

Similarly, any child with severe anxiety would be at risk for an exacerbation of anxiety with the use of a stimulant medication. This group would include those who seem biologically predisposed to simply have high levels of anxiety and those who are highly anxious or worried due to situational circumstances. An example might be the child who lives in a chaotic family environment or one who has been emotionally traumatized by significant abuse or neglect. As in the case of psychotic disorders, both anxiety and depressive disorders will tend to present themselves with symptoms of poor concentration and attention, and thus can either be mistaken for ADHD or be present with ADHD and exacerbate the ADHD symptoms. In these cases stimulants may, at best, appear to only mildly improve symptoms of inattention, since stimulants by themselves are not considered to be appropriate treatment for either depressive or anxiety disorders. In the case of the anxious child with ADHD, the stimulant has the potential to help with the ADHD, but the stimulant will also have the potential to worsen ADHD symptoms by exacerbating the anxiety. Likewise for depressed children with underlying ADHD, stimulants may at times appear mildly helpful, but if the depressive disorder is significant, then the child's symptoms will not likely improve to any meaningful degree until the depression is adequately treated.

Other situations in which treatment with stimulants might not be helpful are with children who appear to have ADHD-like symptoms associated with intrauterine drug exposure, in those with traumatic brain injuries, or those with pervasive developmental disorders such as autism. These are not hard and fast rules, since some children in these groups may respond positively to stimulants, but children in these categories appear to be at higher-than-average risk for a worsening of their behavioral problems with the use of stimulants.

Stimulants are also not likely to directly improve learning disabilities or oppositional-defiant disorders, but may help if ADHD is clearly present, too. The use of stimulants in children with substance abuse problems is another category in which there is a relative contraindication, as was discussed in question #12 ("Can stimulants lead to problems with abuse of other drugs?").

14) My child's teacher says that my child should only be on Ritalin for school, and my doctor says he needs it daily. Whom should I believe?

While there is no correct answer to this question, Dr. Rosenthal's own philosophy is to recommend Ritalin or Dexedrine every day for those children whose impulsivity or hyperactivity leads to emotional outbursts or behavioral problems that improve whenever the stimulant is taken. In these children, withholding medication on weekends doesn't make sense if the inevitable outcome is eruption into chaos.

On the other hand, many children have no unusual behavioral problems. The primary reason for their taking the stimulant is to improve attention in the classroom or to complete homework after school. Consequently, unless there is some unusual activity that requires a great deal of attention, they won't need their stimulants on weekends or holidays. Additionally, since there is no identified set of symptoms associated with abrupt discontinuation of stimulants, i.e., a *withdrawal syndrome,* then there should be no problem withholding the medication on weekends and restarting it again on Mondays for school.

15) Are there problems with adverse drug interactions if my child is on a stimulant?

There are very few problematic drug interactions with stimulants. Antidepressants called monoamine oxidase inhibitors (MAOIs) do have to be used with great caution with the stimulants, but these are rarely used in the general population and are almost never used in children. Perhaps the most common interaction would be with other stimulating drugs such as caffeine or cocaine, in which case an enhanced stimulant effect would likely occur. Generally, if a person is already consuming large amounts of caffeine before starting the stimulant, Dr. Rosenthal recommends slowly decreasing the daily dosage of caffeine over time to avoid withdrawal symptoms that can come from abrupt discontinuation of caffeine.

Stimulants will tend to counteract the sedating effects of antihistamines or other sedating drugs, but this is often more of a benefit instead of a problem. Lithium may interfere with the stimulating effects of Ritalin and Dexedrine. The effects of the tricyclic antidepressants such as imipramine or nortriptyline can be enhanced when combined with stimulants, and the stimulant effects may be enhanced as well. Occasionally, this might necessitate a decrease in dosage of either one or both of these medications. Stimulants have also been noted at times to interact with the anticonvulsant drugs Dilantin, phenobarbital, or Primidone to increase anticonvulsant activity, yet, by themselves, stimulants may actually increase seizure potential in those with seizure disorders.

Another important interaction that often goes unrecognized is the combination of stimulants with what are known as organic acids, such as ascorbic acid (vitamin C) or citric acid (orange or grapefruit juice). These acids can interfere with proper absorption of the medication and are best avoided for at least 45 minutes before or after taking the medication if a consistent response to a particular dosage of a stimulant is desired. Once the medication begins to take effect it should no longer matter if the person then consumes organic acids.

16) I've heard that kids can become psychotic on stimulants.

It is first necessary to understand that when an individual becomes psychotic it means that he has signs or symptoms of withdrawing from reality. Symptoms may include hearing nonexistent voices or seeing imaginary shapes or objects. The individual may have paranoid ideas or other false beliefs called delusions that are not reality-based. Thoughts may be illogical or bizarre in nature and may seem to make little sense. The most common severe psychotic disorder is known as schizophrenia, but people with bipolar disorder (also known as manic-depressive disorder), severe depressive disorders, or personality disorders can have psychotic symptoms at times.

Individuals with psychotic disorders may present with symptoms of inattention or distractibility, and without a thorough evaluation they could mistakenly be given an initial diagnosis of ADHD. If stimulants are prescribed in the presence of psychotic symptoms, however, one may see further loss of connection with reality, so stimulants should not generally be used in individuals with schizophrenia where psychotic symptoms are continually present. In patients with depressive or bipolar disorders in conjunction with ADHD, the stimulants should not be used in the presence of psychotic symptoms. They can, however, be added if needed to other medications used in the treatment of these mood disorders once the psychotic symptoms are completely gone and, ideally, once the mood is relatively stable.

Stimulants used appropriately in the absence of pre-existing psychotic disorders will not normally cause psychotic symptoms. In rare cases it may be possible to induce temporary psychotic symptoms in susceptible individuals by administering stimulants far in excess of their recommended dosages. Prolonged abuse of stimulants at many times their recommended dosage may eventually lead to a schizophrenic-like presentation, but this is simply not an issue with judicious use of the medication and really has only been identified with the chronic abuse of illicit stimulants.

17) Can stimulants be used in children under age five?

Theoretically the answer is yes, but with several caveats. First, stimulant use is not well-studied in children this young, although no unique medical problems have been identified in children under age five that would absolutely contraindicate stimulant usage. A more important reason to withhold prescribing in very young children, however, is that it is difficult to be certain in this age group whether the ADHD diagnosis is accurate. The majority of children who later turn out to actually have diagnosable ADHD in grade school do historically manifest symptoms prior to first grade. In such young children it can be difficult to fully evaluate other problems that can mimic ADHD, e.g., developmental disabilities or simple immaturity. Additionally, most of the psychological tests used in an educational setting to assess for the presence of learning disabilities are simply not available for use in such young children.

A further complication is that children this age generally metabolize medications very rapidly, so much so that regular Ritalin or Dexedrine often only seem to work for one to two hours at a time. Obviously, administering the medication this frequently would simply not be practical in most cases.

Yet another complicating variable is that commercially available dosages of stimulants may be too potent for such small children, and it can be difficult to divide Ritalin or Dexedrine into small enough fractions of a pill to be practical. If larger pill fragments are used for convenience, but the resulting dosage is too high and of short duration, then rebound effects may become a problem and may occur several times daily (see question #8—"What side effects might I expect my child to have from stimulants?"). Under these circumstances both the child and parent may feel like the child is on a mood roller coaster.

Dr. Rosenthal's advice is to try to wait until grade school if possible. If the severity of the problem is such that you can't wait, then discuss other options with your doctor, such as trying Tenex or the clonidine patch (see question #22—"Are there medications used to treat ADHD other than the stimulants?").

18) My child seems to do better after drinking soda or a cup of coffee. Is there anything wrong with using caffeine instead of Ritalin?

Yes. As noted in question #11 ("Are stimulants addictive?"), caffeine may initially seem to be helpful for the treatment of symptoms, but as many readers of this book are all too aware of from personal experience, tolerance to the effects of caffeine can develop over several days or weeks so that progressively larger dosages may eventually be required to achieve the desired response. In addition, if even moderate dosages of caffeine are used daily, withdrawal headaches and rebound symptoms from skipping a day or two of caffeine can be quite severe. While caffeine may literally be the world's most commonly used drug to medicate ADHD symptoms, its use is far from problem-free.

19) Can stimulants bring out bipolar disorder (manic-depression)?

Now better known as bipolar disorder, manic-depression, as the name implies, is a mood disorder that is characterized by distinct depressive periods alternating with distinct manic periods. Such phases typically last for days or weeks, and may be interspersed with periods in which the mood seems relatively normal. When present, depressive symptoms might include, but are not limited to, depressed mood, diminished interest or pleasure in most activities, weight or appetite changes, sleep disturbance, low energy or fatigue, feelings of worthlessness, and suicidal thoughts. Manic episodes are generally characterized by abnormally and persistently elevated, irritable, or expansive moods in which several of the following signs and symptoms will also be present: inflated self-esteem, decreased need for sleep, increased talkativeness or pressure to keep talking, racing thoughts or thoughts jumping from one subject to the next, severe distractibility, abnormally increased productivity, severe irritability and agitation, and impulsive behavior. If severe, then one may even experience hallucinations or paranoia.

Readers might notice the similarity in some of these manic symptoms to those associated with ADHD (i.e., impulsivity, distractibility, irritability, talkativeness, and racing thoughts). Understandably, then, it may be difficult to accurately diagnose bipolar disorder in individuals who initially present with ADHD symptoms. To further complicate the issue, children and teens with bipolar disorder often cycle very rapidly between depression and mania, and may even have a mixture of depressive and manic symptoms at the same time.

It is also possible to actually have ADHD and bipolar disorder concurrently, and most children or teens who are eventually diagnosed with bipolar disorder will have previously been diagnosed with ADHD.

Fortunately there are certain clues that experienced clinicians can use if they are trying to establish that the ADHD-like symptoms a child is experiencing actually represent bipolar disorder instead. For instance, the presence of a strong biological family history for bipolar disorder would greatly increase one's suspicion. Any suggestion that the ADHD symptoms disappear and then reappear would support the presence of a mood disorder as the actual diagnosis. Often in children with bipolar disorder, violent fantasies and aggressive behavior are completely out of proportion to any identifiable precipitant. The presence of hallucinations or severe paranoia also suggests that simple ADHD is not the correct diagnosis. Periods of low energy with excessive sleeping, alternating with periods of extreme hyperactivity, euphoria, and wildly increased impulsivity or hypersexuality associated with a need for only minimal amounts of sleep, would be strongly supportive of a bipolar diagnosis as well. On-again, off-again responses to stimulants would also strongly suggest the possibility of an underlying mood disorder.

Once bipolar disorder is established as a valid diagnosis, medication management should then shift to the use of mood stabilizers such as lithium, Depakote, or Tegretol to control the problem, rather than the use of stimulants. If mood stabilizers are very helpful at controlling the mood swings and the child is significantly better but still demonstrating problems with distractibility and inattention, at that point one could consider restarting a stimulant for the ADHD symptoms. If a stimulant is used in these cases, however, without the concurrent use of a mood stabilizer, then a worsening of symptoms may occur, since stimulants have the potential to exacerbate manic symptoms in individuals with bipolar disorder.

In summary, stimulants will not cause bipolar disorder, but they can exacerbate behavioral symptoms temporarily in cases where the diagnosis of bipolar disorder is present but has not yet been identified.

20) My child used to do well on Ritalin but now it doesn't work. What is going on?

As noted in the previous question, if the issue is an on-again, off-again response to stimulants where the medication seems to work well at times and then not at all, then the possibility of an underlying mood disorder is suggested. Mood disorders usually interfere with one's ability to attend and to concentrate so that ADHD symptoms will appear to be at their worst when mood symptoms are prominent. If ADHD symptoms tend to disappear completely when one's mood is normal while other home and school variables are unchanged, then the actual diagnosis of ADHD becomes doubtful. If ADHD symptoms are merely a bit less pronounced than usual when one's mood is stable, then ADHD and a mood disorder are likely to both be present.

If the issue is not an on-again, off-again problem but rather is simply that the medication no longer is as helpful as it used to be, then a slight dosage increase may be indicated. It is possible that either due to the child's growth or to a developmental change in metabolism, the medication is simply no longer effective at its current dosage. Another possibility is that some tolerance to the medication has developed over time (*tolerance,* as discussed in question #11, refers to either the need to take progressively higher dosages of medication to achieve the desired effect, or to a diminished effect with continued use of the same amount of the medication.) If this is the case, the stimulant can simply be discontinued for several days and then restarted at the former dosage. Once the stimulant has been out of the body long enough for the tolerance to diminish, the former dosage should once again be effective. If tolerance keeps reoccurring with this approach, and the child cannot afford to be without the medication for even brief periods of time, then it may make more sense to change to a different stimulant or to periodically alternate stimulants, as there tends to be little cross-tolerance among different stimulants (i.e., a tolerance to one stimulant will not automatically mean that there will be a tolerance to the second stimulant).

If tolerance does seem to develop, it is worth looking at how the medication is being administered. In Dr. Rosenthal's experience, it is more common to see development of tolerance when the stimulant is being used at high dosages multiple times daily, particularly with the use of long-acting stimulants. It seems that the greater the daily stimulant blood level and duration of that blood level, the greater the chances of some tolerance developing over time. Unfortunately, it may not always be practical to decrease either the individual milligram dosage or the number of doses per day if the child's behavior is unmanageable with less medication.

21) Are there any good natural remedies available?

The term *natural remedies* generally refers to those substances used for medicinal purposes which are found in relatively unaltered states in the environment—as opposed to the unnatural pharmaceutical drugs which are synthesized in laboratories. Natural remedies are popularly thought of as safe, and synthetic unnatural drugs are often considered by the lay public to be potentially hazardous. The problem with what seems to be a simple distinction, however, is that natural remedies are not always safe or adequately tested, and many are processed in unnatural ways before they reach the consumer. Furthermore, many pharmaceutical drugs are actually purified or extracted from natural sources, and may be chemically identical to those synthesized in a laboratory. In other words, the boundaries between natural and unnatural remedies are fuzzy at best.

Nonetheless, using the definition above, there may be some useful natural remedies available for treating conditions that mimic ADHD or conditions that may co-exist with ADHD, such as depressive or anxiety disorders. Dr. Rosenthal, however, has yet to see any clear treatment responses to herbal medicines, homeopathic treatments, or vitamin therapies for the treatment of the core symptoms of ADHD. Many dramatic claims have been touted for the use of remedies such as blue-green algae, fish oils, or other potent antioxidant preparations from pine bark or grape seed extract, but the transient mild benefits noted by some parents in his practice seem to have ultimately amounted to little more than brief placebo responses (see chapter 1 in the "Myth or Fact" section for a discussion of diet, sugar, and possible medical contributors to ADHD).

One possible exception is with the use of those herbal formulations that contain natural stimulants such as ephedra. They should generally be avoided, however, since they are not always safe. Ephedra in particular can be very toxic in high dosages and its use has been responsible for at least 15 well-documented deaths to date in the United States alone. Additionally, some herbal remedies can have significant and potentially serious drug interactions when combined with prescription medications. If you are using any of these along with traditional pharmaceutical medications, inform your doctor, who may or may not be familiar with the potential for problematic drug interactions with these herbs.

The temptation to find a natural approach to treatment can be very strong. Most of us would like to use approaches to treatment that offer the greatest benefit with the fewest risks, but unfortunately, as in the ephedra example, natural or herbal does not always mean safer. Additionally, many parents feel that they can somehow avoid the stigma associated with either the ADHD diagnosis or the use of stimulants by using alternative therapies instead.

Even if these approaches do not end up being toxic, they may have adverse consequences for your child if they significantly delay the usage of more thoroughly researched medications where potential risks versus benefits are better known. There is at least one important reason why natural treatments are often less-well-studied than are more traditional medications. Since natural remedies are by definition found in nature, these substances cannot, generally speaking, be easily patented by companies wishing to package and promote their use. The patent system was designed to give a person or company exclusive rights to research, develop, and market a product for a predetermined period of time. Once a patent is obtained, a company no longer needs to worry (for several years) that their own research and development dollars will allow a competing second or third company to borrow and profit from that research by marketing the same product with minimal investment. Without the ability to patent an herbal remedy, there has been little incentive for private companies to spend money on research. However, due to dramatic recent increases in the general public's interest in herbal remedies in the United States, there is increasing movement by both private enterprise and the government to fund research in this area.

Although Dr. Rosenthal has not seen any truly effective alternative medicines for ADHD thus far, that does not exclude the possibility that safe and effective alternative approaches will eventually be discovered. There are some very knowledgeable practitioners who strongly assert, after their own careful review of the literature, that such approaches are available now. Taylor (2001), in his book *Helping Your ADD Child,* states that significant improvements in behavior can be seen with safe dietary interventions if they are made in a thoughtful, comprehensive manner.

22) Are there medications used to treat ADHD other than the stimulants?

As previously noted, stimulants like Ritalin, Dexedrine, and Adderall appear to be uniquely effective at targeting symptoms of inattention and distractibility. In most affected children, however, the stimulants are less effective at decreasing impulsive and hyperactive behaviors than they are at improving attention. Other medications are often used to target these other behaviors and are used either with stimulants or by themselves. Until recently, if a low-dosage stimulant was effective at treating symptoms of inattention only, then it had been the preferred practice to simply increase the dosage more and more in a sometimes futile attempt to effectively target impulsivity and hyperactivity. This approach does work for some children, but in many cases this just leads to the emergence of more side effects from the medication with little further improvement in symptoms. Despite concerns about using more than one medication at a time, many practitioners and parents have found that two medications used together at low dosages may yield a dramatically greater response and treat more of the child's symptoms with fewer associated side effects than does using a high-dosage stimulant alone.

Clonidine (Catapres) and guanfacine (Tenex)

These two adrenaline-blocking medications have traditionally been used to regulate blood pressure for patients with hypertension, but they are also used to target hyperactive, aggressive, and intrusive behaviors seen with ADHD. Additionally, they can help decrease the severity of tics, and due to their relative safety they have become the medications of choice for treating Tourette syndrome. Both of these medications are taken orally, but the clonidine is also available as a patch that can be placed on the skin and changed once every five to seven days, like a medicated Band-Aid. The advantages of this transdermal patch are simplicity of weekly administration, and the elimination of rebound symptoms due to the constant release of medication into the system 24 hours a day. Clonidine can be sedating at high dosages, but most children tolerate clonidine well if the dosage is slowly increased over several weeks until a therapeutic level is attained. The oral preparation of clonidine can be used for children whose skin is highly sensitive and reactive to the adhesive in the patch. Unfortunately, oral clonidine is very short-acting and often needs to be given four or more times daily to provide a steady level of medication in the bloodstream. Unlike the stimulants, however, clonidine *cannot* be started and stopped abruptly, since it may take a few weeks before the ideal dosage and response are attained. Significant increases in blood pressure are also theoretically possible if oral clonidine is abruptly discontinued, although this is rare in patients without pre-existing problems with high blood pressure.

Guanfacine (Tenex), by contrast, is also given orally but is a longer-acting medication. There is less sedation associated with its use and its longer half-life (i.e., the time it takes for half of the medication to be metabolized or broken down by the body) minimizes any need for it to be given more than two, or at most three, times daily. Guanfacine and clonidine rarely cause significant reductions in pulse rate or blood pressure when used in low dosages despite their use in treatment of hypertension in higher dosages. With these medications there is a small risk of exacerbating depression in children with ADHD who are also depressed. For depressed children many of the same benefits of guanfacine or clonidine can be attained by using tricyclic antidepressants instead.

Tricyclic antidepressants

Tricyclic antidepressants (TCAs), similar to the adrenaline-blockers clonidine and guanfacine, have been shown to decrease hyperactivity, impulsivity, and aggression for some children. They may at times help with inattention, but generally tend to be less effective in this area than the stimulants. They are frequently used when stimulants are not tolerated or are not effective, or when symptoms of anxiety, depression, or enuresis (involuntary urination) co-exist with ADHD. They can be used along with stimulants or by themselves. They are also generally not known to be drugs of potential abuse, so they may be considered as alternatives to stimulants in those who have a history of substance abuse problems. Also, like clonidine and guanfacine but unlike the stimulants, they require gradual dosage increases until therapeutic levels are attained, since this approach tends to lessen the occurrence of annoying side effects like drowsiness, blurry vision, constipation, or dizziness. Their therapeutic effects have a gradual onset, so it may take three to six weeks on the correct dosage to assess how well they are working. TCAs appear to benefit approximately 70% of people who don't respond well to the stimulants.

The most commonly used TCAs for treatment of ADHD are imipramine (Tofranil), desipramine (Norpramin), and nortriptyline (Pamelor). TCAs have some potential for affecting heart rate, blood pressure, or heart rhythm, so most prescribing physicians will recommend occasional monitoring of cardiac function, particularly with dosage increases and particularly with desipramine. Also, accidental or intentional overdoses of TCAs can be quite dangerous, and though problems with cardiac function are rare with normal dosages, these potential complications, along with the other side effects previously listed, relegate the use of tricyclics to second-choice status behind the stimulants.

Wellbutrin (bupropion)

Wellbutrin is another antidepressant that has been gaining popularity in the treatment of ADHD in recent years, particularly with coexisting depression. This is because Wellbutrin is an antidepressant that forms a stimulant when it is metabolized, or broken down, by the liver. The side effects and potential benefits are generally similar to those noted with stimulant medications, although it has less abuse potential than stimulants, since it may cause seizures if abused at higher than the prescribed dosages. Fortunately, this is not a problem at normal dosages unless the patient has a pre-existing seizure disorder, a history of severe head injury, or is a female with active anorexia nervosa or bulimia—conditions that place the patient at greater-than-normal risk for seizures. In these patients the drug should either not be used, or used with great caution. In addition to its use for ADHD, it is also marketed under the name Zyban for use in tobacco smoking cessation.

Neuroleptics

The neuroleptics, such as haloperidol (Haldol), thioridazine (Mellaril), risperidone (Risperdal), olanzapine (Zyprexa), or ziprasidone (Geodon), are normally used in the treatment of psychotic disorders, but they also have an important place as adjunctive treatments in children with ADHD when severe aggression, bipolar disorder, or Tourette syndrome co-exist. Generally the potential side effects of these medications, such as drowsiness, weight gain, dystonic reactions (muscle spasms), and tardive dyskinesia (abnormal involuntary movements) greatly limit their usefulness for the average child or adult with ADHD.

Mood stabilizers

Lithium, Tegretol, Depakote and Neurontin are occasionally used in children with ADHD. While these medications generally have no direct effect on ADHD symptoms, they have a primary role in treatment if bipolar disorder is present (see question #19: "Can stimulants bring out bipolar disorder [manic depression]?") and they are often useful when severe aggression is present in a person with ADHD.

New ADHD drugs on the horizon

There are at least two new investigational drugs on the horizon that are showing some promise for the treatment of ADHD. One is currently being referred to as *GW320659* (hopefully it will be given a better name at some point in the future). This drug looks very promising and is structurally similar to bupropion (Wellbutrin), but appears to have less seizure potential than bupropion. A second new medication is called *atomoxetine.* Thus far it appears to be as effective as the stimulant medications for the treatment of ADHD, and research demonstrates it improves social functioning. It is a nonstimulant that works on the *norepinephrine neurotransmitter system,* and it appears to have little potential to be a drug of abuse, so it might eventually prove to be a better choice than the stimulants for those who have ADHD along with substance abuse problems. Early reports also indicate it may have antidepressant effects in this population.

There are many additional adjunctive medications currently available to treat symptoms or disorders that co-exist with ADHD. Please discuss the possible benefits and risks of these medications with your prescribing physician.

23) When should drugs like Prozac be used?

Prozac (fluoxetine) is in a class of medications known as the *SSRIs* (selective serotonin re-uptake inhibitors). Other medications in this class are Zoloft (sertraline), Paxil (paroxetine), Luvox (fluvoxamine), and Celexa (citalopram). All are similar in their mechanism of action in the brain, yet all are slightly different from each other and none will directly target the core symptoms of ADHD. They are frequently used in children with ADHD when significant symptoms or signs of anxiety, depression, or obsessive-compulsiveness are present. Medications in this class can be extremely helpful for improving hyper-reactivity (as opposed to hyperactivity) in that when they are effective they tend to significantly improve a person's ability to take things in stride so that he is less likely to become easily overwhelmed. This may explain recent reports suggesting that adding Prozac, for example, to Ritalin may improve the overall treatment response to the Ritalin. This class of medication should be used cautiously, however, if bipolar disorder is suspected, since the use of antidepressants without first using mood stabilizers could exacerbate manic symptoms in these cases (see question #19: "Can stimulants bring out bipolar disorder [manic-depression]?" for a description of bipolar disorder).

24) Do medications help learning disabilities?

There really are no medications at this point in time that are known to directly improve learning disabilities (also known as *developmental disorders*). Nonetheless, if ADHD symptoms or other medication-responsive problems are present along with the learning disability, then at least the medication can effectively be used to target these areas. Once these associated treatable problems are better, the impairment from the disability itself can be more clearly seen and may appear to be less severe than originally thought.

25) My child is defiant. Will medication help with this?

Not directly. Oppositional defiant disorder (ODD) is frequently seen along with ADHD, especially in cases where the ADHD goes untreated for several years. Children with this disorder are often irritable and angry and often lose their tempers. They regularly argue with parents and teachers and tend to blame someone else whenever they get into trouble. They actively defy rules and, in more severe cases, may eventually end up in trouble with the law.

Occasionally these symptoms are part of an underlying depressive disorder, in which case the use of antidepressant medications will likely reduce the severity of these symptoms. When seen along with ADHD, however, the ODD is not commonly associated with a depressive disorder, in which case the appropriate treatment is to learn as many of the other behavioral management strategies that you can from other sections in this book.

Despite the absence of any universally acceptable medication for this problem, many parents and psychiatrists in desperation will try antidepressants, neuroleptics, or mood-stabilizing agents in their attempt to mitigate the often-associated symptoms of impulsivity or aggression. At times these other medications can be quite helpful (also see question #22, "Are there medications used to treat ADHD other than the stimulants?").

26) My child with ADHD doesn't sleep well—what should I do about it?

Getting children with ADHD to go to sleep at night can be an ongoing challenge. Most of the time the problem is simply that they have trouble winding down to go to sleep. If they are on stimulant medications during the daytime, then the medication has usually worn off by bedtime, making them at least as hyperactive as they would have been with no medication at all.

Non-medication solutions should usually be tried first and continued even if you decide to later add medication at bedtime to facilitate falling asleep. Perhaps the single most important initial step is to establish a nightly routine with a set bedtime and "lights out" time. The routine itself, culminating, one hopes, in sleep, can actually help set the body's biological clock to a specific desired sleep time. A hot bath can be helpful if given approximately one hour before "lights out." The hot water slightly raises body temperature, and the slow decrease in body temperature following the bath can actually facilitate sleep. Most adults who have soaked in a spa are aware of this phenomenon. A bedtime reading routine can be helpful as long as the content is not overly stimulating. Obviously, this requires that you have children who are capable of either sitting quietly enough for you to read to them, or who are old enough and focused enough to read to themselves. Simply the process of holding a book still enough to read may by itself decrease motor activity sufficiently to allow for drowsiness to set in.

If these approaches by themselves are not successful, then medication can be considered. First, for some affected children, a very low-dosage stimulant such as 2.5 to 5 mg of Ritalin or Dexedrine may provide enough calming of motor activity to induce sleep. For some, it may worsen the insomnia but, fortunately, only one or two nights of trying this will determine its effectiveness or failure. If this doesn't succeed, there are a number of over-the-counter medications that might help, such as 25 to 50 mg of Benadryl (diphenhydramine) or other similar antihistamines. Many people report success with small doses of herbal preparations such as valerian root, passion flower, or kava-kava (please consult your doctor regarding the use of these herbs, however, in order to avoid any possible drug interactions with your child's other medications). Low doses of melatonin can be helpful, as can low dosages of medications such as trazodone (Desyrel), imipramine (Tofranil), amitryptiline (Elavil), clonidine (Catapres), mirtazapine (Remeron), or nefazodone (Serzone). The use of the benzodiazepines (e.g., Valium, Ativan, Xanax, Klonopin, and Restoril) is generally avoided due to their addictive potential with long-term use. Again, consult your doctor if you're considering these medications.

27) Are stimulants used to treat adults with ADHD?

Yes! Fortunately by the time your child reaches adulthood, there is a strong likelihood that the hyperactivity and the impulsivity components of ADHD will have resolved or at least improved to a large degree. The inattention and distractibility components, however, often continue to be a problem for adults with ADHD except for those who have found a niche for themselves in society and in the job market in which having a problem with distractibility is simply not a major concern. Fortunately, stimulant medications are useful in treating both children as well as adults with ADHD, and responses to medication are generally similar in both groups.

Summary

The decision to medicate your child can be a difficult one, but medication has a very important role to play in the treatment of ADHD. The decision to withhold medication in a child with ADHD carries its own set of risks. This chapter's intent was to inform you about the usefulness as well as the limitations of using medication for your child, and to try to answer some of the most common questions that parents and teachers have about the actual use of specific medications for ADHD.

We discussed the various medications used to treat ADHD and the most common side effects and complications associated with the use of stimulant medications and discussed the various options for managing problems that might arise in treatment.

8

If It Works, Try Again,
but It Won't Work for Long

Interventions that work for most children don't work as effectively with with children with ADHD. A mother described the difference in compliance between her affected child and his younger unaffected brother: "Bobby is told time after time not to wear his skates in the house. Even when punished, he doesn't seem to learn. I only had to tell his younger brother once or twice, and it's never happened again. What works for his younger brother, doesn't work for Bobby." Like many mothers of these children, she was puzzled, frustrated, and often angry with her child because nothing she did, from punishment to rewards, seemed to work for long.

As a parent of an affected child, recognize that interventions require many changes. You need to change both rewards and punishment to keep the attention of your child. As mentioned in an earlier section, we encourage parents to hang this suggestion on their refrigerator: *Use Whatever Works, but It Won't Work for Long.* We call this our *W-W Theory.* Try whatever seems to work for your child within reason, but understand it won't work for long. This chapter will give you interventions that often work and ideas that can be helpful in further understanding the challenges presented by your child.

What Works for His Younger Brother
Doesn't Work for My Child with ADHD

Commonly understood interventions such as time-out and token systems will work, but not for long or as consistently. The reasons can be explained by understanding common ADHD traits.

They don't learn from their mistakes as consistently as other children. This important concept has been covered a number of times in earlier sections.

Affected children will repeat the same mistakes more often than other children, which can be partly explained by their difficulty with inhibiting behavior (see chapter 1). The ability to inhibit behavior affects areas of life from interacting positively with people to performing well on the job. Because of possible developmental delays in the brain circuitry that underlie inhibition and self-control, these children have greater difficulty deferring immediate rewards for future gain (Barkley 1998, 67).

They have difficulty ignoring both internal and external distractions. Their minds jump from one thought or distraction to another, and they're frequently controlled by the moment. If much of your day was governed by trying to minimize internal and external distractions, you too would find it difficult to learn from your mistakes.

Children with ADHD often do not pay attention to what is important. One writer, quoting an affected adult, writes, "You don't mean to do the things you do, and you don't do the things you mean to do" (Hallowell and Ratey 1994). The child, unable to stay focused for any length of time, will jump from one thought or action to another. Since focused attention is poor, he will often not make the connection between what he has done and what happens later. Consequently, he will generally have more difficulty in learning from his mistakes, so interventions that are successful for your unaffected child will be less successful with your affected child. So, you ask, what can I do?

First, remind yourself that your child has a neurodevelopmental disorder that makes remembering to remember, following directions, or stopping before he acts more difficult. His disorder presents a problem, but is not your fault or his. It makes successful parenting more difficult, but not impossible.

Second, behavior interventions that work with other children *do* work with children with ADHD. The interventions, however, need to be changed more often, and your affected child may not respond as consistently as your other child. Rewards are usually not as effective as with other children, but rewards can reinforce positive behavior and change a negative relationship between child and parent.

The relationship between the child and the parent can often be very negative, with little attention paid to what the child is doing right during the day. The parent may be more demanding, critical, and impatient with the affected child than with his siblings. Recognize and reward positive behavior in the child with ADHD so he may have a positive interaction with the parent. The relationship between parent and child is bi-directional— each other's choices and responses affect the child's and parent's behaviors.

Third, attach or hang on a wall our motto for working with these children, *Use Whatever Works, but It Won't Work for Long.* Change consequences and rewards regularly. By changing the intervention regularly, your child will stay motivated longer and not get bored as quickly.

Fourth, don't measure success or lack of success in parenting your child by whether his younger or older sibling does better. Your affected child has an identified disorder that often makes for more conflict, failure, and stress in raising him. Also, remember, an intervention may not work all the time, but that doesn't mean it's not appropriate.

Review and Tips

- What works for your child without ADHD may not work as effectively for your child with ADHD. This doesn't mean your affected child cannot be more successful in following directions or completing tasks.

- These children don't perform as consistently as others— there will be good times and bad times.

- Try not to compare or measure your affected child's success with that of his siblings.

Medication Helps, but I Need More

One of the most common assumptions made by parents is that medication alone will somehow fix their child with ADHD. Doctors as well as teachers and other caretakers often look to the pill as the solution to a child's misbehaviors, yet research suggests that utilizing medication along with a behavioral management program can best minimize behaviors.

Some children's behaviors can be helped by medication alone, without additional interventions. However, the typical child benefits most when medication, psychotherapy, and educational interventions are used together. Medication, however, is often the primary vehicle for delivering health care to these children because it is less costly than psychotherapy and special education. Psychotherapy, unfortunately, is often limited because of financial restrictions set by both private and non-private medical plans, so these children, therefore, are often not provided the needed therapy to address the many associated disorders seen in the ADHD population, such as depression, anxiety, and conduct disorders.

A child will often not be diagnosed until after he is in school. Psychotherapy is then needed to help correct negative patterns of inter-actions between the child and parent. Sometimes, they have developed interactive behaviors can be very destructive to the family unit. A child can become so intensely negative that the parent begins conceding to his demands. This pattern, if not corrected, often leads to *learned helpless-ness,* where the parent makes few efforts to enforce commands, and the child learns that he can do as he pleases. The parent, beaten down by the situation, believes that there is no way to stop the child's misbehaviors and may, at this point, become clinically depressed, have very low self-esteem, and have as few interactions as possible with the child, either positive or negative (Barkley 1981). Unfortunately, if the child is allowed to continue to coerce the parent, the misbehaviors will continue and often escalate.

Educational interventions and accommodations often are necessary to minimize learning challenges, as well as to provide social and emotional support to the child while he is in school. With large classroom pupil-teacher ratios, teachers find it difficult to attend to the individual needs of the special-needs child. Also, large classes produce more distractions and permit less flexibility, leaving the affected child in an unfavorable environ-ment. Generally, he requires close monitoring and immediate reinforcement for good or bad behavior, but a teacher in a classroom of 35-plus children simply doesn't have the time or energy to effectively implement this level of intervention. Many children, therefore, are placed on medication to make them both more manageable and attentive in the classroom, but medication alone is not enough.

There is continuing dialogue and research on the most effective behavior interventions for children with ADHD, but most research suggests that affected children, like all children, need structure, consistency, and acceptance, because they don't learn from their mistakes as consistently as other children and display a number of problems from antisocial behavior to learning difficulties. Proper treatment for most of them requires a range of interventions that include the efforts of doctors, teachers, and parents.

The three most important providers of care for a child are the parents, doctor, and school. Unfortunately, communication between these parties is not always consistent, and in many situations, doesn't take place at all. We use the metaphor of the "three-legged stool" to describe the need for communication.

Each leg of a stool is needed for strength and stability. Similarly, a triad of support (family, doctor, and school) is needed to provide the best possible treatment, and the child, like a three-legged stool, has less support if one leg is missing. One role a therapist can play is to facilitate better communication between the parties who are working with the child.

Review and Tips

- Medication is often important in the treatment of a child with ADHD; however, it's not enough for many children. They often need additional support through behavioral management, educational accommodations, and, for some children, therapy to address associated problems such as depression and oppositional defiant behaviors.

- ADHD is a disorder that presents itself in varying degrees in children. Some have few challenges; others require a multitude of services to be successful.

- Families dealing with ADHD often need additional support. The ideal treatment environment requires a triad of support services, including the school and doctor, as well as family counseling when necessary.

- Don't feel inadequate or pushy if you request additional support from your child's school or doctor. Schools are required to make accommodations for children with special needs if the need is great enough.

There Will Be Good Moments and There Will Be Bad Moments

There are times when things run more smoothly in raising an affected child. One moment your child probably seems no different from his sibling, and the next moment or day you wished you could take a vacation from home. You may have asked yourself, "Why is my child compliant and attentive one moment and at other times is his usual self—inattentive, forgetful, and argumentative?" The answer to this question can be explained by understanding some common ADHD traits.

These children can be attentive, compliant, and generally a delight to be with when involved in activities that are of high interest to them. Most present few difficulties when playing Nintendo, listening to their stereo, or playing with a favorite toy. In fact, when involved in high-interest activities, they usually don't stand out from other children. They can be delightful, entertaining, and loved by those around them.

An affected child at the park is less a problem than when in a grocery store or at a photo shoot. A child at the park is generally self-directed and finds things to entertain himself. He is not asked to stay seated, follow directions, or do tasks that are stressful for him. The park is a place where he can run, jump, and climb without getting into trouble. He can pick and choose what to do with little outside interference or direction from other people. In the grocery store, however, he is asked to keep his hands to himself and walk along with mother. This can often be a difficult task for a disinhibited child.

These children will sometimes have fewer problems at school than at home, where structure and routine are common, and positive peer recognition is desired. The child responds best in environments that are structured and routine. Like all children, he wants to be liked by his peers and be asked to play games at recess. This desire to be liked can often enable the impulsive child to be more sensitive to others' space and property. Generally, however, with more active and impulsive children, desire alone is not enough. Behavioral management plans, combined with medication, are often needed to help them be more successful in making and keeping friends, avoiding trouble at recess, and keeping up with schoolwork.

The school environment can also be stressful, leading to misbehavior both at school and at home. The curriculum may be too hard, the school may not be supportive or knowledgeable about ADHD, and the child may have a bad fit with his teacher. Some teachers and schools are more understanding and knowledgeable, which often leads to a good fit, while in other school settings a bad fit will create more problem behaviors.

These children have difficulty modulating their emotions. The time between impulse and action may be very short, so if the child is enjoying something and is asked to stop, he will react quickly, not considering the negative consequences of his actions. He may throw a game board across the room, for example, when asked to come to dinner, or if bored with the game, will have no problem coming to dinner. The parent, not being a mind reader, is given different reactions with no rhyme or reason throughout the day.

There will be times when things run more smoothly than at other times. This pattern needs to be understood as normal for parents raising children with ADHD. The following ideas can help you cope with this sometimes puzzling and frustrating pattern.

- Remind yourself that your child will be more attentive and compliant at some times than at other times. His reactions are not always a reflection of what you have or have not done.

- His inconsistent pattern of reacting to pleasant and unpleasant events is often a manifestation of his disorder; a developmental delay in impulse control is usually the primary factor in his inconsistent behavior.

- Prepare your child for any changes that are coming. Remember that these children often have great difficulty transitioning from one activity to another, such as being asked to turn off the TV and come to dinner (see "He's So Emotional—Is This Normal?," chapter 4, for further discussion).

- Make a mental note when your child is compliant and attentive. Give him praise or tokens to reinforce these behaviors. Even so, he will encounter more difficulty than other children in learning from his mistakes. There will be times when he will be more successful than at other times.

- Make time to refuel your emotional tank. If you are angry most of the time because of your child's behavior, you probably need time apart from him. This time apart doesn't have to be for a long period. If you're a single parent, find an outside person to watch him for short periods of time (see chapter 5, "I Am a Single Parent—Help!"). Activities that can refuel your emotional tank are exercising regularly, meeting a friend for coffee, taking a short walk, and if married, letting your spouse take over some day-to-day responsibilities until you feel less anxious or agitated. Your spouse can monitor homework, follow up on discipline, and find ways to entertain your child while you find respite.

Review and Tips

- Your child will have his good times and bad times. You are not always the cause for his moodiness or poor choices. He will have challenges to deal with that cause internal stresses.

- Try not to personalize your child's inconsistent behaviors. Sometimes it is not you but character traits in these children that can present themselves. Remember that they have both difficulties in disinhibiting behavior and remembering to remember.

- Take time to take care of yourself. If you don't have the patience or energy to deal with your child, it will be damaging to both of you.

I Am Tired of Yelling

Yelling at your children is not fun, makes you feel guilty, and often creates more problems than it solves. You don't enjoy being yelled at and neither do your children. It is normal for a parent to get upset and yell at times, and children are generally forgiving of it. They understand that everyone loses their temper at one time or another. However, when yelling seems the rule rather than the exception, there is usually a problem, and family counseling is often needed.

Parents yell because it can be effective—yelling gets the child's attention and often stops negative behaviors. However, it generally becomes less effective over time. Children begin to tune out their parents or deduce that "Mom yells more than she does anything else." Unfortunately, it can often increase both the child's and parent's negative interactions, and sometimes both will move beyond yelling and become physically abusive. If it is not good and generally not effective over the long run, what can you do to get out of this pattern, or what can you do to stop it?

You have control over your voice. Yelling is a voluntary act that you can change. Anger, in the form of yelling, is your response to your child's actions, and you choose how you will respond to anger-producing situations. You usually don't yell at other adults, which shows that you can control this behavior—you find other ways to deal with angry and frustrating feelings. The first step in stopping begins with you. Your child is not responsible for your yelling, you are.

Take time to evaluate your anger. It may often be justified, but at other times it can be *displaced anger*. Displaced anger is when one is angry about one thing, but takes it out on another person not connected to the anger. Many times something else is being annoying, rather than the present problem, so one can overreact, making the other person feel confused and victimized. We use the "Kick the Cat" story to describe displaced anger with families. The story goes something like this. Dad comes home from work and is angry because he didn't get the promotion he wanted. He sees toys scattered on the living room floor and yells at his wife. His wife, feeling unfairly picked upon, runs up stairs to find the children who left their toys on the living room floor. When entering their room, she finds them wrestling on the bed. Mom, still upset at her husband, yells and threatens to ground the children for their behavior. She yells at them to go downstairs and pick up their toys. The youngest child, in anger, kicks the cat as he goes out of the room. The poor cat wasn't responsible, but was the recipient of displaced anger. Look at the source of your anger if your reactions seem unreasonable. Displaced anger can be harmful to the parent as well as the child.

Third, if you're angry and starting to yell, back away and deal with the problem another time. Most problems don't need to be stopped right away and can wait until you feel calmer. You can tell your child, "I am very upset with your behavior right now. We yell when we're upset, so let's talk about this problem in a few minutes." Walk away until you feel calmer, but let your child understand that you will be discussing his behavior when you calm down. Holding off dealing with the problem right away can also give you time to gather more information. You may assume or perceive certain things are happening when in fact they are not. With new information you may realize that your anger was unjustified. You may be upset with your child because he yelled at his younger sister, but when you investigate, find that she had provoked him. A delay is not always appropriate, especially when your child is out of control, but it can be a beginning step in resolution. Also, holding off talking about a problem can allow your child time to calm down and think about what he has done.

Because he has a difficult time controlling his emotions, try to stay as calm as possible. One method is to visualize ahead of time how you will look, what you will say, and how you will react to your child's yelling, swearing, or hitting. Visualization is a learned activity that can help you deal with confrontational situations more successfully. It's a common practice used by athletes, fighter pilots, and other professionals to help reinforce and strengthen appropriate behaviors. Take a few moments to picture in your mind a common problem behavior. Visualize you and your child talking about the problem. Picture yourself calm, assertive, and in control. Picture how you are standing, how your face looks, and what you are saying to him. See yourself being successful. Visualization can help you gain more confidence and be more successful in dealing with difficult situations.

Make sure you are not a victim of *emotional blackmail* by your child. Emotional blackmail is a concept presented by Susan Forward and Donna Frazier with regard to destructive interactions in adult relationships. This concept can be helpful for parents who have to deal with an oppositional and noncompliant child. Children can be masters at emotionally blackmailing their parents through manipulation and threats, and learn this skill at an early age. "Manipulation becomes emotional blackmail when it is used repeatedly to coerce us into complying with the blackmailer's demands, at the expense of our own wishes and well-being . . . . Once blackmail has touched a relationship, it becomes rigid, stuck in patterns of demands and capitulation" (Forward and Frazier 1997). Children know what buttons to push and how to upset their parents. The reason you want to know whether you are being manipulated unfairly is to assess whether your child is more interested in winning or resolving the problem. When you realize that his goal is to win or to get you mad rather than discuss the problem, talking generally doesn't help. Walk away until you are ready to set consequences without yelling or hitting.

Try not to personalize his anger. You may be saying, "That's easy to say, but when he's calling me names and throwing things at me, it's hard not to take it personally." We are not suggesting that this behavior is acceptable. You are not asked to accept his behavior, but only view it as an attempt on your child's part to get his way. You have asked him to something he doesn't want to do. The aggressive and verbal abuse directed at parents by their children is often not seen in other settings such as school. Many children with ADHD misbehave more at home than in school—why? The teacher sees the behavior as manipulation and generally doesn't take the anger personally. She keeps the emotional interactions to a minimum and keeps her emotions in check. The parent, because of the emotional history with her child, finds this more difficult.

When you get angry and start yelling, your child has probably won the battle. He's made you lose control. Even if you manage to change your child's behavior, he has won by getting you angry. He probably says to himself, "Mom may make me go to my room, but now she's unhappy, too." Misery loves company.

Recognize that you will become angry and yell at times, but if you try these suggestions and better understand your anger, you may yell less.

Review and Tips

- How you deal with your anger is under your control. There have been many situations when you have felt angry but didn't strike out or yell, and you can practice this same level of self-control with your testy child.

- You don't have to deal with the problem now, in most situations. Most problems can wait until you feel more in control and not driven by anger. Stop, count to five, and walk away. Talk with your child when you are calm.

- Try not to personalize your child's anger. Generally, his anger is related more to manipulation and power struggles rather than sincere anger or hatred towards a parent.

- Practice visualization often. Picture how you want to act when confronted by your child's anger or misbehaviors. Visualization can help you develop successful ways to deal with him.

- Don't let your child blackmail you. You are the parent. Set limits and consequences using as few words and emotions as possible. Say what you want and then walk away.

- Everyone yells at times, so forgive yourself when this happens. However, if your yelling seemed inappropriate and out of line, apologize to your child and let him know you are working on this problem. Model for him that people can change how they deal with anger.

I Am Uncomfortable Bribing My Child to Be Good

Many parents are uncomfortable with the idea of rewarding their children for doing something they should do anyway. One parent asked, "Why should I bribe my child to be good? I worry that he will learn that every time he does something good, he should be rewarded." This is a legitimate concern. Children shouldn't be rewarded every time they do something good. As they grow, they need to learn that doing chores or helping a neighbor or friend is something people should do for each other. Social and personal responsibility is a value that needs to be taught and reinforced by parents, and children who don't learn this lesson often have great difficulty making friends and reaching goals.

Affected children need to be taught by their parents appropriate ways to deal with social and personal conflicts. They can learn these important social lessons, but it's often difficult because they are driven by the moment. They will need extra attention and reinforcement when making appropriate choices. The purpose of material rewards is to reinforce these positive behaviors.

When you bribe someone, you are giving something to induce that person to do something illegal or wrong. When you reward your child with a token or treat, you are not bribing him, but rewarding him for doing the right thing. Rewards are not bribes, and can be a positive reinforcement. Bribes come *before* a deed is done; a reward or reinforcement comes *after* the desired goal has been achieved. Even though rewards are generally less effective with children with ADHD when compared to unaffected children due to developmental delays in impulse control, they help reinforce positive behaviors, and rewards can strengthen positive interactions between a parent and child.

Other children learn ways to delay their actions and thoughts, allowing them to reach goals and not repeat old mistakes. One important way this is done is by self-directed talk. Affected children often don't talk through a problem before acting on their thoughts. For example, the child may not stop and say to himself, "If I get out of my seat, the teacher will take recess away." More often than not, he will be driven by the momentary thought of getting out of his seat, get up, and lose recess. Self-directed talk is less developed in affected children (see chapter 1), and only when taught and reinforced by a parent or teacher can it become more automatic. Verbal and/or material rewards can help reinforce this activity.

Children with behavioral problems often need more than verbal praise to motivate them to follow commands, do their chores, or do their homework. Reward systems, such as tokens, can be very effective in reinforcing good behavior. Children under the age of 12 generally respond well to tokens. A token is a concrete reinforcer that reminds and rewards the child for making good choices. A token, for example, can be a star, happy face, poker chips, or point system. Stars, poker chips and happy faces are especially successful for children ages four through nine, because schools often use them for reinforcement. Children ages nine to 12 respond better to point systems. The tokens can be put on a chart or in a jar for the child to quickly see his progress. Set up a token system that is appropriate for your child's age.

Because these children often become bored quickly, you may want to interchange various tokens intermittently. With stars, you can use different colors (red, yellow, and green) that keep a young child's interest. The same stars can be given different weight (red = 1, yellow = 2, and green = 3) when used with older children. When using the stars in a point system, the points are added up and go towards a special privilege or reward. When using tokens like stars and happy faces, paste them on a chart and hang in an open area for the child to see (front of the refrigerator, bathroom mirror, or bedroom wall). Reinforcement is enhanced when the child put the tokens on his chart and decorates the chart himself.

Older children respond best to point systems. Points are tied into jobs such as making the bed, taking a bath or shower without a reminder, or getting dressed and ready for school on time. Each job is given a point and each reward has a fixed-point value. For example, getting dressed and ready for school on time earns five points, and watching a video costs 40 points, riding the bike after school costs four points, etc. Set up your point system around jobs that your child does daily, such as getting dressed, washing his face, and brushing his teeth. You can add additional jobs that seem most problematic for your child, such as picking up his toys, not fighting with siblings at the dinner table, and telling the truth when there is a problem. The harder jobs can be given higher points to motivate the child to do them.

You assign a certain number of points to each job, and these points apply to rewards that your child enjoys (playing video games, going out to lunch at a fast food restaurant, talking on the phone, etc.) Rewards that are most expensive or require special time are given the most points (miniature golfing, renting a video game, or having a friend over for the night).

Do not tie the point system into family activities. A child should not feel he has to earn time to be with his family. He needs to know that he is still loved and accepted even when he misbehaves. Your goal is to change his inappropriate behaviors, not make him feel alienated from his family.

Many books and journals discuss proper procedures for setting up a successful token or point system for children (see Appendix I: *Recommended Reading*). You often can find them in a local library or bookstore. One important source for parents is CHADD (Children and Adults with Attention-Deficit/Hyperactivity Disorder). CHADD groups often have monthly support group meetings and books and literature to help you with setting up a reward system.

The simpler the reward system, the more successful it seems to be. If a reward system requires too much of your time and is too complicated, you and your child will find it difficult to manage—*Keep it simple* is our motto. Remember, if it doesn't work all the time, that doesn't mean it isn't working. Try a reward system for at least one month before abandoning it. One month gives you and your child time to understand the program and to make changes in both of your behaviors.

A good reward system can help minimize the yelling and blame sometimes experienced in affected families. Your child can see his progress in concrete ways, as well as what it takes to earn certain privileges. You will no longer be a policeman, but a scorekeeper who helps him recognize when he makes good decisions. Like a coach, you will give support and advice, but success on the field ultimately depends on his effort. You can also see that your child often makes the right choice. He will be seen in a different light—not always forgetful and noncompliant, but a child who can make real progress towards meeting behavior goals both at school and in the home.

Try to understand that you are not bribing your child when you reward him for good behavior. View your rewards in a positive light, not something that will be damaging to your child.

Review and Tips

- Rewarding your child for something he did well is not bribery. Bribery is giving something to someone to induce that person to do something illegal or wrong. When you reward your child, you are rewarding him for something he did well.

- Set up a reward system that is appropriate for your child. Younger children generally respond to token systems such as stars, poker chips, beans in a jar, and happy faces. Older children generally do better with point systems. Token systems are usually not effective with children over the age of 12.

- Give your token system time to work. Try a reward system at least one month before abandoning it. Both you *and* your child will need to make changes, which is difficult and requires both effort and successes to make it seem real.

- Find a system that works for you. If the token system or reward system is too involved, you may not find it manageable. Keep it simple so you and your child can use it. Very difficult children often require an outside specialist, such as a behaviorist, to work with a family.

- Don't take away family time when your child acts out. He needs to know that he is loved and accepted even when he misbehaves.

My Adolescent Is Too Old to Place in Time-Out

When children reach a certain age, they are too old to put in time-out and too strong to restrain. Adolescents can still present many behaviors seen at younger ages that challenge their parents: impulsiveness, inattentiveness, noncompliance, and violent outbursts. This problem upsets many affected families, and finding some satisfactory solution sends many parents to the therapist's office. Exhausted and furious parents are at a loss as to what to do.

No one enjoys the thought of confronting a 165-pound adolescent, ADHD or no ADHD. There comes a time when your children are stronger than you, bigger than you, and smarter, too. What can you do to limit a teen's aggressive and noncompliant behaviors?

Understand that any adolescent can present challenges to their parents from time to time. As one writer, Frank Pittman (1987), comments, "Adolescence is a period of normal psychosis. At no time in a person's life is there such awareness of crisis and change." Adolescents are self-conscious and acutely aware of personal deficiencies. They are constantly aware of peer status, and their moods change quickly. Pittman goes on to write, "Every moment, every mood seems forever. And there is little ability to act contrary to one's impulses or moods, even in the interest of one's survival, much less in the interest of one's future." Both parent and child can make each other feel inadequate, unhappy, and frustrated with the relationship. The parent wonders if she deserves this acting-out adolescent after years of trying to be the good parent, sacrificing both time and money to make a decent life for the child. Yet, the dialogue must be maintained between the parent and teenager. View adolescence as a road to adulthood and not as a character flaw. "It is the parents who must maintain the overview of the temporary nature of all of this adolescent chaos [because] adolescents view everything as permanent" (Pittman 1987).

Do not confuse normal teenage behaviors for ADHD behaviors—sometimes they are difficult to separate. Any adolescent will present challenges that test a parent's willpower. The *rebelliousness* of adolescence is a necessary stage for healthy development into adulthood, but it's a natural process that challenges parents of teenagers.

Keep things in perspective. You will have crises with your adolescent. No matter how much you try to foresee all possibilities from drugs to sex, you have less control over him than when he was younger. See these crises as a way to help him and not as intentional behavior to make you miserable.

Adolescents are often very self-involved, and you probably enter their mind only briefly when they are making important decisions for themselves. Again, view your teenager's selfish behavior as developmental in most cases, and not as a character flaw. We are not saying a parent's feelings aren't important to an adolescent, only that his looks and friends also play an important role in his decision-making.

The family, even if it doesn't seem so for your teenager, is important to adolescents. Whether the relationship is good or bad, there still is that deep bond that ties him to his family. What Mom and Dad feel about him is important—teenagers seek out and often want parental advice and support, but struggle to balance parental needs with adolescent issues: everything from whom they can have as friends to what music they listen to. They want their parents' advice, but only when they ask for it! They often keep decisions private out of fear of hurting their parents and not because they feel alienated or angry at the parent. Experimentation with drugs, masturbation, and other activities that would be frowned upon are often hidden. Obviously, some adolescents have been abused and abandoned by one or both parents and feel great anger towards their parents. This pain is so great and the wound so deep that it cannot be fixed without much expense and time.

Keep communication open with your adolescent as much as possible. Some families deal with conflict with their teenager better than others. Some families are deeply troubled by any deviation from family values, and view their rebellious offspring as emotionally disturbed—these families often come for therapy.

It is hard for some parents to understand or like the child in his imperfect state. Fears and anxieties often retard the recognition that adolescence is a stage usually passed through with minor cuts and bruises, and most teenagers end up becoming well-adjusted young adults.

Keeping communication open with your teenager—as much as can reasonably be expected—is very important. Even the "normal" adolescent (which is probably an oxymoron) is obsessed with privacy. He doesn't want you asking questions, probing, or looking through his room without first asking. He sets the boundaries for communication, making you feel defensive and uncomfortable with his behavior, so you may push and probe to check if your child is using drugs or alcohol. You may come to see your adolescent as imperfect and "become obsessed with some real or imagined imperfection" (Pittman 1987). This perception often creates more distancing and escalates the division.

When there is poor communication with a parent, the adolescent will often go "underground." The *underground adolescent* may live at home and receive telephone calls there, but avoids involvement with people there. He rarely talks to his parents, going to his room when he gets home. Even more upsetting to a parent is the *rebellious adolescent.* The rebellious adolescent will follow societal rules but stay in open conflict with his parents. "The conflict is not between the child and the adult world, but specifically between the child and the parents . . . [and] their emotional life is primarily consumed by fierce battles with their parents over rules and punishment" (Pittman 1987). The rebellious adolescent often ends up in the therapist's office with anxious and angry parents.

Now that you have some sense of "normal" adolescence and the challenges often confronting parents in raising a teenager, let's talk about specific suggestions that can help minimize conflicts with your adolescent with ADHD.

- Project a posture that says, "I am the parent and I am in charge." You don't have to yell, but have a strong tone or demeanor that projects authority, not defeatism. Your teenager will confront you and challenge you, so be prepared to face him. Practice visualization. Picture him confronting you about something and how you will look and what you will say. This activity can help you be better prepared when you are confronted with your angry and noncompliant teenager. Let him know by your demeanor and actions that you are not only prepared to talk, but are ready to act.

- Don't confront your adolescent when you are angry, if possible. Not all problems need to be confronted immediately. When you speak in anger, often only the anger is heard by the child, and it can escalate an already volatile situation. If you are very upset, let your child know that you will get back with him about your feelings.

- If your teen is very upset, don't push him. Tell him, "We are both upset, so let's meet when things are calmer." A mother confronted her volatile and impulsive 16-year-old adolescent over having cigarettes in his bedroom. Holding them in her hands, yelled at him about her discovery. He yelled back, "You had no right to look in my room! Give them back!" Anger escalated with more yelling and threats. The hostility finally came to a climax when he pushed his mother against the bedroom wall, grabbed his cigarettes, and ran out the front door. This mother had escalated the situation by taking her teen by surprise. She knew that he was not good at surprises or controlling his anger. He was wrong for pushing his mother; however, she escalated the situation by not stopping when she saw he was angry. She could have handed him his cigarettes and later talked with him about her concerns—this problem was not life-threatening. She could have backed away and dealt with her son at another time.

- Don't anticipate the worst if your adolescent forgets his homework or fails a class. Barkley notes that parents of affected children often anticipate ruination (Barkley 1995). They often have such a strong sense of fear that their child will end up on welfare or be unemployable that they can exaggerate the consequences of his behaviors. The danger with this overreaction is that it can be self-fulfilling. Your adolescent picks up on your lack of trust in his judgment, thinks, "Why try?" and ends up doing those very things you fear most.

- Your goal should be to change your teen's behavior, not punish him. Punishment may be the method you choose to create change, but it shouldn't be the goal. If you are looking to change his behavior concerning curfew, for example, by limiting his weekend activities, you can be successful, but it often depends on how the intervention is presented, as much as the intervention itself. If he feels it is unjust punishment made in an angry moment, and not as the result of his poor choices, he often will dismiss it as mean-spirited and blame you. Successful interventions are built on the shoulders of a healthy relationship between a parent and child. If you have had problems in communicating with your adolescent since an early age, you may need outside support to implement effective interventions.

- Keep the conversation on the problem. Do not let your teenager direct the focus away from the problem. His goal will be to change the emphasis or put the problem back on you. Go back to the original issue: "The problem is that *you* came home at two in the morning. Let's not talk about Bobby's curfew." When he admits there is a problem, only then can you find solutions so it doesn't happen again. He may have legitimate concerns or suggestions, so don't dismiss them outright. Talk *with* him, not *at* him. If he is not willing to work with you, you have the final word.

- Your teen's anger is his own, not yours. It is unrealistic to set limits with him and then expect he will always understand. Don't expect him to say, "Gee, Dad, I understand what you mean. It could be dangerous being alone on the street after 11 p.m.—that makes sense." Expect that he will be angry when you set limits; however, setting fair and safe limits is your parental responsibility. Find ways to deal with his anger and not avoid problems that it causes.

- Don't protect your adolescent from natural consequences stemming from noncompliant behaviors. Noncompliant behavior is purposeful and willful, and a teen needs to be held accountable for it. However, incompetent behaviors in adolescents with ADHD, like forgetting to remember, often are a manifestation of their disorder, and they needs to be taught ways to minimize these behaviors (see chapter 4, "Is My Child Noncompliant or Just Incompetent?" for more explanation). If your teenager forgets to call when he's going to be late, after a number of reminders, this may be incompetence and not noncompliance. You could provide him a pager, and if he is not home when he should be, you could page him to call you.

- Teenagers seem to respond well to contracts, which is a mutually developed verbal or written agreement between a parent and child. Don't force an agreement upon your adolescent, though. If you do, it is not a contract. Also, intimidation and threats are not good stepping-stones for building mutual respect. If the contract is not mutually agreed upon, the chances are it will not work. A good example of a contract would be that your teenager agrees to perform routine chores around the house and you agree to let him stay out an additional hour Saturday night when the chores are completed. Both parties have to agree to the contract. If you are not willing to live up to the contract, don't agree to it. If you say yes and then reneg, you have broken a promise. Also make sure your teenager understands and is willing to live with the contract. He has equal responsibility to abide by his word. Contracts are effective because the rules are discussed and mutually agreed upon before any action needs to be taken. However, teenagers in general do not always stick with their agreements. When yours doesn't, then that is an important issue for discussion and learning. Just because it doesn't work all the time, however, doesn't mean it is not a good idea.

- If you are married make sure there is agreement between you and your spouse about major decisions in raising your teenager. Teamwork is essential. Teens are experts at dividing and conquering, so both parents have to set up a united front. If agreement between you and your spouse has never been good, it is never too late—see a counselor to come together. If you are single, seek out the aid of someone you can consistently count on for support.

- Reach out for help if your situation seems unbearable. An affected teenager is difficult to raise. Sometimes it is advisable to seek out professional help. Adolescents with ADHD tend to be moodier and have more difficulty tolerating frustration or considering consequences for their actions. This difficulty in modulating emotion can frequently lead to arguments and even physical confrontations. A professional can help the family work through those identified areas that seem to create the most conflicts and noncompliant behaviors. However, the therapist should have some understanding of ADHD and how it may be contributing to the problem.

Your teenager is too old to be put in time-out, obviously, but not too old to be guided and held accountable for inappropriate behaviors. Raising him requires the understanding that conflict is a natural process and making mistakes is to be expected. Very few conflicts are so serious or consequences so damaging that they cannot be corrected. Teenagers are more understanding and forgiving than parents care to acknowledge.

Review and Tips

- Adolescence is a natural developmental stage to adulthood.

- These adolescents often present more problems than other children their age. They are often seen as more immature and, because of their behaviors, have more conflicts with adults and peers.

- Try to be a good listener. You don't want your teen to go "underground." Be firm and set clear guidelines, but also speak in a tone that shows respect and understanding. You may be right most of the time, but age and experience has given you this wisdom. Try not to push this awareness in your teen's face. Show him respect and leave room for forgiveness.

- Remember, you want your children to come home for Thanksgiving and other holidays when they are older. You will want to spend time with your grandchildren, so don't develop a feeling of "ruination" which often leads to overreaction and alienation between a parent and child.

Summary

It is very important for parents of children with ADHD to understand that any intervention will present more challenges for these children. Because of their disorder, they find it more difficult to do the right thing. Parenting an affected child requires imagination, perseverance, and understanding. You need a "Survival Guide" of references covering various interventions that can be drawn upon when needed. We advocate a few simple interventions that can be implemented easily and require minimal effort or time. Overly involved and complicated procedures generally end up failing because a parent is too busy or the intervention requires outside monitoring that can be both costly and time-consuming. Empathy through education is the best "pill" for dealing with affected children.

Any intervention you try will need to be changed more often than with unaffected children. Affected children, for reasons discussed in this chapter and in other sections, need more monitoring, changes, and support from parents.

9

I Would Love to Help as a Teacher, but I have 35 Children in My Classroom

The teacher is one of the most important persons in a child's social, emotional, and educational development. By graduation from high school, the average American child will have spent more waking time with teachers than with any other adults except parents. You are critical to the child's success.

A parent sends her child to school hoping he will learn social and educational skills that will prepare him for life. Unfortunately, you are often asked to perform this important job, often alone, with limited resources—a finite number of classroom books, outdated or small selections of art or music materials, as well as limited classroom support for students with special needs. In addition, you are asked to teach students having a wide range of academic and social skills.

Some students present few challenges and advance through their grades with little attention; others, like children with ADHD, present daily challenges that can make the school experience an unhappy one for both you and the child. Parents must understand the difficulties you face when teaching an affected child. You sometimes have to deal with angry parents who want to blame someone or something for their child's unhappiness and lack of academic success, while you try to motivate the unmotivated student who seems to have written off school as a meaningless part of his life.

This chapter presents concerns commonly brought to our attention by teachers. The interventions suggested should not be viewed as a final solution. They should be seen, rather, as ideas to better understand and minimize problem behaviors; not interventions that will erase them. Parents reading this section can benefit by increasing their awareness of the difficulties their children present in the classroom and reviewing interventions that are helpful at school.

I Have Too Many Other Responsibilities

A caring but frustrated teacher shared, "I would love to help as a teacher, but I have 35 children in my classroom." She was not really complaining but was frustrated that she could not meet the needs of two boys with ADHD in her classroom. She understood that school was hard for them, but sending them to the office when they were disruptive, or marking down their papers when turned in late, was not helpful. She asked the school psychologist to give her suggestions that would make the school day a more positive experience for her and the two boys.

The Challenge Presented Teachers

You must try to meet the educational needs of affected students, while at the same time not take away important teaching time from others. You are often faced with this dilemma. These students demand more of your time than seems reasonable, and more often than not, you are expected to address their educational and behavioral needs with limited support.

Some school districts provide aides to help the teacher, but generally this time is limited to part of the day. Normally, the teacher is left to her own skills and effort. After many attempts to minimize behaviors, teachers may blame the students, others, and themselves.

Blame Doesn't Help

Sometimes it is difficult not to blame the student who doesn't seem to try, disrupts others, and creates chaos in the classroom. Like the parent, you may view him as a "Bolt from the Blue" and try to find something or someone to blame. You understand that you will always have problem students; however, an affected student's behavior will at times be so outrageous and disruptive that your patience and fondness for him evaporates. You feel victimized by his behaviors and may fall into the blame trap.

Blame seldom helps and often diminishes the possibility of a positive relationship with him. It often originates from frustration and sometimes guilt. You are probably successful in managing most students, but when faced with one with ADHD, you may be less successful and blame yourself for his lack of success. However, there is not an ideal or complete intervention that will eliminate ADHD behaviors. Teachers should develop a mindset that accepts that ADHD is a disorder that makes certain tasks in the classroom challenging, such as sitting still, following directions, finishing and/or turning in completed assignments, and staying out of trouble during free time. The student hasn't asked for these problems. His disorder is the primary reason behind his difficulties, and neither you nor he is to blame.

Teachers Need Not Feel Guilty

The majority of classroom teachers do more things right than wrong when teaching affected students. Don't feel guilty because you cannot always meet their educational needs. You are only one person with many responsibilities with limited supports, and you often need the support of others (parents, doctors, and school administrators) to make the students day more successful. Parents often want to help, but they may have limited knowledge of classroom interventions and academic challenges. Doctors are generally responsive to calls from teachers, but seldom initiate follow-up after putting a child on medication. School administrators, depending on their level of knowledge about ADHD, may or may not be helpful. Administrators who support classroom accommodations may provide additional staff support for you, and are open to setting up alternative programs for these students (experience-based/project-oriented learning environments that emphasizes *doing* rather than just listening) that can give you much-needed relief.

Both time and resources limit your effectiveness. Any long-term solution to this dilemma demands more supports, such as on-site alternative classroom settings that can accommodate behavior-disordered students. You need places to send the disruptive student besides home. Ideally, he can use a coach or monitoring person to help him with ways to stay more focused, organized, and compliant. It is unfair and unreasonable to expect you to meet the many needs of students with ADHD or other disorders and still address the educational needs of the others in the classroom without appropriate supports. Because of the lack of appropriate support for both student and teacher, these students are often suspended, expelled, and they drop out of school, and the teachers are often blamed.

Review and Tips

- Students with ADHD can cause additional stress. Educating yourself on this disorder can help you cope with their difficult behavior.

- You cannot guarantee the student will be successful in your classroom, but you can offer him more opportunities for success by recognizing his special needs.

- Try to stay away from blame, which doesn't help and often makes things more difficult. The problem is not you or the student, the problem is his disorder.

My Students Find Some Curriculum Especially Difficult

These children may struggle in a number of curriculum areas: reading comprehension, spelling, written language, and math calculation. You may be unaware of the associated learning difficulties of ADHD. A large percentage of children with ADHD are learning disabled (LD), receiving special education services, or are underachievers performing significantly below their cognitive ability. Research suggests that "inattention may be associated in some unique way with learning disabilities" (Marshall et al. 1999, 240). An attention dimension such as selective attention may arise from a primary impairment in a cognitive process (stimulus filtering) that may underlie associated learning deficits in language, reading, and math that occur more frequently in the ADHD population.One recent study looking at eight- to 16-year-old children suggested that "learning and attention problems are on a continuum, are interrelated, and usually coexist" (Mayes et al. 2000, 417, 419). This same study reported that the presence of one or more types of learning disabilities was more common in the 86 children in the study with ADHD-C (68.8%) than in the 33 children without ADHD (39.4%). The study also found a disproportionate number of children with ADHD-C had a learning disability in written expression (65.1%) when compared to those not diagnosed with ADHD-C (27.3%); and children with ADHD-C showed more delays in spelling (30.2%) than those without ADHD-C (6.1%). The authors go on to recommend that in light of their study, children with ADHD-C should be assessed in written expression. This is especially important, they suggest, because written expression is the most amenable to compensatory accommodations (word processors, spell checkers, and oral or dictated performance) when compared to other learning disabilities.

Because of deficits in internal cognitive processing, a student with ADHD will present more difficulties both in regulations of movement and interlinking of ideas. They can exhibit diminished fine motor control (poor handwriting and impaired visual-motor coordination) as well as difficulties in articulation and language impairments because of decreased control of the tongue. Also, because of impulsivity, these children do not self-cue or prompt themselves before acting. Because of overarousal, they are flooded with irrelevant stimuli, impacting both selective and sustained attention. Excessive arousal overwhelms the attentional filters, causing too many events to be deemed important (Hunt et al. 1994, 106–112). Excessive arousal is often observed in their difficulty with attending to what is important at the time. Instead of working on a math paper, they are focused on a fly crawling across a classmate's desk.

Some authors suggest that there is little overlap between learning disabled (LD) and ADHD. Children who are labeled LD may actually be misdiagnosed students with ADHD. These students, because of underachievement and poor classroom productivity, are labeled LD and placed in special education. The danger of not correctly identifying ADHD is that other treatments unique to ADHD may not be considered (Morriss 1990).

Whatever the nature of the LD-ADHD relationship, experience tells us that some types of schoolwork are especially difficult for many students with ADHD. These include the areas below.

Written Work

These students often will have difficulty with written work. The student with ADHD-I (Inattentive type) may be slower than the average student in doing paper and pencil tasks, taking measurably longer to complete written work. This is supported by findings showing affected students do worse than others on tests involving motor speed and hand-eye coordination. The student with ADHD-HI (Hyperactive/Impulsive), unlike the student with ADHD-I, can have trouble synchronizing motor movements with his fast-moving thoughts. He can produce interesting ideas at a rapid rate, but his poor motor ability prevents him from keeping pace with his fast-flowing thoughts. Consequently, his writing is disorganized and does not represent his knowledge of the subject (Levine 1987). Recent research is divided over whether stimulant medications improve fine-motor functioning; however, one writer reports that stimulant medication may increase the student's capacity to delay responding, thus improving general motor skills (Brown and Sawyer 1998). Affected students are often not visually aware of patterns in words, can be careless in their writing and spelling, often forget to include headings and margins, and their cross-outs and erasures are not neat (see "Writing Assignments Are Especially Difficult for My Child," chapter 6).

Arithmetic

Affected students often have difficulty properly aligning numbers, leading to incorrect answers because of carelessness. They often lag behind their classmates in learning their multiplication tables and facts, especially higher numbers (sevens and eights). Measures of math ability, however, improve when a child is placed on Ritalin. It is suggested that Ritalin improves concentration and attention. Earlier studies suggested that lower dosages were more effective in improving cognition, and that higher dosages were thought to be most effective in improving behavioral problems. However, more recent research indicates that both learning and behavior may reach their peak effect with higher dosages of stimulants. Both cognitive tasks and classroom behavior improved as a function of increasing the dosage, particularly if they were in the low-to-moderate ranges (Brown 1998).

A recent study found that students with ADHD-I might be at risk for arithmetic calculation difficulties. Their diminished attentional capacity (especially selective attention) may impair their ability to focus on and master basic math facts during the primary grades. Consequently, because they failed to master these facts, they must allocate at the early-middle grades an "already diminished attentional capacity to calculation" (Marshall et al. 1999, 244). Again, medication, such as stimulants, has been found to improve arithmetic performance in children with ADHD-I for short periods of time. Well-controlled studies on long-term effects of stimulants on arithmetic performance are not available (Marshall et al. 1999, 245).

Reading Comprehension

Some affected students have difficulty with reading comprehension, which can be symptomatic of a learning disability and may not necessarily be because of ADHD-based behaviors. Reading comprehension combines two interactive skills: word identification and language comprehension. When word identification is adequate, reading comprehension depends on adequate language comprehension. However, a deficiency in word identification is one of the most important causes of a reading disability. This difficulty is thought to be caused by weaknesses in auditory-related skills, such as identifying individual sounds with words (phonemic awareness) and associating those sounds with written letters (sound-symbol relationships). Research reports that stimulants exert little specific influence on childhood

learning disabilities, but medication can help address the attentional disturbance. Any learning disability must be addressed through educational remediation (Brown and Sawyer 1998).

These children often have difficulty with reading comprehension
because they do not attend to what they are reading and their mind drifts,
focusing on something else they did, or something they want to do (focused
attention). This can happen to any person, but affected students often have
greater difficulty refocusing on the reading passage. One student said that
when he was reading, he would sometimes daydream. He looked like he was
reading, but his mind was focused on something unrelated to his reading
material. Another student spoke of reading the passage, "It snowed last
night" and discovering his mind drifting to a family outing in the snow the
weekend before. Consequently, these students often have to reread the material until it is retained. Homework requiring extensive reading material can
add many minutes to a student's study time, making homework a frustrating experience both for child and parent.

We have chosen the above curriculum areas because they seem most problematic for many students with ADHD, and you may need to make academic
accommodations in these areas. Accommodations could be extra time for
written work, and outside monitoring to increase accuracy and completion of
school assignments (see "What Interventions Seem to Work Best in the
Classroom?" in this chapter for more suggestions). All children avoid doing
schoolwork at times because they find it boring and simply don't want to do it.
However, don't dismiss too quickly the possibility that their avoidance of certain classwork may be because the curriculum is too laborious and difficult.

Review and Tips

- Students with ADHD are at risk for learning problems.

- Their difficulties with many core curricula often stem from
cognitive processing delays.

- Accommodations are often suggested to help them be more
successful, such as additional time for written work and
math assignments.

- These students need more monitoring to assure they are on
task when involved in classwork.

I'm Angry That I'm Responsible for His Medication

You may understandably feel uncomfortable and sometimes annoyed when required to administer medication at school. Some teachers worry they will be sued if something happens to a student when they give him the medication, that the student could have an adverse physical reaction to the medication and they will be held responsible. Other teachers have strong personal beliefs against medicating children for ADHD and feel it is unfair that they have to participate. The most common complaint is that the student, especially an older student, should remember to take his medication without reminders from the teacher.

These concerns are understandable; however, teachers and/or schools have both a legal and a professional responsibility to administer medication to students who require it during the school day. Schools should provide procedural guidelines for administering medication. Sometimes the child will take his medication in the classroom or be sent to the school office where the medication is given. Whatever guidelines are followed in your school district, schools are required to put in place a program to assure the student's medical needs are met.

You cannot be held legally responsible for any possible side effects from the medication if procedures are followed. You are not a physician, and as long as you and the school have followed the doctor's guidelines outlined on the prescription bottle or permission slip signed by the doctor, you have met your legal responsibility.

The reason these students are taking medication is because they have a neurodevelopmental disorder that makes remembering to remember difficult, so it is unreasonable and often unfair to expect primary grade students to remember to take their medication. Those in middle school and high school are often more responsible; however, even students in this age group need reminders at times. If the student refuses to take his medication, the parent needs to be informed immediately of his refusal.

You play an important role in the treatment of an affected student. You can provide information to the child's physician on any possible side effects from the medication, as well as observed behavioral changes while on the medication. See your role as an important team member who can provide ongoing monitoring that is essential for any treatment of children on medication, and not someone who is simply the "pill dispenser."

It is in your best interest and the interest of other students to ensure the affected student in your classroom has taken his medication. Medication helps him be more focused and generally more receptive to verbal directions and requests.

Review and Tips

- You have both a legal and professional obligation to facilitate the administration of medication to students.

- You are an important participant in a student's treatment, and your observations are valued by both parents and treating professionals.

- Make sure the student receives his medication, which helps him be in control and less impulsive, distractible, and hyperkinetic.

He Is on Medication, So Why Isn't He Doing Better Academically?

Many teachers and parents ask this question. Medication can minimize problem behaviors, but medication alone does not correct or eliminate academic problems or social behaviors.

We do not currently know a lot about how medication affects academic performance because many studies are done in a laboratory and not in a classroom, and those studies have not been good predictors of a student's response to medication in the classroom. However, medication can make some important differences in the classroom for student's who respond positively to medication (Garber, Garber, and Spizman 1996).

Stimulants

Stimulants are most often used to test the effects of medication on academic performance, so we have focused on stimulants and their reported impact on school performance.

The psychostimulants currently most commonly prescribed to children with ADHD are methylphenidate (Ritalin), dextroamphetamine (Dexedrine), and dextroamphetamine/amphetamine (Adderall). As discussed in chapter 7, psychostimulants take effect and wear off quickly. Behavioral effects can be observed in these medication within 30 minutes The behavioral effects of Ritalin and Dexedrine normally peak two hours after ingestion and disappear by the end of three to four hours. With

Adderall, behavioral effects begin to plateau, rather than peak, at two hours, but often persist at this level for six hours or more before trailing off. Effects disappear at around eight hours in most people, but Adderall may last for up to 12 hours in some individuals, particularly with higher dosages. The time-response pattern has important implications for students medicated in classroom settings. For example, if a student has trouble at recess with peers or with classwork, the medication would have no beneficial effect if the pill was taken more than four hours earlier in the morning.

Short-Term Effects of Stimulants on Academic Performance

Although stimulants like Ritalin are effective in the short term in controlling problem behaviors, there still remains a concern about their effect on academic performance. In fact, the effect of stimulants on learning is still controversial and continues to be debated. In contrast to teachers and parents reporting marked improvement in students' classroom performance when on medication, several studies found no improvement on standardized tests. A number of suggestions were presented to try to explain this discrepancy. These hypotheses included the variability of dose response on learning, inadequate time on medication, and use of instruments that are insensitive to the effects of medication (Brown 1998). In another publication, one writer suggests that one factor that may be adding to this functionality variability is that physicians rarely evaluate the effects of stimulant medication on academic performance. This is partly due to time restraints on the doctor and logistic difficulties. Consequently, the positive effects of medication on academic performance may not be reliably tested in the school environment (Carlson and Bunner 1993, 184–195). However, current opinion suggests that stimulants probably do help improve a student's classroom performance.

Many studies have proven that Ritalin, for example, produces immediate improvement in various academic tasks (Carlson and Bunner 1993, 185). Medications such as Ritalin are very likely to improve a student's impulsivity, attention, academic efficiency, organization, and possibly fine-motor coordination. Classwork, in terms of completion and accuracy, has been found to improve when a student is on stimulant medication. The improvement seems to be associated not simply with the amount of time spent on the work, but the efficiency of time spent.

Ritalin, like other stimulants, is not likely to directly improve a student's score on a test, because school tests measure what the student has learned. Studies do find, however, that students with ADHD who are on medication are often able to persevere in the face of a frustrating task, such as test taking or classwork (Garber, Garber, and Spizman 1996). Because of difficulty in modulating his emotions, the student can quickly become frustrated with a task that is challenging. Those who are medicated are better able to temper their emotions, allowing them more opportunities for success.

Long-Term Effects of Stimulants on Academic Performance

It is more difficult to draw any conclusions about the long-term effects of Ritalin on academic performance. There are methodological problems that, if corrected, may show that stimulant medication increases what is actually learned. At present, we just don't know.

There appear to be methodological problems in studies that have failed to support long-term benefits of stimulant use on school performance (Carlson and Bunner 1993, 186–189). For example, the failure to see long-term academic gains could have been because the dosage level prescribed was not conducive to improved cognitive performance—dosage level has been found to be an important determinant of the drug's effect on learning. Another possibility that may account for difficulty in measuring long-term benefits of stimulants on school performance is that several weeks or months are not sufficient to measure long-term change in student performance, and most long-term studies do not last for years. Lastly, achievement testing that has been used to measure achievement gains tend to be insensitive to slight changes in achievement (Carlson and Bunner 1993, 193–195). Most studies, when looking at efficacy of medication on behavioral and academic performance, lacked a control group. One author notes that this is an important omission because children placed on medication may have presented more severe symptoms than their peers not treated with medication. Consequently, "What seems to be a discouraging picture of long-course treatment with stimulant medication may be more a reflection of the initial severity of symptoms rather than a true lack of long-term efficacy" (Brown and Sawyer 1998). Until more information is available, decisions about treatment must be made on an individual basis.

What Stimulants Cannot Do to Improve Performance

Research suggests that stimulant medication alone is not enough to improve academic functioning to a normal range, especially when the primary problem relates to learning and not behavior (Carlson and Bunner 1993, 192–193). This continues to surprise many teachers and is a disappointment to parents.

Studies have suggested that medication, coupled with psychosocial and psychoeducational interventions, is the most effective treatment for children with ADHD (Carlson and Bunner 1993, 192–193). A student who is on medication can still have academic and behavioral problems. Medication does not teach a student academic skills or fill gaps in learning—he cannot do what he doesn't know. However, when on medication, he will be more receptive to material presented by you. Medication does not address learning disabilities, and will not correct basic psychological processing disorders, but the student will be more receptive to educational interventions that attempt to address processing disorders.

Not all children respond to stimulant medication. Approximately two-thirds of children with ADHD show benefits from stimulants, and the other third show either no response or an adverse response. Only a minority of children who do respond to the medication show sufficient improvement for their behavior to fall within the normal range, and for the rest, additional interventions are needed. Further, children's responses can vary depending on the task and the dosage of stimulant. A student who is on a low dosage may demonstrate good classwork completion, but still make negative comments in class, so you may think the medication is not effective, whereas in fact, it *is* addressing the classwork but not negative behavior. Age can also affect the response level of a child on medication—preschoolers and kindergartners show less response than elementary-age students do (Carlson and Bunner 1993, 206–208).

Other Reasons Why He Is Not Doing Better

A child with ADHD is more than his disorder. Other factors can contribute to his difficulties in school. As mentioned in other sections, he can have a learning disability in addition to ADHD, which can contribute to his difficulties in school. He can experience personal stresses from moving or a parental divorce, or be experiencing levels of trauma that make it difficult for him to attend to schoolwork. A personality conflict between a student and you can sometimes contribute to classroom difficulties. You are human and cannot be expected to relate to all students in your classroom.

A student on medication can show improvement in a number of behaviors that lead to better academic performance, but medication alone will probably not be the only intervention needed to sustain positive interactions with staff and peers and promote academic growth. A successful intervention often combines medication with social and educational accommodations.

Review and Tips

- Medication will improve classroom performance and behavior for students who respond positively to medication.

- Medication helps them perform more efficiently. Classwork completion and accuracy has been found to be better when the student is on medication.

- It is more difficult to draw any conclusions about long-term effects of medication on academic performance. However, some researchers suggest methodological factors have made long-term studies more inconclusive than short-term research.

- Research suggests that the most effective method to address academic performance is to combine medication with social and educational interventions.

He Is Disrupting the Education of the Other Children—I Can't Allow That

Affected students can and often do interrupt the education of others. A class lesson often stops while you address disruptive behavior, and this stop-and-go interaction between you and the student can slow a lesson plan, break up continuity, and distract the other students' attention from you. You probably quickly tire of the affected student's actions and will send him to the office, or out of desperation, seat him outside the classroom door for a short period of time. His antics can also invite disconcerting comments from classmates and add to his difficulties in making and keeping friends.

You are trying to balance the educational and emotional needs of the student with ADHD with those of his other classmates. You were hired to teach all the students, so you should not be required to spend an unreasonable amount of time addressing the misbehaviors of the affected student. Unfortunately, he requires more attention than the average student in a classroom. How you address his disruptions can make a big difference in minimizing misbehaviors. Below are some ideas for dealing with disruptive students in your classroom.

Have a Plan

We have said that parents should never leave the house without a plan; this is true for teachers in the classroom. These students are not self-starters, they have difficulty with free time, and they often need monitoring when transitioning from one activity to another. Don't expect the student to automatically follow rules or to start on classwork without reminders. Set up a daily program to deal with affected students in your classroom. It doesn't necessarily have to be complicated, but it needs to be followed each day. Teachers will often start a program with a student, be successful for a while, and stop it. Special programs take extra time and effort, but these students generally need a continuous daily plan to minimize problem behaviors. A classroom behavior program will help the affected student be more manageable and give you more time for other students.

Set Firm Limits and Follow Them

All children function best when they know their limits. They can be master manipulators, and children with ADHD are no different. Set firm limits and follow them. Reminding the student at the start of each day of classroom rules and expectations can be very helpful in minimizing disruptive behaviors. He can verbalize the rules that are especially difficult for him to follow. Remember, he is driven by the moment, and the more often he is reminded, the more successful he will be.

Pick Your Battles

Behaviors that are not too disturbing should be ignored. Affected students will often talk to themselves, make funny noises, and fidget in their seats. If you find that these behaviors are not too disturbing to other classmates, ignore them. Often a quiet reminder, such as a light touch on the shoulder or a whisper in the ear, can help them stop the distracting behavior.

These students will hardly ever sit quietly or line up for recess as consistently as others, so if you focus on all the misbehaviors, the exchanges with them will be generally negative. The pattern of exchanges becomes one of demands or commands, with little focusing on more positive interactions. Focus only on those behaviors that are obviously disruptive or possibly dangerous to others. An example of a disruptive, but not dangerous, behavior in the classroom is that of a third-grade student seen in counseling who made clicking sounds with his mouth while working at his desk. The teacher reported this behavior was especially a problem in the afternoon during quiet reading time. This student was only taking medication in the morning, so it was not helping him during afternoon reading. The parents were opposed to an afternoon dose, so it was recommended that the teacher put in place a behavior plan to help minimize this behavior. She was encouraged to use a nonverbal signal to help the student stop the clicking sounds when they became disruptive. She put a sticker on the student's desk, and when he started to make clicking sounds, she quietly walked up to his desk and touched the sticker with her finger. This nondisturbing reminder helped him manage his behavior. His teacher also used the sticker to help refocus him if other disturbing behaviors at his desk were observed. It worked pretty well.

An example of a potentially dangerous behavior was that of a student who was running around at recess poking classmates with a stick. This behavior was dangerous and needed to be stopped, so he was put on a bench for time-out and missed his next two recesses.

Catch Him Being Good

All students need to be recognized when they are good. When the affected student is working at his desk, waiting in line without pushing, or turning in his homework without reminders, he should be praised. He responds best to immediate recognition, so try to attend to his proper behaviors as soon as possible. It's hard sometimes to catch an affected student being good, so don't pass up those moments. You are not expected to stop a lesson or go to his desk each and every time, but make an effort to compliment him throughout the school day. These students often have low self-esteem, as well as feelings of victimization, so they need more attention than the average student in a classroom.

Recognize that even with the best of plans, the student's inappropriate behaviors will never disappear. You can minimize many of them through good classroom management, but the job will never be easy or without frustration and disappointment. As discussed in chapter 1, these children are *Hunters,* not *Farmers.* They usually get bored easily, are not cautious, and are easily distracted by outside noises and events. Add the excessive body movements, and one can appreciate why they are more disruptive than their classmates.

Review and Tips

- Students with ADHD are more disruptive than others in the classroom.

- Try to ignore behaviors that are not too disturbing. Focus on those behaviors that are very disruptive or can be harmful to the student or his classmates.

- Have a daily plan to address the student's primary disruptive behaviors.

- Reward the younger student through verbal praise or tokens when you see him following school rules. Both praise and special privileges, such as extra time on the computer, can encourage older students.

What Interventions Seem to Work Best in the Classroom?

Any discussion of interventions requires an understanding of the primary behaviors presented by ADHD. Once you have a general understanding of these behaviors, you can better evaluate appropriate classroom interventions. First, we will begin by briefly reviewing the primary areas that present problems for affected students (see chapter 1 for more discussion).

What Activities Give Students with ADHD Difficulty?

They have the greatest difficulty when they are required to make plans, organize themselves, and carry out complex behaviors over a long period of time. To be successful in these activities, a person must have self-control. Affected students lack self-control or have difficulty inhibiting their behaviors. Behavioral inhibition is an essential ingredient for goal-directed behaviors.

Activities required in school to be successful are difficult for these students in large part because of deficits in self-control. Activities such as following your directions, remembering to turn in homework, raising the hand before speaking, not marking on a paper until told to do so, or standing in line without pushing all require levels of self-control. Any activity that requires self-control, goal setting, and organization will generally be more difficult for the affected student than other students.

Interventions that target some broad areas of concerns teachers find most challenging for these students are given below. There are other areas and interventions not covered in this section that you could access through recommended readings and books suggested at the end of this book. An especially helpful resource is Stephan McCarney's *The Attention Deficit Disorders Intervention Manual* (1989).

He Always Needs to Be Reminded

These students need help to stay focused on what is important. As mentioned in earlier sections, they are often paying attention, but to the wrong things. They will watch the custodian sweep the hall rather than focus on the writing assignment due at the end of the period.

The suggestions below can be helpful and require minimal monitoring.

Primary Grades (Kindergarten through Sixth Grades)

- Place a sticker at the top edge of a student's desk. Explain to him that when he is observed off task, you will quietly walk up and touch the sticker with your finger.

- Each morning before the start of school, review with the student problem behaviors that he especially finds difficult to master. Have him repeat these rules to you. Praise him as often as possible when you observe him following a rule—the more immediate the reinforcement, the better. He will perform better with immediate rewards or praises rather than with intermittent or delayed reinforcement.

- Have him write on a 3x5 card one or two behaviors that he will work on improving during the school day. Review his progress mid-morning and remind him of the card at the beginning of afternoon studies. If he goes to another room, he can take the 3x5 card with him. The new teacher is informed of the card and its purpose. These behaviors can be tied into a reward system. It may sometimes take time to get him to use the card, so don't become discouraged if he initially rebels or forgets.

- Set up a *study buddy system* to help the affected student stay on-task. Make sure you first have his permission. He can be seated next to a classmate with good study habits who can help model on-task behavior. Change the "buddy" intermittently to avoid burning out helpers.

- Seat the student at the front of the room where he can be monitored more closely and where there are fewer distractions.

Secondary Grades (Seventh through Twelfth Grades)

- Affected students generally act younger than their chronological age, so they will often respond to behavior interventions meant for younger students.

- Seat the student at the front of the room where there are fewer distractions and where he can be given reminders without bringing too much attention to himself.

- Touch base with the student throughout the period to reinforce on-task behavior. He will know after a period of time that you will be checking up on him. Make sure he is not the only one you approach during the period.

- Quietly remind him of expected behaviors during classwork.

- Remind him that you will be coming back to check on his progress.

He Wastes Time During Class

Students with ADHD often waste time during class. They will play with a pencil, daydream, or pester a classmate rather than work on an assignment. They can be highly distracted both internally and externally. Here are some suggestions that can lessen distractions.

Primary Grades

- Praise the student for attempting to complete class assignments during the study time. You can give a tangible reward such as a sticker or extra time on the computer, or an intangible reward such as praise, a smile, etc. (see Appendix G: The *Daily Student Rating Card*).

- Make sure he understands the work and that it is not too difficult for him.

- Assign a classmate to help him during study time. The classmate can help him stay focused and provide appropriate modeling of good study habits.

- Monitor his progress during study time. Affected students are not self-starters and often need ongoing reminders during study time.

- Allow him additional time for task completion.

- Give him shorter tasks (five math problems rather than 10) and slowly increase the number of problems over time.

Secondary Grades

- Write up a behavior contract outlining expected behaviors during study time. The contract can have built-in rewards for successful completion (for example, no homework on Wednesday, extra time on the computer in the library).

- Provide a *study buddy* to help the student stay focused during study time.

- Seat him in front of the classroom where there are fewer distractions. Monitor him during the class period to measure his progress.

- Establish a checksheet that goes home weekly or bi-monthly to the student's parent indicating his progress.

- Allow additional time for completion. These students often have difficulty with written assignments.

He Fails to Remember to Turn in His Schoolwork

Affected students often forget to turn in their schoolwork. They will often complete an assignment in class, but become distracted and fail to turn it in. Sometimes they complete a homework assignment and leave it on the kitchen table. We have found this ADHD trait common throughout their education.

Primary Grades

- Have the student seated near your desk or at the front of the row, so when work is passed up front, you can easily check to see if it is included.

- Select a *study buddy* to remind him to turn in his schoolwork, but ask the student with ADHD for permission. Rotate "buddies" to avoid burning out helpers.

- Assign the affected student as a helper to pick up classwork, and let him know that he is to put his work on top of the pile. Check to see if he has followed your instructions.

- After giving instructions to the class to turn in classwork, stand next to the student's desk. Your physical presence can sometimes help him remember to turn in his work.

- Place all homework in one manila folder or pocket folder. The student can more easily access it when reminded to turn in homework.

- Set up a weekly monitoring system (see Appendix F: *The Weekly Report*).

Secondary Grades

- Select a *study buddy* to remind the student to turn in his classwork.

- Seat him up front so you can closely monitor his classwork. When you ask for work to be turned in, check to see if he is putting his material together.

- Establish a binder reminder to help him better self-monitor his completion of schoolwork. The binder reminder can be used along with concrete rewards to help increase task completion (see chapter 6).

- Communicate closely with parents regarding his progress so accommodations can be made at home to increase or reward positive steps.

- Have him keep a record of assignments so he can begin to self-monitor his progress. Any missing assignments are to be completed over the weekend and turned in the following Monday without penalty.

Written Work Seems Especially Difficult

Written assignments are often difficult for these students. The child with ADHD-I (Inattentive) may be slower than the average child in doing paper-and-pencil tasks, and the child with ADHD-HI often has trouble synchronizing motor movements with his fast-moving thoughts. This child can produce interesting ideas, but his poor motor ability prevents him from keeping pace. The child with ADHD-I , on the other hand, can take measurably longer to complete written work than his classmates.

Written work difficulties seem so common with these children that the school psychologist should recommend classroom accommodations such as the one below to address this difficulty.

Primary Grades

- Writing neatly is often a problem. Make sure the student, if on medication, is consistently taking his medication during school hours. Stimulants, in particular, seem to help him with handwriting and written output. If written expression is in the afternoon, make sure he has his afternoon dose.

- Teach him your expectations on how a proper paper should look when turned in for grading.

- Some students may continue to need larger-spaced and larger-lined paper beyond what would be expected for their age.

- Encourage the student to proofread his written work. You can have specific areas for him to edit, such as capital letters at the beginning of each sentence, etc.

- Provide additional time for completion of written work.

- Provide alternative ways for the student to demonstrate his knowledge if writing seems especially difficult.

- Introduce word processing/keyboarding skills to him. A variety of software programs are available to teach students proper keyboarding.

- If homework requires a lot of writing, encourage the parent to write down answers given by the child. Another accommodations is for the child and parent to share in writing answers required in the assignment.

Secondary Grades

- Provide additional time for written work. Tests that have essay answers may need accommodations, such as using a computer or allowing the student to tape-record his answers. He could be sent to the library or into another room where no one will be disturbed.

- Allow him to use spell-check devices such as Spellmaster, Speaking Dictionary, or Wordmaster—standard electronic aids—if he has difficulty accessing regular reference materials.

- Allow the student to use voice-activated computer software if available. Voice activated software allows students with writing delays to verbally communicate their thoughts into a computer, which in turn, prints the essay.

- Monitor written work during class time to help him gauge his progress. Remember that these students are poor self-starters and can become easily distracted.

He Gets Out of His Seat Without Asking

Students with ADHD are fidgety and impulsive. They know they should stay in their seats, but lack self-control, so they often get out of their seat without asking. Driven by the moment, they get into trouble because of this behavior.

The suggestions below may help your student stay in his seat longer.

Primary Grades

- Reward him for staying in his seat. Give tangible rewards such as tokens, classroom privileges, or short periods of free time during the day.

- Maintain visibility with the student. Try to make eye contact on a regular basis as a reminder that you are monitoring his behavior.

- Keep open communication with the parents (regular calls to home, notes, etc.) so they can work on reinforcing desired classroom behaviors.

- Give verbal praise intermittently to other students about your pleasure in seeing them seated.

- Monitor to make sure classwork is not too easy or difficult. Boredom, stress, or anxiety will often make affected students more fidgety.

Secondary Grades

- Utilize some of the suggestions given above with seventh- to twelfth-grade students.

- Place student in the front of the classroom where he can be monitored more closely.

- Remind the student at the beginning of the period that he is only to leave his seat with your permission. Students with ADHD need reminders on a daily basis, such as, "Bobby, class is about to get started. Remember, don't leave your seat without my permission. I know you can do it."

He Gets Angry and Upset Too Quickly

These students have great difficulty modulating their emotions. If they are happy, they're really happy; if they are angry, they can be really angry. They have difficulty inhibiting their feelings or thoughts and they seldom reflect upon the consequences of their actions. The time between impulse and action can be very short. They respond poorly to change, which can cause unwarranted reactions such as mood changes and emotional outbursts—unfortunately, you and your other students are often victims of these outbursts.

The interventions below can be helpful in minimizing emotional outbursts and mood swings in the classroom.

Primary Grades

- Communicate classroom rules to the student. Let him know what behaviors are acceptable and which behaviors are not, and maintain consistent expectations. Display the rules in the front of the room and quickly draw them to the student's attention.

- Provide him with positive feedback when he controls his emotions more appropriately. "Bobby, thank you for walking away from Jimmy and going back to your seat when he called you a name. I will talk with Jimmy before recess."

- Monitor him on a regular basis to assess his mood (see the *Green, Yellow, Red* intervention in chapter 4) and let him know by your presence that he is being monitored. Regular physical proximity can be enough to temper any possible outbursts.

- Provide a quiet place in the classroom for him when he seems to need time by himself.

- Set up a daily token system to reinforce positive behaviors. Pick one or two behaviors he will work on during the day.

- Provide self-management skills such as *Stop, Think, Look, and Do* and *Counting to Five Silently* (see chapter 4). Teach alternative ways to deal with anger or frustration.

- Make sure other staff members are aware of his difficulties in controlling his emotions. Provide suggestions that work for you when he becomes upset.

<u>Secondary Grades</u>

- Implement many of the above suggestions.

- Try to make environmental accommodations to limit frustrating situations. Separate the student from peers who upset him the most.

- Maintain a calm and positive environment. Quietly tell him which positive behaviors you've noticed. Let him know where he can go when he is upset (library, vice principal's office to calm down, or a quiet spot at the back of the classroom).

- Try different groupings or seating arrangements to minimize emotional outbursts.

He Turns in His Schoolwork, but It Is Sloppy

Affected students often do work quickly without attention to detail or neatness. They turn in work that is illegible and sloppy. Provide interventions and accommodations to address this common ADHD behavior.

<u>Primary Grades</u>

- Assign shorter assignments but require quality work.

- Provide additional time to do written work with the expectation that more effort will be put into the finished product.

- Make sure the student knows what he did incorrectly. Be specific and give him suggestions for improvements.

- Supervise him while he is doing the schoolwork. Monitor for neatness, spelling, etc.

- If he seems distracted, provide a quiet area for him to work on his assignment (study carrel, resource room, back of the room, library, etc.).

- Provide a *study buddy* to help model appropriate samples of acceptable work.

- Make sure he has all the necessary materials to complete the assignment (pencil, eraser, scissors, and paper).

- Provide time for exercises to improve handwriting skills.

- Use graph paper to teach spacing skills.

Secondary Grades

- Apply some of the suggestions above.

- Provide other means besides paper and pencil to demonstrate knowledge of a subject area (word processor, tape recorder). Affected students often have difficulty with paper/pencil tasks. Accommodations to address these concerns are appropriate.

- Provide incentives for turning in work that is legible and ready to grade (no homework on Thursday, bonus of 20 points on the next examination, etc.).

The goal of any classroom management program is to get students to do what needs to be done conscientiously and independently. Many of these interventions are suggested with the purpose of reinforcing independent work habits in the classroom. As in any good lesson plan, *structured practice* is an important component in mastery of a new skill and reinforcing appropriate school behavior (Jones 1987). You will be primarily responsible for providing the structure needed for performance mastery. Carefully prompt the student to help build skill performance in positive classroom behaviors. Recognize that skill mastery will come slowly. Don't expect these interventions to suddenly turn the distracted, inattentive, and impulsive child into a cooperative and self-directed student. Though you will initially have to do the hard work, you should find significant improvement in his classroom behavior.

Review and Tips

- Remember that many school activities required for success can be challenging to these students.

- Affected children will generally need more monitoring and reminders than unaffected children throughout their education.

- Writing assignments, reading comprehension, and arithmetic calculations often challenge these students. Make accommodations in the classroom to address these problem areas.

- Implement a daily plan to address problem behaviors. Affected students become bored quickly, so change the program on a regular basis.

- Behavior plans will help minimize problem areas, not make them go away permanently.

Section 504 Worries Me

Section 504 (the Rehabilitation Act of 1973) prohibits discrimination against any person with a disability in any program in school districts receiving federal financial assistance. Under the act, an individual with a disability is anyone who has a mental or physical impairment that substantially limits one or more major life activities. Learning is considered one such life activity.

Section 504 shouldn't worry you—it simply formalizes good teaching. Teachers worry sometimes when required to implement a Section 504 plan for an affected student. They may, however, have already been implementing interventions that are effective; all the plan does is to formalize these and other suggested interventions.

A Section 504 plan provides support and direction for a student with ADHD as he advances in grades. For example, a student who is transitioning from the sixth grade into middle school can be supported by a Section 504 plan. It flags him and makes incoming teachers and staff aware of his special needs. Obviously, if he does not present problems and is doing well in school, the plan is not recommended or appropriate.

A Section 504 plan can give you added information and suggestions for working with a student. There is no need to reinvent the wheel. You can access suggestions by previous teachers that can be helpful. These students struggle with common challenges throughout their education, such as task completion, organization, time management, written language, and impulsivity.

One important step in utilizing a Section 504 plan is to understand its purpose. We discuss Section 504 and IDEA (special education legislation) as it relates to children with ADHD in chapter 6, and have included below legal issues and guidelines teachers should be familiar with.

Section 504, like IDEA, requires that schools receiving federal funds address the needs of students with ADHD when their disorder substantially limits their learning. Included in the U.S. department of education regulations for Section 504 is the requirement that handicapped students be provided a Free Appropriate Public Education (FAPE). These regulations require identification, evaluation, provisions, and procedural safeguards in every public school in the United States.

Schools are required to draw up a Section 504 plan at the local school site. In a school district near our town, the *student study team* is the educational body that implements the plan. It is important to understand that Section 504 is not a special education program, but is enforced by the federal Office of Civil Rights (OCR) and is a general public education responsibility.

Under Section 504 procedures, the parent or guardian must be provided with notice of actions affecting the identification, evaluation, or placement of the student and are entitled to an impartial hearing if they disagree with the school district's decisions in these areas. Section 504 is a formalized act with procedural safeguards to protect the student from discrimination because of his disability.

Even though the information above can seem ominous and threatening, it should be viewed as a positive act meant to protect the civil rights of your students and give you support in the classroom. If you had a child or grandchild with a disability, you would want him protected from discrimination because of his disability. If you view the affected student in the classroom as "my child" or "grandchild," you may look at Section 504 in a different light—no longer an obstacle to good teaching, but a support to the student and a vehicle to help you better focus on his educational challenges.

Review and Tips

- Section 504 is part of the Rehabilitation Act of 1973 that gives legal protection to people with disabilities.

- It can give you support by providing a history of behavior interventions that have been successful.

- You are probably using positive interventions that can be formalized at a Section 504 plan meeting. Don't feel intimidated by the procedure.

How Should I Tell Parents I Think
Their Child Has ADHD?

You have a student in your classroom that you think could have ADHD, but you're unsure as to how to share this concern with his parent. How you approach this matter with a parent can have serious consequences if not done correctly. ADHD is not a life-or-death disorder, but can have serious implications for a child. As stated throughout this book, these children often experience a wide range of social and educational challenges, so the earlier a diagnosis is made, the better it is for everyone.

You have an important role to play in the evaluation of a student for ADHD. He spends a large part of his day at school; you see him daily and can compare his behavior with other students of similar age and gender. Physicians often perceive the teacher's observations as more balanced than that of the parents. This observation is made not to put down parents, but to point out that because teachers see such a large number of children, they are often more observant of aberrant behaviors. The parent generally has only siblings, cousins, or neighborhood children with whom to compare their child's behavior. Your advice is important and valued by physicians, psychologists, and other professionals who work with children outside the school setting.

You are probably thinking, "What then can I say to parents about my suspicions that her child has ADHD without getting her angry or upset?"

First, don't attempt to label or tell a parent her child has the disorder. Educators are not qualified or licensed to diagnose a child with a medical or psychological disorder. Any diagnosis must be left up to a qualified person licensed or trained in neurological or psychological disorders. This person doesn't necessarily have to be a physician, but it is advisable that a physician be involved in any diagnosis of ADHD.

Second, when talking to a parent about your concerns, be sensitive to her reactions. No parent wants to hear disturbing things about her child. Parents often initially react with disbelief or anxiety that may present itself as anger, blame, or denial. You may receive their anger, so prepare your reactions. You may want another professional familiar with the child present to give you support.

Third, share your concerns in a private and nonthreatening manner, not in a moment of frustration or anger. What you have to tell the parent is very important, so don't minimize its importance by coming across as bitter or blaming.

Fourth, be clear about your concerns, and when you present them to the parent, give concrete examples to help clarify your concerns. You are making some serious observations and the parent will want examples or situations to support your assertion. Talk about behavior and stay away from labeling.

Fifth, be honest. A large part of your effectiveness in communicating with the parent will be the trust they have in you. Let her know why you requested a conference about her child. You can say, for example, "I wanted to talk with you about Bobby's behaviors. I have observed a number of children whose behaviors are similar to Bobby's who are diagnosed with ADHD. I am not saying Bobby has ADHD, but I wanted to bring my concerns to your attention. If he were my son, I would want him evaluated by his doctor to assess this possibility."

Sixth, if you feel you do not have a good relationship with the parent, but still feel the student could have ADHD, let someone else be the messenger. It could be another teacher or the school counselor, school psychologist, or principal. It is important that they observe the student a few times if they are going to talk about your concerns. They can give credence and validate your observations or suggest other possibilities for his behavior.

Share your concerns in a positive and constructive manner. You will have an important role to play in the child's assessment for ADHD and a positive relationship with the child's parent is important. A diagnosis of ADHD is not simple and often requires close communication between the parent, teacher, and doctor. Your first responsibility and task will be to communicate clearly with the parent, and by following some of the suggestions outlined above, you should find it more comfortable and less stressful for all parties involved.

Review and Tips

- ADHD is a diagnosis that needs to be made by a professional familiar with this disorder. Don't attempt to label or tell a parent her child has ADHD.

- Share your concerns in a private and positive manner. Be sensitive to the parent's reactions. Remember that no parent wants to hear bad things said about her child.

- Have specific examples to help demonstrate your concerns to the parent. Write down your thoughts so the parent can share them with a doctor if the child is evaluated.

- You are doing both the parent and child a good deed by bringing your concerns to the parent's attention. Undiagnosed ADHD can put a child at risk for educational and social difficulties.

How Can I Help the Doctor?

Most doctors value your input and support in the course of treating a child for ADHD. Without regular communication between a physician and you, effective treatment is difficult. It is a disorder that is best treated when important parties involved in the child's life communicate. Often the communication between a physician and teacher is not consistent because of a number of factors. First, a parent may not share with you that the child is under treatment for ADHD. Second, physicians are very busy people, too, or they are not necessarily aware of the importance of close communication with a child's teacher. However, most doctors will return your call if you contact them. Fourth, a physician understands the role of medication in the treatment of ADHD, but may be unfamiliar with treatment methods beyond medication. He may not necessarily understand the importance of a multidimensional approach to treating ADHD, or he is uncomfortable speaking with professionals outside the medical community. Just as you may feel anxious talking with a physician, he too may sometimes be at a loss when talking with you. He may be unsure what role you can play in the child's treatment.

You cannot change or control what the doctor does, but you can take steps to provide closer communication with the child's physician. Ask for a *release of information* from the parent so you may talk with the child's doctor. This is a first step before communication with the doctor can take place. Speak with the parent about the importance of communication between you and the child's doctor. A parent may not understand that you can play an important role in the treatment of her child. You can share your observations of the child before and after medication has been administered. You can provide feedback and implement behavioral management suggestions provided by the physician or other professionals working with the child. You can fill out forms or diagnostic scales often used in both the assessment and monitoring of medication.

Provide regular feedback with the doctor through ADHD scales or personal notes on the child's progress once medication has begun. Include in your notes task performance, impulsive behavior, sustained or focused attention, as well as general moods such as irritability or agitation. Medications such as stimulants can cause side effects such as increased irritability or loss of appetite. Regular feedback can help the doctor monitor the dosage levels and/or decide on the appropriateness of the medication.

Make sure the medication is administered as indicated by the doctor if required during school hours. A log must be kept on the administration of the medication at school (date/time). You can fax or have the school office fax to the doctor a copy of the log along with any comments you have on the child's behavior. We recommend that this be done weekly for the first six weeks a child is placed on medication. Normally any changes in dosage will happen during this six-week period of time. Also, some children are on antidepressants, and it may take four to six weeks to get a full response to the medication.

Ask for information on possible medication side effects. Physicians will generally cooperate by mailing or faxing an overview of possible side effects. Read information on what medications are used in the treatment of ADHD and be knowledgeable on what the medication will and will not do in addressing ADHD behaviors. You will find that chapter 7 answers many of these questions.

You can play an important role in the treatment of the child in your classroom. Establish close communication with the child's physician. Your information is an important part of a physician's recommendations to a parent. A child may not need medication at home, but will continue to need its support during school hours.

Review and Tips

- Most physicians value your observations about a child. Try to facilitate communication with the doctor. If the doctor is very busy, you can often work with the office manager or the doctor's nurse.

- Help the parent understand that your close communication with the child's doctor is important for proper treatment. This is especially the case when a child is first placed on medication. Understand that you or the medication may not always be successful.

- Make sure the child's medication is administered during school hours as indicated by the doctor. If a child refuses to take his medication, remind him that you will have to call his parents immediately.

Summary

The student with ADHD creates many challenges for you, the teacher. When provided with appropriate accommodations, he will be more successful. Understand that ADHD is a neurodevelopmental disorder, and no amount of environmental accommodations will make up for biologically based dysfunctions. Environmental accommodations can lessen problematic areas in the classroom, but will never eliminate them. Medication can minimize impulsive and inattentive behaviors, but it cannot eliminate associated behaviors such as organizational difficulties, poor motivation, and noncompliant and oppositional behaviors. These issues require behavioral management interventions and classroom accommodations to minimize the impact on a student's educational progress.

As mentioned often in this book, you are one of the most important people in a student's social, emotional, and educational development. Don't minimize your importance in the treatment of the student in the classroom. You can provide accommodations that can make a significant difference in his school success. An important component to success is both knowledge and empathy for the challenges that are presented to these students. Remember, many behaviors displayed are not purposeful, but are symptomatic of the disorder.

We end this chapter by quoting from an adult with ADHD who expresses a common experience shared by children and adults with ADHD: "You don't mean to do the things you do, and you don't do the things you mean to do" (Hallowell and Ratey 1994). Remember this line when confronted with frustrating and seeming inexplicable behaviors by students with ADHD in the classroom.

10

From Frustration to Hope— A Summary

We have emphasized throughout this book that raising a child with ADHD is hard work and often challenges the best in a parent. ADHD traits, even with medication, cannot be eliminated—they can only be tempered. You may have become frustrated when you first realized that medication alone did not address your child's needs. As much as you wanted medication to be the answer to his problems, you soon found out that it alone was not enough. You have probably also realized that environmental changes cannot eliminate all his problems. We counsel parents that the most effective intervention for minimizing ADHD behaviors is to combine medication with a behavioral management program, and we have tried to present this partnership throughout our discussions and suggestions.

We have tried to keep a balanced approach when presenting information on medication. Medicating a child for ADHD is often a very difficult decision for a parent. Contrary to popular belief, our experience is that most parents don't jump quickly into medicating their child. They are generally driven to medication because of the daily conflicts with their child and/or pressures from their child's school and other care providers. Often medication is their last choice, only made after trying other suggested interventions. They discover, however, that medication is often the most helpful intervention in minimizing core ADHD symptoms.

There are writers who suggest that medications such as Ritalin have potentially serious side effects and are being overprescribed by doctors at the expense of children (Breggin 1998). However, the American Medical Association, in a recent news release, reported that there is "little evidence found of incorrect diagnosis or overprescription for ADHD" (Goleman 1998). Any medication has possible side effects; however, so does being in trouble with your parents, failing in school, and not being invited to birthday parties. As suggested throughout this book, most important decisions we make in life are neither simple nor conflict-free. For some children, medication is an important and necessary intervention to help them be more successful in life.

Your decision to use or not use medication should be supported. There are many factors that went into your decision, and we know that you did not come to your decision alone, quickly, or easily. If you change your mind from time to time, that's okay. There will be times when you may want to take your child off medication or put him back on medication. As your child gets older, you may find that he can be successful without it, or he may continue to need its support.

Our sections on school activities have tried to help you better understand and deal with an often-stressful experience for affected children. We have spent much time covering school-related areas because school can be an important contributor to your child's self-esteem. Children not only learn to read and write in school, but they learn how to socialize. However, those traits that are important for being successful in school and keeping friends are less developed in children with ADHD, such as paying attention, being patient, controlling emotions, following directions, taking turns, and being self-directed. The consequence is that these children will be challenged by school, and they will often be frustrated and discouraged. They may be underachievers who do not reach their potential.

The dilemma for many children is that schools are often not ready for them and they are not ready for school. Options are generally limited for affected children when it comes to classroom accommodations. Schools, we suggest, are generally not providing the educational setting needed for these children to be more successful. Those who act out or are aggressive are often expelled from school rather than provided with classroom environments that can better address their special needs. Aggressive behavior, however, cannot be tolerated in school, and sometimes children with ADHD need to be removed from school. For the majority of affected children who are not aggressive, minor educational accommodations can provide much-needed support. Generally, however, schools have been slow in implementing accommodations.

The primary explanation, often understandable, for not implementing more accommodations is lack of money. Seldom is there additional money in regular education funding to address children with special needs, so schools are often challenged to find creative ways to deal with difficult children without the benefit of additional money to support smaller class size, housing, and teaching staff. Federal legislation such as IDEA, which is partially federally funded, can be helpful, but some children do not qualify for IDEA, and accommodations are not quickly offered or are resisted because of monetary considerations and school staff disapproval. State and federal reimbursement for special education services covers only a percentage of school district funding, so school districts are very careful to keep special education costs down, because any additional costs come out of general district funds. Section 504, legislation that is federally required but not federally funded, is sometimes viewed by some teachers as "more work," and not as a vehicle of support for them and the student. Parents, consequently, often have to advocate for themselves or find an advocate (often at great cost), or be fortunate their child is in a school that is sympathetic and knowledgeable about legislated requirements.

Finally, ADHD continues to be viewed as a questionable disorder by some educators, resulting in many problem children not receiving the necessary educational support they deserve. Educators who continue to deny or minimize this disorder, unfortunately, can contribute to the low self-esteem and negative escalating behaviors seen in these children. Any long-term educational solution for dealing with difficult children must include additional funding for schools, as well as school programs that reflect a wide range of learning styles. Many promising children with ADHD are dropping out of school because schools are not meeting their educational, social and emotional needs.

Schools need to convey compassion, understanding, respect, and interest in the needs of affected children and their families. Schools should address the strengths and talents of these children. Educators should expect the best from affected children, both behaviorally and academically; however, they also need to offer the necessary educational support for them to succeed.

Even though schools cannot prevent the underlying neurological impairment found in children with ADHD, or "fix" bad parenting, they can do a better job preventing these impairments from causing academic and social failure. They can be more effective in teaching these children better ways to control their impulses and emotions. Daniel Goleman (1995) suggests schools can be more proactive in "schooling the emotions." Schools can partner with parents in helping affected children find better ways to deal with their emotions. "Emotional lessons" can merge naturally into daily academic curriculum. This is a daunting task, but for schools to meet the needs of difficult children such as these, they must see their role as beyond their traditional mission of teaching reading, writing, and arithmetic. "The larger design requires," in the words of Daniel Goleman (1995), "apart from any specifics of curriculum, using opportunities in and out of the class to help students turn moments of personal crisis into lessons of emotional competence."

A further problem is that mental health coverage for ADHD treatment is limited. Insurance coverage for long-term or any treatment of ADHD is often not available. Some insurance plans limit medication choices by denying financial coverage for certain drugs. Proper treatment requires not only coverage of medication but often ongoing psychotherapy for the family. Many affected children have associated mental health concerns, such as depression, anxiety, and conduct disorders that require mental health intervention.

We have addressed a common dilemma of parents of children with ADHD: separating ADHD behaviors from normal childhood behaviors. We have presented important concepts and interventions that will help you better understand this difference. Your child is diagnosed with ADHD, but ADHD is not your total child. When you find yourself having doubts, take time to find a section that comes close to your question and read it for suggestions and clarity.

An important theme presented in this book is that the relationship between a child with ADHD and a parent can often be more conflictual than with an unaffected sibling. This has probably not been news to you; however, we feel it is important to underline this concern. In some ways, the relationship between a parent and her affected child can be a "good-enough" relationship, borrowing from Mark Karpel's description of couple relationships (Karpel 1994). The love a parent has for her child is obviously different and more unqualified than for a mate; however, it helps for parents to have realistic expectations of their child's challenges. Just as in marriages, periods of contentment can be disrupted by periods of extreme tension and discord. A "good-enough" couple relationship is not problem-free, but there develop patterns of communication that help the couple maintain a sense of fairness in the relationship.

Maintaining a sense of fairness in the relationship with your child is very important for the health of the relationship. Learn to listen sympathetically to your child's frustrations and be open to the idea that you may at times be a contributor to his anger. Sympathy does not mean agreeing all the time with your child, but being open to looking at his challenges in other ways. Try to maintain a sense of fairness so you do not become closed to hearing his words.

No intervention will work all the time, but don't stop trying an intervention just because it doesn't work consistently. Remember that these children have difficulty learning from their mistakes. Also, change takes time. Have our motto *Try Whatever Works, but It Won't Work for Long* nearby, so you can be reminded that behavioral plans need to be changed often with these children.

Our wish is that you have gained more understanding and confidence in parenting your child after reading this book. We hope you have moved from frustration to hope. Hope comes when you begin to see yourself more content and successful in your interactions with your child. The dictionary defines hope as "a feeling that what is wanted will happen; desire accompanied by expectation." Knowledge provides the foundation for maintaining a more positive and less stressful relationship with your child. Hopefully this book has given you the hope that is necessary for your positive mental health and his health.

We wish you the best of luck and encourage you to use this book as you would a "Survival Guide"—a resource to help you raise your child. Implement the suggested interventions and begin to listen with more confidence to your inner voice. Your newfound knowledge and confidence should shelter you from storms that come your way. Now put this book in a safe place and pick it up when you feel you need it.

Appendices

Appendix A

DSM-IV-TR Criteria for
Attention-Deficit/Hyperactivity Disorder

A. Either (1) or (2):

(1) inattention: six (or more) of the following symptoms of inattention have persisted for at least 6 months to a degree that is maladaptive and inconsistent with developmental level:

(a) often fails to give close attention to details or makes careless mistakes in schoolwork, work, or other activities

(b) often has difficulty sustaining attention in tasks or play activities

(c) often does not seem to listen when spoken to directly

(d) often does not follow through on instructions and fails to finish schoolwork, chores, or duties in the workplace (not due to oppositional behavior or failure to understand instructions)

(e) often has difficulty organizing tasks and activities

(f) often avoids, dislikes, or is reluctant to engage in tasks that require sustained mental effort (such as schoolwork or homework)

(g) often loses things necessary for tasks or activities (e.g., toys, school assignments, pencils, books, or tools)

(h) is often easily distracted by extraneous stimuli

(i) is often forgetful in daily activities

(2) hyperactivity-impulsivity: six (or more) of the following:
Reference symptoms of hyperactivity-impulsivity have persisted for at least 6 months to a degree that is maladaptive and inconsistent with developmental level:
Hyperactivity
(a) often fidgets with hands or feet or squirms in seat

(b) often leaves seat in classroom or in other situations in which remaining seated is expected

(c) often runs about or climbs excessively in situations in which it is inappropriate (in adolescents or adults, may be limited to subjective feelings of restlessness)

(d) often has difficulty playing or engaging in leisure activities quietly

(e) is often "on the go" or often acts as if "driven by a motor"

(f) often talks excessively

Impulsivity

(g) often blurts out answers before questions have been completed

(h) often has difficulty awaiting turn

(i) often interrupts or intrudes on others (e.g., butts into conversations or games)

B. Some hyperactive-impulsive or inattentive symptoms that caused impairment were present before age 7 years.

C. Some impairment from the symptoms is present in two or more settings (e.g., at school [or work] and at home).

D. There must be clear evidence of clinically significant impairment in social, academic, or occupational functioning.

E. The symptoms do not occur exclusively during the course of a Pervasive Developmental Disorder, Schizophrenia, or other Psychotic Disorder and are not better accounted for by another mental disorder (e.g., Mood Disorder, Anxiety Disorder, Dissociative Disorders, or a Personality Disorder).

Code based on type:

314.01 Attention-Deficit/Hyperactivity Disorder, Combined Type: if both Criteria A1 and A2 are met for the past 6 months

314.00 Attention-Deficit/Hyperactivity Disorder, Predominantly Inattentive Type: if Criterion A1 is met but Criterion A2 is not met for the past 6 months

314.01 Attention-Deficit/Hyperactivity Disorder, Predominantly Hyperactive-Impulsive Type: if Criterion A2 is met but Criterion A1 is not met for the past 6 months

Coding note: For individuals (especially adolescents and adults) who currently have symptoms that no longer meet full criteria, "In Partial Remission" should be specified.

Appendix B

Developmental Stages of ADHD
(Author Unknown)

Developmental Stages

Infancy
>   Poor task completion
>   Difficulty in staying on schedule (sleeping and eating)
>   Having a low threshold level, difficulty adjusting to changes in schedule
>   Very active
>   Irritability (i.e., cry and fuss more than gurgle and coo)

Preschool Age
>   High activity level
>   Noncompliance
>   Poor attention span
>   Reckless behavior (injury prone)
>   Easily distracted

Elementary School Age
>   Poor attention span
>   Difficulty concentrating and/or finishing schoolwork
>   Impulsiveness/lack of self-control
>   High frequency of off-task behavior
>   Poor social skills
>   Increase in conduct problems (aggression, destructive, oppositional behavior, if hyperactive symptoms are present)
>   Disorganized/messy

Adolescent
>   Low self-esteem
>   Social skill deficits
>   Learning problems
>   Poor problem solving skills
>   Difficulty concentrating
>   Disorganized/messy

Adults
>   Low educational achievement
>   Poor social skills
>   Low self-esteem
>   Increase in anxiety
>   Continued problems with restlessness/poor attention span

Appendix C

Nerve Cell

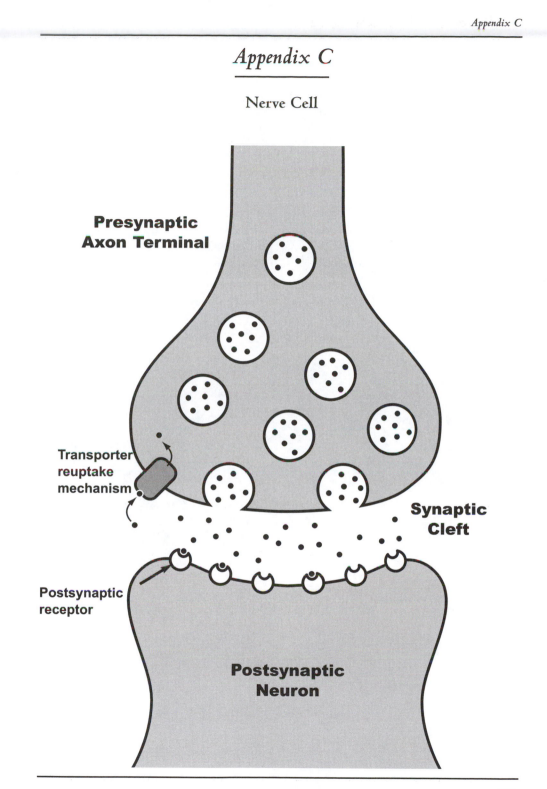

Presynaptic Axon Terminal

Transporter reuptake mechanism

Synaptic Cleft

Postsynaptic receptor

Postsynaptic Neuron

Appendix D

Disorders That Can Mimic ADHD

The disorders below have been found to mimic ADHD and are sometimes mistaken for ADHD.

Unidentified learning disability
Reactive attachment disorder
Child abuse (sexual, physical, mental)
Adjustment base disorders (Home, school changes)
Depression
Bipolar disorder
Tourette syndrome
Pervasive developmental disorder
Anxiety disorder
Oppositional defiant disorder
Separation anxiety disorder
Mild seizure disorder
Auditory processing disorder
Language-based disorder
Sensory deficits
Sensory integration dysfunction
Mild cerebral palsy
Malnourished or sleep-deprived children (including sleep apnea)
Reaction to medication
Hyperthyroidism
Pinworm infection
Bad fit with the environment (temperament)

Appendix E

Stimulant Medications Used in Treatment for ADHD

David K. Rosenthal, M.D.

Generic Name	Trade Name	Typical Dosage Range	Onset of Behavioral Effect	Duration of Action
Methylphenidate	Ritalin	5-20 mg/dose	20-30 minutes	3-4 hours
Methylphenidate SR (sustained-release)	Ritalin SR	20-40 mg/dose	45-60 minutes	6-8 hours
Methylphenidate ER (extended release)	Concerta	18-54 mg/dose	20-30 minutes	10-12 hours
Methylphenidate SR (sustained-release)	Metadate ER	10-40 mg/dose	45-60 minutes	6-8 hours
Dextroamphetamine	Dexedrine	5-20 mg/dose	20-30 minutes	3-4 hours
Dextroamphetamine (sustained-release)	Dexedrine Spansules	5-40 mg/dose	45-60 minutes	6-8 hours
Dextroamphetamine saccharate/sulfate	Adderall	5-30 mg/dose	20-30 minutes	8-12 hours
Dextroamphetamine saccharate/sulfate	Adderall XR	10-30 mg	20-30 minutes	10-14 hours
Pemoline	Cylert	37.5-112.5 mg/dose	45-60 minutes	6-12 hours

Appendix F

The Weekly Report

THE WEEKLY REPORT
(Grades 4-8)

Name: _____ Date: _____

Scores:	
3 = Often	Class: _____
2 = Sometimes	Period: _____
1 = Rarely	Teacher: _____

	M	T	W	Th	F
Works independently	AM / PM	AM / PM	AM / PM	AM / PM	AM / PM
Is prepared for school work	AM / PM	AM / PM	AM / PM	AM / PM	AM / PM
Completes work in class	AM / PM	AM / PM	AM / PM	AM / PM	AM / PM
Follows teacher's directions	AM / PM	AM / PM	AM / PM	AM / PM	AM / PM
Turns in Homework	AM / PM	AM / PM	AM / PM	AM / PM	AM / PM
Stares excessively or looks "spaced out"	AM / PM	AM / PM	AM / PM	AM / PM	AM / PM
Fidgets at desk	AM / PM	AM / PM	AM / PM	AM / PM	AM / PM
Talks excessively	AM / PM	AM / PM	AM / PM	AM / PM	AM / PM
Stays out of trouble during free time	AM / PM	AM / PM	AM / PM	AM / PM	AM / PM

Parent Signature: _____ Date: _____

Run for four weeks or as needed. Show copies to doctor if child is on medication.

Appendix G

Daily Student Rating Card

THE DAILY REPORT
(Grades K-3)

Name: _____ Date: _____

```
┌─────────────────────────────────────────┐
│ Token:                                    │
│     Green Star   =   Good                 │
│     Yellow Star  =   Fair                 │
│     Red Star     =   Needs Improvement    │
└─────────────────────────────────────────┘
```

	AM	PM
☆ Stays seated during circle time/class discussion		
☆ Finishes table/desk work in class		
☆ Plays cooperatively during free time		
☆ Respectful to others		
☆ Raises hand before talking		

Teacher Signature: _____

Run for four weeks or as needed. Show copies to doctor if child is on medication.

Appendix H

Web sites offering information about ADHD

www.c4.com

www.ixquick.com

www.brightgate.com

www.dogpile.com *(look for ADD/ADHD Information Library)*

http://www.nlci.com/nutrition *(ADD/ADHD Online Newsletter)*

http://www3.sympatico.ca/frankk/contents.html *(ADD: FAQ)*

http://www.signasoft.com/adult *(adult recovery)*

http://www.usask.ca/psychiatry/CPADDC.html *(Canadian Professionals ADD Page)*

http://www.chadd.org *(CHADD)*

http://www.feingold.org (Feingold Association Dietary Connection)

http://www.mindspring.com/ ~ staywell/add.html *(Nutritional Supplemental for ADD)*

http://www.mentalhealth.com/book/P40-gtor.html *(Tourette Syndrome)*

http://www.tourettesyndrome.org *(site for Tourette Spectrum Disorder Association—information on ADHD, Tourette syndrome, and other associated disorders, and advocacy issues pertaining to IDEA and Section 504)*

http://www.tourettesyndrome.net *(a goldmine of information about Tourette syndrome, ADHD, and advocacy issues pertaining to IDEA and Section 504)*

http://www.hopepress.com (information, reasearch, books)

Appendix I

Recommended Reading

For Parents and Teachers

1,2,3, Magic, Effective Discipline for Children, (ages) 2-12, Phelan, T., Ph.D. (1996), Glen Ellyn, Illinois: Child Management Inc.

ADD Success Stories: A Guide To Fulfillment for Families with Attention Deficit Disorder [focus primarily on adults with ADHD], Hartmann, T. (1996), Grass Valley, CA: Underwood Books.

All About Attention Deficit Disorder, Symptoms, Diagnosis and Treatment Children and Adults, Phelan, T., Ph.D. (1996), Glen Ellyn, Illinois: Child Management Inc.

Answers to Distraction, Hallowell, E., M.D., & Ratey, J., M.D. (1996), Bantam Books.

Attention Deficit Disorder, A Different Perception, Hartmann, T. (1996), Grass Valley, California: Underwood Books.

Attention Deficit Disorder and Learning Disabilities: Realities, Myths, and Controversial Treatments, Ingersoll, B. & Goldstein, M. (1993), New York: Doubleday.

Driven To Distraction: Recognizing and Coping with Attention Deficit Disorder from Childhood through Adult, Hallowell, E., M.D., & Ratey, J., M.D. (1994), New York: A Touchstone Book, Simon & Schuster.

Dr. Larry Silver's Advice to Parents on Attention-Deficit Hyperactivity Disorder, Silver, L. (1993), Washington, D.C.: American Psychiatric Press.

Helping Your Hyperactive/Attention Deficit Child, Taylor, J., Ph.D. (1994), Rocklin, California: Prima Publishing.

How To Reach and Teach ADD/ADHD Children, Rief, Sandra, F. (1993), New York: The Center for Applied Research and Education.

Hyperactivity: Why Won't My Child Pay Attention, Goldstein, S. & Goldstein, M. (1992), Salt Lake City: Neurology, Learning and Behavior Center.

Maybe You Know My Kid: A Parents Guide to Identifying, Understanding, and Helping Your Child with Attention-Deficit Hyperactivity Disorder, Fowler, M. C. (1990), New York: Berch Lane Press.

Parents and Adolescents Living Together, Forgatch, M., & Patterson, G. R. (1989), Eugene, Oregon: Castalia.

Setting Limits, How To Raise Responsible Independent Children by Providing Reasonable Boundaries, MacKenzie, R., Ed.D. (1993), Rocklin, California: Prima Publishing.

Taking Charge of ADHD: A Complete, Authoritative Guide for Parents, Barkley, R., Ph.D. (1995), New York/London: The Guilford Press.

The ADD Hyperactive Workbook for Parents, Teachers, and Kids (2nd. ed.), Parker, H. (1988), Plantation, Florida: Specialty Press.

Think Fast: The ADD Experience, Hartmann, T., & Bowman, J. with Burgess, S. (1996), Grass Valley, California: Underwood Books.

Tourette Syndrome and Human Behavior, Comings, D., M.D. (1990), Duarte, California: Hope Press.

What Every Parent Wants To Know: Attention Deficit Hyperactivity Disorder, Wodrich, D. (1994), Baltimore: Brookes.

Your Hyperactive Child, Ingersoll, B. (1988), New York: Doubleday.

For Children

ADD and the College Student, Quinn, P. (1994), New York: Magination Press.

All Kinds of Minds, Levine, M., Educators Publishing Service, Inc.

Eagle's Eyes: A Child's View of ADD, Gehret, J., Verbal Images Press.

I'm Somebody Too, Gehret, J. (1992), Verbal Images Press.

I would If I Could, Gordon, M. (1992), De Witt, New York: GSI.

Jumpin' Johnny Get Back To Work! A Guild's Guide To ADHD/Hyperactivity, Gordon, M. (1992), De Witt, New York: GSI.

Keeping A Head In School, Levine, M., Educators Publishing Service, Inc.

Learning To Slow Down and Pay Attention, Dixon, E. & Nadeau, K. (1991), Chesapeake Psychological Services.

Making the Grade: An Adolescent's Struggle with Attention Deficit Disorder, Parker, Roberta (1992), Impact Publications.

My Brother's A World Class Pain, Gordon, M. (1992), De Witt, New York: GSI.

Otto Learns About His Medicine: A Story About Medication for Children (Rev. Ed.), Galvin, Michael, Ph.D. (1995), New York: Magination Press.

Shelly the Hyperactive Turtle, Moss, Deborah. (1989), Woodbine House.

Survival Guide for College Students with ADD or LD, Nadeau, K. G. (1994), New York: Magination Press.

Putting on the Brakes: Young Peoples' Guide to Understanding Attention Deficit Hyperactivity Disorder, Quinn, P. & Stern, J. (1991), New York: Magination Press.

Reference List

Abikoff, H., Ganeles, G., Reiter, G., Blum, C., Foley, C., and Klein, R. G. 1988. Cognitive training in academically deficient ADHD boys receiving stimulant medication. *Journal of Abnormal Child Psychology* 16:411–432.

Abramowitz, A. J. and O'Leary, S. G. 1991. Behavioral interventions for the classroom: Implications for students with ADHD. *School Psychology Review* 20:220–234.

Aman, M. G. 1980. Psychotropic drugs and learning problems: A selective review. *Journal of Learning Disabilities* 13:87–97.

Anastopoulos, A. D. and Shelton, T. L. 2001. *Assessing Attention-Deficit/Hyperactivity Disorder.* Kluwer Academic/Plenum Publishers, New York.

Archer, A. and Gleason, M. 1990. *Skills for School Success.* North Billerica, MA: Curriculum Associates.

Atkins, M. S. and Pelham, W. E. 1991. School-based assessment of attention deficit-hyperactivity disorder. *Journal of Learning Disabilities* 24(4):197–204.

August, G. and Garfinkel, G. D. 1990. Comorbidity of ADHD and reading disability among clinic-referred children, *Journal of Abnormal Child Psychology* 18:29–45

Barkley, R. A. 1981. *Hyperactive Children: A Handbook for Diagnosis and Treatment.* New York: The Guilford Press.

———1987. *Defiant Children: A Clinical Manual for Parent Training.* New York: The Guilford Press.

———1989. Ritalin treatment for hyperactivity. *CHADDER Newsletter* (Summer) 3–4

———1990. *Attention-Deficit Hyperactivity Disorder: A Handbook for Diagnosis and Treatment.* New York: The Guilford Press.

———1991. *Attention-Deficit Hyperactivity Disorder: A Clinical Workbook.* New York: The Guilford Press.

———1992. Is EEG biofeedback treatment effective for ADHD children? *CHADDER Newsletter* (April) 5.

———1993. Pseudoscience in treatments for ADHD. *The ADHD Report* 1(6):1–3.

———1995. *Taking Charge of ADHD: The Complete Authoritative Guide for Parents.* New York: The Guilford Press.

———1997. *ADHD and the Nature of Self-Control.* New York: The Guilford Press.

———1998. Attention-Deficit Hyperactivity Disorder. *Scientific American* (September) 6–71.

Barkley, R. A. and Cunningham, C. E. 1979. The effects of methylphenidate on the mother-child interactions of hyperactive children. *Archives of General Psychiatry* 36:201–208.

Barkley, R. A., Grodizinsky, G., and DuPaul, G.J. 1992. Frontal lobe functions in attention deficit disorder with and without hyperactivity: A review and research report. *Journal of Abnormal Child Psychology* 20:163–168.

Barkley, R. A., Karlsson, J., Pollard, S., and Murphy, J. V. 1985. Developmental changes in the mother-child interactions of hyperactive boys: Effects of two doses of Ritalin. *Journal of Child Psychology and Psychiatry* 26:705–715

Barkley, R. A., McMurry, M. B., Edelbrock, C. S., and Robbins, K. 1990. Side effects of methylphenidate in children with attention deficit hyperactivity disorder: A systematic, placebo-controlled evaluation. *Pediatrics* 86:184–192.

Bentz, K., Steward, M., Hansen, R., and Barton, K. 1995. Cognitive development of preschool children prenatally exposed to stimulant drugs: A neuropsychological study. *CASP Today* (Summer) 6–12.

Biederman, J., Wilens, T. E., Mick, E., Faraone, S. V., Weber, W., Curtis, S., Thornell, A., Pfister, K., Jetton, J. G., and Soriano, J. 1997. Is ADHD a risk for psychoactive substance use disorders? Findings from a four-year follow-up study. *Journal of the American Academy of Child and Adolescent Psychiatry* 36:21–29

Bowen, J., Fenton, T., and Rappaport, L. 1991. Stimulant medication and attention deficit-hyperactivity disorder: The child's perspective. *American Journal of Diseases of Children* 145:291–295.

Breggin, P. R. 1998. *Talking Back to Ritalin: What Doctors Aren't Telling You about Stimulants for Children.* Monroe, ME: Common Courage Press.

Brown, R. T. and Sawyer, M. G. 1998. *Medications for School-Age Children: Effects on Learning and Behavior.* New York: The Guilford Press.

Brown, R. T., Jaffe, S., Silverstein, J., and McGee, H. 1991. Methylphenidate and adolescents hospitalized with conduct disorder: Dose effects on classroom behavior, academic performance, and impulsivity. *Journal of Clinical Child Psychology* 20:282-292.

Brunk, D. 2000. Federal report spotlights issues in ADHD diagnosis. *Clinical Psychiatry News* (February) 1, 5.

Burnett, K. 1996. ADD and delinquency: Myths, pathways, and advice. *Attention!* (Winter) 20–26.

California Education Code. 1976. Section 49423.

Carlson, C. and Bunner, M. 1993. Effects of methylphenidate on the academic performance of children with attention-deficit hyperactivity disorder and learning disabilities. *School Psychology Review.* 22(2):184–198.

Carlson, C., Rapport, M. D., Kelly, K. L., and Pataki, C. S. 1992. The effects of methylphenidate and lithium on attention and activity level. *Journal of the American Academy of Child and Adolescent Psychiatry* 31:262–270.

CASP Today. March/April, 1991. Attention deficit disorders: Suggested classroom accommodations for specific behaviors. *(Reprinted data from the ADHD Task Force of the Anchorage, Alaska, School District.)*

Comings, D., 1990. *Tourette Syndrome and Human Behavior.* Duarte, CA: Hope Press.

Cunningham, C. E. and Barkley, R. A. 1979. The interactions of hyperactive and normal children with mothers in free play and structure tasks. *Child Development* 50:217–224.

Diagnostic and Statistical Manual of Mental Disorders, Fourth Edition, Text Revision. 2000. Washington, D.C.: American Psychiatric Association.

Douglas, V. I., Barr, R. G., Desilets, J., and Sherman, E. 1995. Do high doses of stimulants impair flexible thinking in attention-deficit hyperactivity disorder? *Journal of the American Academy of Child and Adolescent Psychiatry* 34:877–885.

Douglas, V. I., Barr, R. G., O'Neill, M. E., and Britton, B. G. 1986. Short-term effects of methylphenidate on the cognitive, learning and academic performance of children with attention deficit disorder in the laboratory and the classroom. *Journal of Child Psychology and Psychiatry* 27:191–211.

Dreikers, R. 1964. *Children: The Challenge.* New York: Hawthorn Books.

DuPaul, G. J., Guevremont, D. C., and Barkley, R. A. 1992. Behavior treatment of attention deficit hyperactivity disorder in the classroom: The use of the attention training system. *Behavior Modification* 16:204–225.

DuPaul, G. J. and Hennington, P. N. 1993. Peer tutoring effects on the classroom performance of children with attention deficit hyperactivity disorder. *School Psychology Review* 22:134–143.

DuPaul, G. J. and Rapport, M. 1993. Does methylphenidate normalize the classroom performance of children with attention deficit disorder? *Journal of the American Academy of Child and Adolescent Psychiatry* 32:190–198.

Erenberg, G. 1999. The clinical neurology of Tourette syndrome. *CNS Spectrums* (February) 49.

Federal Register. 1999. Rules and Regulations. March 12, 64(48):12422, 12542–12543.

Forward, S. and Frazier, D. 1997. *Emotional Blackmail: When People in Your Life Use Fear, Obligation, and Guilt to Manipulate You.* New York: Harper Perennial.

Friedman, R. 1998. Distinguishing between attention deficit disorder, learning disabilities, and conduct disorder. *CHADDER Newsletter* (Fall/Winter) 3–4.

Gadow, K. D. and Nolan, E. E. 1993. Practical considerations in conducting school-based medication evaluations for children with hyperactivity. *Journal of Emotional and Behavioral Disorders* 1:118–126.

Gadow, K. D., Nolan, E. E., and Sverd, J. 1992. Methylphenidate in hyperactive boys with comorbid tic disorder: II. Short-term behavioral effects in school settings. *Journal of the American Academy of Child and Adolescent Psychiatry* 31:462–471.

Gadow, K. D., Nolan, E. E., Sverd, J., Sprafkin, J., and Paolicelli, L. M. 1990. Methylphenidate in aggressive-hyperactive boys: I. Effects on peer aggression in public school settings. *Journal of the American Academy of Child and Adolescent Psychiatry* 29:710-718.

Garber, S., Garber, M., and Spizman, R. 1996. *Beyond Ritalin.* New York: Harper Perennial.

Gittelman, R., Klein, D. F., and Feingold, I. 1983. Children with reading disorders: Two effects of methylphenidate in combination with reading remediation. *Journal of Child Psychology and Psychiatry* 24:193–212.

Goldman, L. (April 7, 1998). News Release. American Medical Association.

Goldstein, S. and Goldstein, M. 1990. *Managing Attention Disorders in Children: A Guide for Practitioners.* New York: John Wiley and Sons, Inc.

Goldstein, S. and Ingersoll, B. 1992. Controversial treatments for children with attention-deficit hyperactivity disorder. *CHADDER Newsletter* (Fall Winter) 19-22.

Goleman, D. (1995). *Emotional Intelligence: Why It Can Matter More Than I.Q.* New York: Bantam Books.

Gomez, R. and Condon, M. 1999. Central auditory processing ability in children with ADHD with and without learning disabilities. *Journal of Learning Disabilities* 32(2):150–158.

Goodwin, F. and Ghaemi, S. N. 1998. Understanding manic-depressive illness. *Archives of General Psychiatry* (January) 23–25.

Green, W. 1991. *Child and Adolescent Clinical Psychopharmacology.* Baltimore: Williams & Wilkins.

Hallowell, E. and Ratey, J. 1994. *Driven To Distraction: Recognizing and Coping with Attention Deficit Disorder from Childhood through Adult.* New York: A Touchstone Book, Simon and Schuster.

Halperin, J. M. and Gittelman, R. 1982. Do hyperactive children and their siblings differ in I.Q. and academic achievement? *Psychiatry Research* 6:253–258.

Halperin, J. M., Matier, K., Bedi, G., Sharma, V,. and Newcorn, J. H. 1992. Specificity of inattention, impulsivity, and hyperactivity to the diagnosis of attention-deficit hyperactivity disorder. *Journal of American Academy Child and Adolescent Psychiatry* 31:190–196.

Hanker, B. and Whalen, C. 1989. Hyperactivity and Attention Deficits. *American Psychological Association* 44(2):216-223.

Hartmann, T. 1993. *Attention Deficit Disorder: A Different Perception.* Grass Valley, CA: Underwood Books.

Hartmann, T., Bowman, J., Burgus, S., eds. 1996. *Think Fast: The ADD Experience.* (Interview of Louis B. Cady by Carla Berg Nelson in chapter, "How Doctors May Differ about ADD.") Grass Valley, CA: Underwood Books.

Harvard Mental Health Letter. 2000. Is Ritalin underused? 16(9):6–7.

Harvard Mental Health Letter. 1989. What happens to hyperactive children when they grow up? (Discussion with Gabrielle Weiss, M.D., and Lily Hechtman, M.D.) 8.

Harvard Mental Health Letter. 1988. Does diet affect behavior and learning in hyperactive children? (Interview with C. Keith Connors) 5(5):23–25.

Hinshaw, S. P. 1991. Stimulant medication and the treatment of aggression in children with attention deficits. *Journal of Clinical Child Psychology* 20:301–312.

Hinshaw, S. P., Buhrmeister, D., and Heller, R. 1989. Anger control in response to verbal provocation: Effects of stimulant medication for boys with ADHD. *Journal of Abnormal Child Psychology* 17:393–407.

Hynd, G. and Obrzut, J., eds. 1981. *Neuropsychological Assessment and the School Age Child: Issues and Procedures.* Boston: Allyn and Bacon.

Ingersoll, B. 1988. *Your Hyperactive Child.* New York: Doubleday.

Ingersoll, B. and Goldstein, S. 1993. *Attention Deficit Disorder and Learning Disabilities: Reality, Myths, and Controversial Treatments.* New York: Doubleday.

Jensen, P. S. 2000. The National Institutes of Health Attention-Deficit/ Hyperactivity Disorder Consensus Statement: Implications for practitioners and scientists. *CNS Spectrums* 5(6):29–33.

Johnson, C. and Fine, S. 1993. Methods of evaluating methylphenidate in children with attention-deficit hyperactivity disorder: Acceptability, satisfaction, and compliance. *Journal of Pediatric Psychology* 18:717–730.

Jones, F. A. 1987. *Positive Classroom Instruction.* New York: McGraw-Hill Book Company.

Jordan, D. 1991. Whatever happened to ADD without hyperactivity? *CHADDER Newsletter* (May) 5–6.

Kaplan, B. J., Crawford, S. G., Dewey, D. M., and Fisher, G. C., (September/October 2000). The I.Q.s of children with ADHD are normally distributed. *Journal of Learning Disabilities* 33(5):425-432.

Karpel, M. 1994. *Evaluating Couples: Handbook for Practitioners.* Scranton, PA: Norton Press.

Kasten, E. F., Coury, D. L., and Heron, T. E. 1992. Educators' knowledge and attitudes regarding stimulants in the treatment of attention-deficit hyperactivity disorder. *Journal of Developmental and Behavioral Pediatrics* 13:215–219.

Kinsbourne, M. 1992. Quality of life in children with ADHD. *Challenge: A Newsletter of the Attention Deficit Disorder Association* 6(1):1–2

———1991. Overfocusing: An apparent subtype of attention deficit-hyperactivity disorder. *Pediatric Adolescent Medicine, Basal, Krager* 1:18–35.

Kramer, J. R., Loney, J., Ponto, L. B., Roberts, M. A., and Grossman, S. 2000. Predictors of adult height and weight in boys treated with methylphenidate for childhood behavior problems. Journal of the American Academy of Child and Adolescent Psychiatry 39(4):517–524.

Kupietz, S. S., Winsberg, B. G., Richardson, E., Maitinsky, S., and Mendell, N. 1988. Effects of methylphenidate dosage in hyperactive reading-disabled children: I. Behavior and cognitive performance effects. *Journal of the American Academy of Child and Adolescent Psychiatry* 27, 1:70–77.

Levine, M. 1987. Attention deficits: The diverse effects of weak control systems in childhood. *Pediatric Annals* 16(2):117–130.

Levine, M., Busch, B., and Aufesser, C. 1982. The dimension of inattention in children with school problems. *Pediatrics* 70, 387.

Littman, E. 1999. ADHD underdiagnosed in girls. *Clinical Psychiatry News* 27(12):15.

Liu, C., Robin, A. L., Brenner, A., and Eastman, J. 1991. Social acceptability of methylphenidate and behavior modification for treating attention-deficit hyperactivity disorder. *Pediatrics* 8:560–565.

Lyon, R. 1994. *Frames of Reference for Assessment of Learning Disabilities.* Baltimore: Paul H. Brookes Publishing. (referencing Baddeley, A. D. 1986. Working Memory. New York: Oxford University Press.)

Mackenzie, R. 1996. *Setting Limits in the Classroom: How to Move Beyond the Classroom Dance of Discipline.* Rocklin, California: Prima Publishing.

——1993). *Setting Limits: How To Raise Responsible, Independent Children by Providing Reasonable Boundaries.* Rocklin, California: Prima Publishing.

Marks, D. J., McKay, K. E., Himelstein, J., Walter, K. J., Newcorn, J. H., and Halperin, J. M. 2000. Predictors of physical aggression in children with attention-deficit/hyperactive disorder. *CNS Spectrums* 5(6):52–57.

Marshall, R. M., Schafer, V. A., O'Donell, L., Elliot, J., and Hardwic, M. L. 1999. Arithmetic disabilities and ADD subtypes: Implications for DSM-IV. *Journal of Learning Disabilities* 32 (M/J): 240.

Mattes, J. A. 1980. The role of frontal lobe dysfunction in childhood hyperkinesis. *Comprehensive Psychiatry.* 21:358–369.

Mayes, S. D., Calhoun, S. L., and Crowell, E. W. 2000. Learning disabilities and ADHD: Overlapping spectrum disorders. *Journal of Learning Disabilities* 33(5):417–424.

McCarney, S. B., The Milich, R., Carlson, C. L., Pelham, W. E., and Licht, B. G. 1991. Effects of methylphenidate on the persistence of ADHD boys following failure experiences. *Journal of Abnormal Child Psychology* 19:519–536

Mitchell, A., Steffenson, N., Hogan, H., Gibson F. H., and Steffenson, M. 1996. Tics, Tourette, and attention deficit hyperactivity disorders: Connections and treatment. *American Journal of Maternal Child Nursing* 21:294–300.

Morriss, R. 1995. *Students with Attention Disorders: Real Versus Pseudo ADD.* Carmel Valley, CA: Village Press.

——1990. *Attention Disorders in School-Age Children: The Role of the School Psychologist in Diagnosis and Treatment.* Carmel Valley, CA: Village Press.

National Institute of Mental Health: Questions & Answers. (Update: December 14, 1999). NIMH Multimodal Treatment Study of Children with ADHD.

Neilans, T. H., and Israel, A. C. 1981. Towards maintenance and generalization of behavior change: Teaching children self-instructional skills. *Cognitive Therapy and Research* 5:189–196.

Papolos, D. F. and Papolos, J. 1999. *The Bipolar Child.* New York: Broadway Books.

Parker, H. C. 1996. Helping adolescents with ADD perform in school. *Attention!* (Winter) 38–44.

Pelham, W. E. 1993. Pharmacotherapy for children with attention-deficit hyperactivity disorder. *School Psychology Review* 22(2):199–227.

Pelham, W. E., Vodde-Hamilton, M., Murphy, D. A., Greenstein, J., and Vallano, G. 1990. The effects of methylphenidate on ADHD adolescents in recreational, peer group, and classroom settings. *Journal of Clinical Child Psychology* 20:293–300.

Pennington, B. F., Grossier, D., and Welsh, M. C. 1993. Contrasting cognitive deficits in attention deficit hyperactivity disorder versus reading disability. *Developmental Psychology* 29:511–523.

Phelan, T. 1996. *All About Attention Deficit Disorder Symptoms, Diagnosis and Treatment: Children and Adults.* Glen Ellyn, IL: Child Management, Inc.

Phelan, T. 1995. *1-2-3- Magic: Effective Discipline for Children 2-12.* Glen Ellyn, IL: Child Management, Inc.

Pisterman, S., Firestone, P, McGrath, P., Goodman, J., Webster, I., Mallory, R., and Goffin, B. 1992. The role of parent training in treatment of preschoolers with ADHD. *American Orthopsychiatric Association* 62 (3):397–407.

Pittman, F. S. 1987. *Turning Points: Treating Families in Transition and Crisis.* New York: W. W. Norton & Company.

Quinn, P. 1997. *Attention Deficit Disorder, Diagnosis and Treatment from Infancy to Adulthood.* New York: Brunner/Mazel.

Rapport, M. D. and Kelly, K. L. 1991. Psychostimulant effects on learning and cognitive function: Findings and implications for children with attention-deficit hyperactivity disorder. *Clinical Psychology Review* 11:61–92

Rapport, M. D., Quinn, S. O., DuPaul, G. J., Quinn, E. P., and Kelly, K. L. 1989. Attention deficit disorder with hyperactivity and methylphenidate: The effects of dose and mastery level on children's learning performance. *Journal of Abnormal Child Psychology* 17:669–689.

Rief, S. 1993. How to Reach and Teach ADD/ADHD Children. Nyack, NY: The Center for Applied Research in Education, Simon and Schuster.

Ross, R., Hommer, D., Breiger, D., Valey, C., and Radant, A. 1994. Eye movement task related to frontal lobe functioning in children with attention deficit disorder. *Journal of the American Academy of Child and Adolescent Psychiatry* 33:869–874.

Safer, D. J., Zito, J. M., and Pine, E. M. 1996. Increased methylphenidate usage for attention deficit disorder in the 1990s. *Pediatrics* 98:1084–1088.

Sandson, T. A., Bachna, K. J., and Morin, M.D. 2000. Right hemisphere dysfunction in ADHD: Visual hemispatial inattention and clinical subtype. *Journal of Learning Disabilities* 3(1): 83–90.

Schultz, K. P., Himelstein, J., Halperin, J. M., Ph.D. (June, 2000). Neurobiological models of attention-deficit/hyperactivity disorder: A brief review of the empirical evidence. *CNS Spectrums* 5(6):34–44.

Sherman, C. 2000. ADHD patients may have oral comprehension problems, *Clinical Psychiatry News* (December) 22.

———2000. Girls with ADHD have more psychosocial issues. *Clinical Psychiatry News* (December) 22.

Shue, K. L. and Douglas, V. I. 1992. Attention deficit hyperactivity disorder and the frontal lobe syndrome. *Brain and Cognition* 20:102–104.

Solanto, M. V 2000. The predominantly inattentive subtype of attention-deficit/hyperactivity disorder. *CNS Spectrums* 5(6):45–51.

Spencer, T. 2000. *Point—Counterpoint: ADHD.* (Interview with Thomas Spencer) 2(3):16.

Spencer, T. J., Biederman, J., Harding, M., O'Donell, D., Faraone, S. V., and Wilens, T. E. 1996. Growth deficits in ADHD children revisited: Evidence for disorder-associated growth delays? *Journal of the American Academy of Child and Adolescent Psychiatry* 35(11):1460–1469.

Stanford, L. and Hynd, G. 1994. Congruence of behavioral symptomatology in children with ADD/H, ADD/WO, and learning disabilities. *Journal of Learning Disabilities* 27(4), 243–253.

Summers, J. A. and Caplan, P. J. 1987. Lay people's attitudes toward drug treatment for behavioral control depend on which disorder and which drug. *Clinical Pediatrics* 26:258–263.

Taylor, J. 1994. *Helping Your Hyperactive Attention Deficit Child.* Rocklin, CA: Prima Publishing.

Teeter, P. A. 1998. *Interventions for ADHD: Treatment in Developmental Context.* New York: The Guilford Press.

Voeller, K. K. S. and Heilman, K. M. 1988. Attention deficit disorder in children: A neglect syndrome? *Neurology* 38:806–808.

Weiss, G. and Hechtman, L. T. 1986. *Hyperactive Children Grown Up.* New York: The Guilford Press.

Wender, E. 1986. The food additive-free diet in the treatment of behavior disorders: A review. *Developmental and Behavioral Pediatrics* 7(1):35–42.

Whalen, C., Henker, B., and Granger, D. 1990. Social judgment processes in hyperactive boys: Effects of methylphenidate and comparisons with normal peers. *Journal of Abnormal Child Psychology* 18:29–316.

Williams, L. 1988. Parents and doctors fear growing misuse of drug used to treat hyperactive kids. *Wall Street Journal* January 15.

Wozniak, J. and Biederman, J. (June, 1996). A pharmacological approach to the quagmire of comorbidity in juvenile mania. *Journal of the American Academy of Child and Adolescent Psychiatry* 35(6):826-828.

Zentall, S. 1993. Research on the educational implications of attention deficit hyperactivity disorder. *Exceptional Children* 60:143–153.

Index

1–2–3 Magic, 119–20
200 Cards, 1, 12

A

abuse, 91, 108–9, 121, 128, 214
    child, 30, 121, 128, 190, 212, 220, 273
    substance (*see also* drug abuse; alcohol),
        177, 188–90, 200–1
academic (*see* school)
accidents, 14–15, 18, 21–22
accommodations (*educational, environ-
    mental, etc.*), 20, 39–40, 44, 115–16,
    132, 138–39, 142–43, 150–1, 159–62,
    164, 166, 171–72, 208–9, 229–30,
    233, 238, 246–47, 250–51, 258,
    260–61
accountability, 68, 72, 78, 223–24
acids (*ascorbic, citric, organic*), 190
acknowledging mistakes (*see* mistakes)
Adderall, 101, 179–80, 188, 198, 235–36,
    275
additives, 32
ADHD-C (Combined), 7, 11, 19–20, 230
ADHD-HI (Predominantly Hyperactive-
    Impulsive), 7, 11, 17, 19–20, 231, 246
ADHD-I (Predominantly Inattentive), 7, 11,
    19–20, 93, 117, 161, 231–32, 246
adjustment base disorder, 273
adolescence, 3, 10, 18, 21, 23–24, 38, 43,
    50, 64, 67, 76, 79–82, 87, 93–94,
    98–100, 106–8, 125, 152, 159, 162,
    172–73, 186, 188–89, 194, 219–25,
    268–69
adoption, 34
adrenaline, 18, 154, 198–200
adults, 10, 13, 18, 20–21, 29, 43–44, 48–52,
    55, 61, 65, 74, 81, 106, 109, 125–29,
    137–38, 140, 155, 158, 163, 168, 173,
    176, 182–83, 188, 201–6, 212, 214,
    217, 219–21, 224, 227, 258, 268–69
adventure programs, 45
advocacy, 55, 116, 128, 143, 164, 166, 261
affect, 25
affection, 61, 111, 121

affective storms, 48–49
age, 1, 10, 15–17, 21–22, 24, 29–30, 33,
    37–39, 42, 51, 55, 70, 72, 79–80,
    88–89, 101, 105, 108, 119–20,
    126–27, 163, 170, 172–73, 182, 193,
    214, 216, 218–19, 222, 224–25, 234,
    238, 243, 247, 254, 268–69
age-appropriate, 11, 22, 40, 61, 80, 127, 135,
    137, 148
aggression (*see also* hostility; violence; emo-
    tions; overreaction; volatility), 20–21,
    36, 40, 48–49, 64, 68–69, 72, 82–83,
    91, 105, 141–43, 167, 169, 180, 195,
    199–203, 214, 219, 260, 269
alcohol, 18, 34, 37–38, 44, 48, 106, 159,
    188, 221
alertness, 154, 165, 181
allergies, 21, 32
American Psychiatric Association, 175
American Medical Association, 176, 259
Americans with Disabilities Act (ADA), 44,
    165
amitryptiline, 204
Anastopoulos and Shelton, 14, 17, 22–23,
    32, 42–43
anger, 2–3, 7, 17–19, 26, 36, 43, 48–49, 54,
    59–62, 65, 67, 69–70, 73–74, 76–77,
    81–85, 88, 93, 102, 108, 111, 114,
    129, 131, 135, 138, 141–43, 159,
    168–70, 175, 202, 205, 211–15,
    220–23, 227, 234, 249, 254, 262
    control techniques, 3
annoyance, 18, 168, 212, 234
anticonvulsant, 191–92
antidepressants, 35, 191, 200, 202–3, 257
    tricyclic, 187, 191, 199–200
antihistamines (*see also* Benadryl; diphenhy-
    dramine; Periactin), 184, 191, 204
antioxidants, 197
antisocial personality disorder, 43
anorexia nervosa, 201
anxiety, 7, 18–24, 43–44, 53–54, 61–62, 68,
    106–7, 115, 126, 132, 138–39, 182,
    186, 190, 200, 202, 211, 220–21, 248,

254, 256, 269
disorders, 20, 190, 197, 206, 262, 268, 272
apnea, 33, 272
apologizing, 3, 53, 73, 75, 215
appetite (*see also* diet), 48, 103–4, 177, 179, 183–85, 194, 257
Archer, Anita, 135
arguing, 16, 18, 24, 68, 73, 168, 202, 209, 224
arithmetic (*see also* math), 30, 232, 251, 261
arousal, 25, 36, 74, 100, 105–7, 168, 231
articulation, 231
artificial sweeteners, 32
aspartame, 33
assessment, 41–42, 46–7, 54–55, 177, 180–81, 193, 200, 214, 230, 249, 254, 256
assignments, 44, 113–16, 131–32, 135, 146, 149–56, 161–62, 229, 232–33, 243–47, 250–51, 267
asthma, 21, 107
Ativan, 204
atomoxetine, 201
attending (*see* attention)
attention (*see also* inattention), 7, 11, 13–19, 22–26, 29–30, 33, 36–37, 45–46, 61, 74, 80, 85, 88, 91, 94, 96–104, 108, 111, 113, 119, 125, 140, 151, 154–55, 160–61, 163, 177–82, 190–91, 195, 198, 206, 208–12, 217, 230–33, 236, 238, 242–43, 249–50, 257, 260, 267–69
    disorder, 15, 24
    divided, 14
    focused, 14, 233
    selective, 14, 230–32
    span, 13, 45
    sustained, 14, 116, 131, 231
Attention Deficit Disorders Intervention Manual, 242
auditory, 3, 129, 189, 232
auditory processing disorder, 273
authority figures, 17–18, 127
autism, 11, 190
avoidance, 18, 115, 233

B

babysitting, 45, 105, 110, 125–29, 147
Barkley, Russell, 10, 13, 19, 24–30, 33–34, 36–39, 41, 53, 56, 59, 70–71, 74, 111–112, 161, 172, 206, 208, 222
bathroom, 15, 27, 45, 52, 64, 86, 94–95, 100, 107, 109–10, 217, 221
bedroom, 14, 52, 82, 86, 88, 94–95, 100, 107, 109–10, 217, 221
bedtime, 3, 71, 96, 100–1, 104–7, 112, 115, 119, 134, 184–85, 203
    rituals, 105, 203
bed-wetting (*see also* enuresis, urination), 15, 100
behavior, 2–3, 7, 9, 11–13, 16–19, 22–34, 36–52, 55, 58–91, 98, 100, 103, 105, 107, 110–12, 115–20, 123, 125–43, 150–53, 158–59, 164, 167–72, 177, 180–84, 188, 190–91, 194–98, 204–207, 210–24, 227–29, 232–44, 248–59
    age-appropriate, 22
    antisocial, 68, 86, 159, 177, 208
    arousal (*see* arousal)
    avoidance, 115
    bias, 54–55, 137, 163, 258–59, 261–63, 269
    biological, 31, 34, 37, 39, 190, 195, 203, 258
    compliant (*see also* compliant), 85, 88–90
    contract, 245
    crib, 21
    dangerous, 26, 241
    disinhibited (*see* disinhibition)
    disorders, 43
    disruptive (*see* disruption)
    effects (235–36, 274
    explosive, 96
    goal-directed (*see* goals)
    high-risk, 44, 154
    history, 93
    hyperkinetic (*see also* hyperactivity), 33
    "I'm sorry," 75
    incompetent (*see* incompetence)
    inconsistent (*see* inconsistency)
    inhibited (*see also* inhibition), 24,

26–27, 69, 78–79, 180, 204, 242
intellectual, 145
interactions, 41, 208
interventions (*see also* intervention), 50,
    68, 140, 172, 206, 208, 243, 253,
    258
intrusive, 198
management, 37, 72, 87, 97, 168, 180,
    196, 202, 207, 209–10, 240–41,
    252, 256
manic-like (*see* bipolar disorder)modifi-
    cation, 29–30
motor, 28
noncompliant (*see* noncompliance)
oppositional (*see* oppositional)
patterns, 10, 152
physical, 145
report, 181
rule-governed, 27, 78–79
sexual (*see also* promiscuity), 36
social, 145, 235
start, 119
stop, 119
thoughtful, 30, 36, 154
training, 42
violent (*see* violence)
behaviorist, 218
Benadryl, 184, 204
betrayal, 114
bike, riding, 18–19, 84, 114, 217
binders, 116, 135, 148–49, 152, 246
biological hazards, 37
biology, 31
bipolar disorder (*see also* manic-depression),
    43, 48–50, 182, 190, 192, 194–95,
    201–2, 273
biting, 21, 81
bladder control (*see also* bedwetting;
    enuresis; urination), 15
blame, 18, 51–55, 58–64, 67–68, 72–73, 86,
    91, 93, 111, 121, 143, 158, 168,
    171–72, 202, 218, 222, 227–30, 254
blood
    flow patterns, 30
    levels, 185, 196
    pressure, 183, 199, 200
    stream, 178, 188, 199
    test, 11, 180

blue-green algae, 197
Bolt from the Blue, 51, 59, 228
boredom, 13, 16, 29–30, 44–45, 70, 98, 127,
    130, 134, 147, 150, 154, 156, 159,
    207, 210, 216, 233, 241, 248, 252
bowel, 15
boys/males, 7, 10, 13, 34, 73, 111, 228
brain, 1–2, 29, 32, 35–36, 71, 133, 180–81,
    202
    basal ganglia, 36
    cerebellum, 36
    chemistry, 1–2, 35, 37, 60, 70, 80
    circuitry, 24, 206
    damage, 32
    development, 9, 14, 24, 31, 37, 52, 66,
        71, 79, 97, 154, 206, 234, 258
    injury, 32–34, 37, 190, 200
    metabolism, 2, 30
    minimal brain damage, 32
    prefrontal cortex, 36
    prefrontal lobes, 2, 30–31, 34, 36, 154
    scan (*see also* positron emission tomog-
        raphy [PET]), 11, 30, 180
    size, 36
    striatum, 36
    structure, 1
    studies, 30
    tissue, 33
    vermis, 36
brainstorming, 64, 110, 140, 171
breakfast, 33, 102–4
Breggin, Peter, 175, 259
bribing, 75, 149, 215–16, 218
brother (*see* siblings)
bulimia, 201
bupropion, 187, 200–1

C

caffeine, 100, 182, 184, 188, 190–91,
    193–94
calculation (*see also* arithmetic; math), 230,
    232, 251
calendar, 53, 64, 98–99, 109–10, 114, 122,
    135–36, 149
California, 144, 175
cancer, 107
candy, 100

carbohydrate, 33, 104
career, 44, 80
cartoons, 45, 101–2
Catapres (see clonidine)
cause, 2, 9–10, 21, 31–34, 37, 39–42, 47, 49,
    58, 84, 107, 179, 183–87, 190, 192,
    199–200, 232, 257
Celexa, 202
central nervous system, 34–35, 37, 39–40,
    183
cerebral palsy, 273
CHADD, 65, 125, 127, 140, 176, 217
change, difficulty with, 18, 36, 77–78, 99,
    105, 107, 126, 211, 218, 249
characteristics, 1, 9, 11, 13, 16, 44, 48, 65,
    117, 136, 138, 167
charts, 75, 89, 91, 99, 101–4, 109, 119, 127,
    186, 216–17
childhood, 10, 20, 26, 34, 49, 65, 93, 105,
    232, 262
child-rearing practices, 37
chores, 13–14, 20, 29, 87, 95–97, 101, 122,
    128, 181, 215–216, 223, 267
Ciba-Geigy (see also Ritalin), 175
citalopram, 202
clinical interview, 42
clonazepam, 187
clonidine, 184, 187, 193, 199–200, 204
coaching, 75, 116, 120, 134–35, 151, 153,
    172, 174, 218, 229
cocaine, (see also drug abuse), 191
coffee, 64, 100, 188, 193, 211
cognitive
    ability (see also intelligence), 163, 173,
        230
    performance, 237
    process, 1, 25, 230, 233
    style, 131
    tasks, 232
cola (see also soda), 100
colds, 21
colic, 21
college, 43, 80, 152, 172
comedies, 45
commercials, 45
communication, 2, 11, 24, 34–35, 40, 42,
    55, 74, 87, 114–17, 132–33, 142, 145,
    150, 153, 208–9, 220–22, 246–49,
    255–57, 262
compliance (see also noncompliance), 26,
    58, 85, 89, 91, 111, 119, 141, 158,
    205, 209–11, 229
comprehension, 113, 136, 138, 146, 198,
    230, 232–33, 251
compulsions, 18, 46, 138, 202
computers, 13, 18, 45, 106–7, 161, 242,
    244–45, 247, 251
concentration, 11, 45, 104, 106, 190, 195,
    232, 269
Concerta, 179, 185, 275
conduct disorder, 49, 208, 262, 269
conscience, 3
consequences, 22, 25–26, 58, 68–70, 76, 79,
    81, 83, 87, 90–91, 109, 118–20,
    129–30, 141, 155, 169, 188, 197, 207,
    210, 214–215, 222–224, 249
consistency, 10, 12, 14–16, 20, 24, 29, 38,
    41, 58, 71–72, 88, 96, 105, 115, 129,
    131, 155–57, 164, 170, 190, 205–8,
    211–12, 240, 246, 249, 256, 263
consoling (see self-consoling)
constipation, 200
contract, 87, 149, 152, 223, 245
contraindications, 186, 189–90, 193
cooperative, 2, 21–22, 68, 91, 181, 251, 257
coping skills, 22, 152, 211, 229
copying, 132, 135, 160
coprolalia, 46
correlates, 1
Council of Scientific Affairs, 176
counseling, 9, 21, 23, 28, 36, 39–40, 42, 56,
    58, 61, 63, 67, 81, 84, 87, 97, 108,
    111–12, 124–28, 131, 139, 148,
    151–52, 157, 159, 173, 209, 212, 224,
    240, 254, 259
Counting to Five, 68, 70, 77, 215, 249
creativity, 9, 25, 110, 126, 148, 260
criminal justice, 10
criticism, 2–3, 31, 33, 90, 121, 128, 134,
    269
crying, 21, 51, 67, 81, 100, 134, 269
cussing (see also coprolalia; swearing), 81
Cylert, 179–80, 275

D

daily plan, 240, 242, 252

dating, 125–29

daycare, 21, 42, 55, 125, 129, 147

daydreaming, 14, 19, 23, 27, 65, 146, 151

death, 48

decision-making, 13, 18, 20, 26, 31, 36, 52, 69–70, 74, 80, 94, 173, 218, 220

decoding, 136

defiance (*see also* oppositional-defiant disorder; noncompliance), 17, 24, 97, 188, 190, 202, 209

delusions, 192

denial, 3, 48, 79, 121, 254

Depakote, 195, 201

depression, 21, 24, 26, 43, 48–49, 107, 128, 155, 159, 182, 184, 190, 192, 194, 197, 199–203, 208–9, 262

desipramine, 200

destructive, 21, 86, 269

Desyrel, 204

determination, 30

developmental (*see also* neurodevelopmental), 9, 11–12, 21–22, 24, 28–29, 33, 36–37, 39–40, 61, 70–72, 76, 79, 107–8, 113, 121, 124, 128, 155, 159, 173, 187, 190, 193, 196, 202, 206, 211, 216, 219–20, 224, 227, 258, 260, 267–69, 273

   history, 48

Dexedrine, 35, 48, 101, 178–80, 188–89, 191, 193, 198, 203, 235, 275

dextroamphetamine, 178–79, 235, 275

diagnosis, 9–17, 22–23, 33, 36, 41–43, 46–50, 54, 62, 94, 111, 131, 138, 165, 175–76, 182–86, 190–97, 205, 230–31, 254–56, 259, 262

Diagnostic and Statistical Manual of Mental Disorders, Fourth Edition, Text Revision (DSM-IV-TR), 13

diet, 32–33, 197

Dilantin, 191

dinner, 23, 77, 96, 112, 115, 125, 147, 183, 185, 211, 217

diploma (*see also* graduation; high school), 134, 173–74

directions (*attending to, following*), 12–19, 22, 68, 85–87, 94–96, 99, 113, 126, 129, 132, 141, 146, 159–60, 206–7,

210, 229, 233, 242, 260

   positive, 85–86, 96

disability (*see also* learning disability), 44, 80, 110–111, 116, 142, 163–66, 187, 193, 202, 252–53

disability center, 80

discipline (*see also* punishment), 3, 27, 58, 67–72, 79, 88, 91, 111, 138, 141, 211

discrepancy model, 163–64

discouragement, 2, 156, 161, 237, 243, 260

disinhibition, 26, 36, 44, 69, 210, 212

disorganization (*see also* disorganization; executive function), 15, 19–20, 38, 123, 138, 148, 161, 231, 269

disrespect, 110, 142

disruption (*behavior*), 16, 90, 102, 126, 131–32, 138, 141–43, 159, 174, 228–29, 239–42

distractions/distractibility, 11–16, 19, 23, 27–29, 35, 43, 47–49, 73, 85, 87, 94–95, 101–4, 116–17, 138, 146–51, 154–55, 164, 181–82, 192, 194–95, 198, 204, 206, 208, 235, 239–45, 248, 250–51, 267, 269

divorce/separation, 42, 121, 142, 177, 238

dizziness, 200

doctor (*see* physician)

dopamine, 35–36

Dreikers, Rudolph, 61–62, 64

drop out of school, 171–73, 229, 261

drug

   abuse/addiction, 18, 38, 44, 48, 56, 159, 188–93, 200–1, 220–21

drugs (*see also* medication; psychopharmacotherapy), 49, 100, 107, 144–45, 178, 187–97, 201–2, 237

   companies/manufacturers, 174, 184

   dependence, 188

   exposure, intrauterine, 190

   generic, 184, 275

   interactions, 191, 197, 204

   insurance coverage, 262

   investigational, 201

   mood-altering, 189

dystonic reactions, 201

E

ears, 21

education/educational (*see also* school), 10,
    20, 22–24, 24, 39–44, 56, 69, 72, 82,
    86, 113, 116, 123, 131–34, 138–39,
    141–42, 144, 151, 159–60, 163–67,
    171–73, 176, 193, 207–9, 225,
    227–29, 233, 238–39, 245, 251–61,
    269
  codes, 144, 166
  department of, 167, 252
  family, 37–38
  history, 145
  records, 145
  review, 116
  secondary (*see also* school, high), 146
  skills, 227
  special, 38, 116, 136, 143, 163–67, 171,
    207, 230–31, 252–53, 261
Elavil, 204
embarrassment, 13, 15, 17, 56, 76, 118, 133,
    175
emotional
  abuse, 128
  blackmail, 214
  development, 39, 71, 128, 227, 258
  disorder, 43
  disturbed, 220
  hijack, 73
  lessons, 261
  outburst, 48–49, 76–77, 81, 130, 180,
    191, 219, 219, 249–50
  scars, 138
  volatility, 18, 40, 67, 81, 123, 221
emotions, 2, 10, 18, 29, 31, 34, 36, 41, 46,
    50, 52–53, 56, 64, 72, 76–77, 81, 84,
    99, 117, 120–22, 136–38, 141–42,
    156, 158–59, 167–68, 173, 190, 208,
    211, 213–15, 221, 235, 239, 249,
    261–62
  modulation, 60, 76, 99, 134, 167–68,
    170, 210, 224, 235, 249, 260
empathy, 82, 258
employment, 12, 24, 44, 79, 117, 124–25,
    142, 204, 206, 222
encouragement, 2–3, 75–76, 82–83, 106–7,
    130, 138, 162, 240, 242, 247
enthusiasm, 9, 48–49, 155
enuresis, 200
environment, 10–11, 13, 16, 26, 28, 31, 34,
    37, 39–40, 42, 61, 63, 72, 85, 90–91,
    104, 114, 116, 128, 139, 142, 146,
    150–51, 154, 159–60, 168, 171–72,
    177, 190, 196, 208–10, 228, 236, 250,
    258–60, 272
ephedra, 197
escalation, 77, 81, 83, 88, 117–19, 140, 208,
    221–22, 261
euphoria, 48–49, 194
excitement, 26, 45–46, 98–99
executive function (*see also* organization;
    planning; self-regulation), 1, 25–30
exercise, 84, 100, 147, 150, 250
expectations, 22, 29, 60, 97–98, 102, 118,
    136, 159–60, 240, 247, 249–50,
    262–63
expulsion, 18, 38, 172, 229, 260
explosive *(behavior)*, 18, 96, 127, 138
eye contact, 96, 248

F

family, 1–3, 7–9, 16–17, 22–24, 32, 34,
    37–45, 51–52, 58–65, 81–83, 87, 93,
    95, 97, 99, 101–2, 108, 111, 113, 116,
    121–27, 136, 139, 143, 145, 157,
    176–77, 190, 208–9, 212–13, 217–20,
    224, 261–62
  blended, 127
  history, 34, 43, 48, 54
  outings, 97, 233
  therapist, 41
Farmer, 16, 241
fatigue, 100, 106, 186, 188, 194
fear, 7, 18, 51, 56, 59–62, 81, 173, 220, 222
federal financial assistance, 165, 252
federal funds, 165, 252, 259
federal law, 44, 142, 163–6, 260
Feingold Diet, 32
Feingold, Benjamin, 32
females/girls, 10, 34, 200
fidgeting, 15–16, 23, 45, 98, 175, 181, 240,
    248, 267
fine-motor function, 180, 231, 236
fine visual-motor coordination (*see* visual-
    motor coordination)
fish oils, 197
fixation, 18, 26, 82, 101

flexibility (*see also* inflexibility), 25
fluency, 74
fluoxetine, 202
fluvoxamine, 202
forgetfulness (*see also* memory; remem-
    bering), 13–14, 20, 23, 77, 80, 86–87,
    89, 94–95, 123, 127, 134–35, 138,
    150–52, 162, 209, 218, 222–23, 231,
    243, 245, 267
forgiveness, 23, 51, 64, 72, 75, 84, 173, 212,
    215, 224–25
formula, 21
Forward, Susan, 214
Frazier, Donna, 214
friends
    child's, 18, 20, 44, 73, 75–80, 82, 86, 93,
        95, 99, 102, 133, 135, 157, 159,
        172–73, 189, 210, 215, 217, 220,
        239, 260
    parent's, 46–47, 51, 58, 64–65, 71, 122,
        126–27, 129, 138, 164, 211, 215
frustration, 1, 8, 12–13, 16–18, 20, 22, 24,
    28–29, 42, 52, 54–55, 58, 65, 67, 80,
    82–83, 85, 93, 99, 105, 108, 117, 126,
    128, 131, 135, 150, 152, 155, 156,
    161, 167, 177, 205, 211–12, 219, 224,
    228, 233, 237, 241, 249–50, 254,
    258–63
Free Appropriate Public Education (FAPE),
    166, 253

G

gambling, 44
Garber, Garber, and Spizman, 35, 95, 235,
    237
genes (*see also* polygenic), 10, 34, 38, 44, 46,
    52, 176, 186
genetic, 31, 34, 38–40, 44, 52, 186–87
Geodon, 187, 201
Gleason, Mary, 135
goal-directed, 25, 30, 155, 242
goals, 16, 25, 27–30, 61–62, 79, 84, 88–89,
    118, 139, 154–56, 166, 171, 214–18,
    222, 242, 251
Goldman, Larry, 176
Goldstein, Sam and Michael, 14, 33, 84–86,
    90

Goleman, Daniel, 73, 155, 259, 261–62
grades, 31, 38, 79, 154–57, 160, 165
graduate degree, 43
graduation, 93, 134, 150, 172–73, 227
grandparents, 12, 42, 55–57, 125
grape seed extract, 197
gratification, 14, 86, 109
Green Cards, 169
Green, Yellow, Red, 83, 249
group settings, 45, 73
growth, 185–86, 196
guanfacine, 187, 199–200
guidelines, 41, 50, 78, 84, 114, 144, 225,
    234, 252
guilt, 17, 52–53, 56–63, 67, 93, 126, 128,
    175–76, 212, 228–29
GW 320659, 201

H

Haldol, 187, 201
half-life, 147, 199
haloperidol, 187, 201
hallucinations, 189, 194–95
hand-eye coordination, 20, 231
Hartmann, Thom, 16, 61, 156
headache, 177, 184, 188, 194
head banging, 21
health care, 10, 207
heart rate, 183, 200
Helping Your ADD Child, 3
herbal medicine, 197
heredity, 34
hitting, 46, 67–69, 79, 83–84, 141–42, 169,
    213–14
home, 1–2, 10, 14, 18, 20, 22, 29, 31, 37,
    39–40, 42–43, 46, 52, 62–63, 65,
    71–72, 80, 91, 94, 97, 108, 110,
    112–20, 124, 126–28, 135, 141–43,
    147–50, 152, 160, 162, 169–72, 195,
    209–10, 213–14, 218, 221–25, 229,
    245–48, 257, 268, 273
homeopathy, 197
homework, 18, 23, 29, 31, 69, 95–96, 98,
    100, 106, 112–19, 129, 131, 134–38,
    144–61, 179, 181, 185, 191, 211, 216,
    222, 233, 241–42, 245–46, 251, 267
honesty, 53, 60, 74–76, 79, 115, 133, 255

hopelessness, 7, 48, 155
hospitalization, 62–63
hostility, 17, 109, 222, 297
*How to Reach and Teach ADD/ADHD
    Children,* 114
Hunter, 16, 61, 241
hyperactivity, 7–8, 10–12, 15–24, 33–35,
    37, 43–44, 49, 65, 94, 101, 105, 117,
    125–26, 140, 158–59, 161, 168, 176,
    178, 182, 184, 191, 195, 198–204,
    217, 231, 267–69
hyperfocus, 13, 154
hyper-reactivity, 202
hypertension, 183, 199
hyperthyroidism, 33, 273
hypnotics, 107

I

I. C.A.R.E., 82–83, 100, 121, 198
illness, 32–34
imaging, 36
imipramine, 191, 200, 204
immaturity, 20, 159, 193, 224
impairment, 1–2, 10–12, 25, 39, 165, 167,
    188, 202, 230–32, 252, 261, 268
impatience, 19–20, 77, 108, 156, 161, 168,
    206
impulsivity, 11–12, 16–17, 19–24, 35–38,
    43–44, 47, 49, 60, 67–70, 76–77,
    85–86, 94, 105, 108, 110, 113, 117,
    123, 127, 131, 133, 138, 141–42, 145,
    158–59, 162, 167–68, 170, 177–78,
    180, 184, 188, 191, 194–95, 198, 200,
    203–04, 210–11, 216, 219, 221, 231,
    235–36, 248–49, 251–52, 256, 258,
    261, 267–69
inadequacy, 2, 58, 209, 219
inattention, 9, 11–21, 37–38, 43–44, 47, 86,
    94–96, 101, 130, 133, 138, 161, 188,
    190, 192, 195, 198, 200, 204, 209,
    219, 230–31, 246, 251, 258, 267–68
independence, 24, 38
independent learner, 113, 132, 158, 160,
    251
indicators, 1, 13, 44, 50
Individuals with Disabilities Act (IDEA),
    142, 162–67, 252, 260–61

infants, 1, 21–22, 104–5, 269
inflexibility, 16
information processing, 13, 19–20, 22, 25,
    35–36, 94
inhibition (*see also* disinhibition), 11,
    24–29, 35, 69, 76, 78–79, 167, 180,
    206, 242, 249
initiative, 26, 43
injury *(bodily)* (*see also* brain injury), 177,
    200, 269
insomnia, 100, 107, 177, 184–85, 204
insurance, 42, 262
intelligence, 12, 23, 44, 145, 158, 163–64
interference control, 26
interrupting, 16, 23, 65, 72, 82, 109–10,
    239, 268
intervention (*see also* behavior), 2, 7, 10,
    23–24, 29–31, 39–40, 50, 52, 57–58,
    62–63, 69–70, 72, 75–77, 80, 82–83,
    86–89, 91, 95–97, 106, 112, 119–20,
    127, 139–43, 147–48, 156, 162, 166,
    168–69, 171–73, 177, 187, 198,
    205–8, 222, 225, 227–29, 233,
    238–39, 242–43, 249–53, 258–63
intruding, 16, 23, 268
irritability, 18, 21, 23, 48–49, 54, 56, 59,
    167, 184, 194, 202, 257, 269

J

jealousy, 108
job (*see* employment)
judgment, 48, 54, 57, 76, 79, 126, 153, 172,
    222
judgmentalism, 20, 53, 112, 138, 140

K

Karpel, Mark, 262
kava-kava, 204
kicking, 81, 213
kindergarten, 21, 238, 243
kitchen timer, 96, 99, 101, 103–5, 109, 119,
    129
Klonopin, 187, 204

L

language, 19–20, 28, 44, 74, 136, 162–63,

230–32, 252, 273

body, 73

lazy, 34, 138

lead poisoning/toxicity, 2, 33–34

learning, 14, 16, 19, 24, 35, 39–40, 52,
57–58, 60, 68, 70–72, 74–79, 81,
83–84, 91, 93–94, 109–10, 113,
116–17, 120–21, 123–24, 126, 129,
132, 135–38, 142, 152, 154, 159–61,
163, 165–67, 203, 205–6, 208, 211,
213–16, 224, 227–28, 232, 236–38,
252, 260–63, 269

learned helplessness, 208

learning disabilities, 2, 20, 22–24, 33, 41,
43–44, 116, 136, 138, 142–43, 150,
156, 158, 162–67, 172, 190, 193, 202,
208, 230–33. 238, 252, 273

legal rights, 145, 160

lethargy, 182

lifeline, 127

limits (setting), 45, 68, 72, 83–84, 86–90,
104, 106, 109–10, 129, 146, 215, 219,
222–23, 240, 250

listening, 14, 17, 19, 27, 80, 82, 87, 94, 110,
115–16, 128, 132, 140, 158, 160, 210,
225, 229, 262–63, 267

lithium191, 195, 201

liver, 179–80

love, 61, 65, 74, 93, 104, 116, 122–23,
127–28, 130, 134, 173, 210, 217, 219,
262

lunch, 103, 133, 181, 183–84

Luvox, 202

M

Magic Cards, 18

making amends, 3, 75

malnourishment, 273

manic-depression (*see also* bipolar-disorder),
43, 48, 192, 194–95, 201–2

manipulation, 11, 112, 214–15, 240

marriage, 3, 9, 41, 44, 93, 111, 121–24, 128,
177, 211, 224, 262

maturation (*see* immaturity)

McCarney, Stephen, 242

meals, 102–4, 106, 127, 183

media, 54, 56

medical disorders, 42, 144

medical problems, 33, 107, 189, 193

medication (*see also* drugs), 2, 11, 21, 35,
37, 43, 47, 49, 50, 56–57, 62, 67–69,
71–72, 77, 100–4, 106–7, 132–34,
140, 144–45, 147, 150, 166, 175–204,
207–10, 229, 231–40, 246, 256–60,
262, 273, 275

log, 144, 257

Mellaril, 201

memory, 25, 36, 95, 138, 161, 180

mental health, 24, 38, 42, 50, 54–55, 58, 62,
128, 262–63

mental status, 38

metabolism, 2, 30, 147, 178, 193, 196,
199–200

Metadate-ER, 179, 275

methylphenidate, 100, 178–79, 201, 235,
275

mirtazapine, 204

misbehavior, 3, 21–22, 60, 88, 118, 120,
141, 143, 207–8, 210, 214–26, 219,
238, 240

mistakes, 3, 16, 19, 28, 52, 58, 60, 62, 66,
74–75, 78–79, 81, 87, 90, 92, 117,
120, 124, 167, 205–6, 208, 211, 216,
224, 263, 267

mnemonics, 95

modifications (*see also* accommodations), 2,
29, 42, 90, 132, 135, 138

monoamine oxidase inhibitors (MAOIs),
191

moods, 18, 20, 36, 43–44, 48–49, 59, 65,
77, 83, 99–100, 102, 105, 108, 139,
159, 167, 184, 189, 192–96, 201–3,
211, 219, 224, 249, 257, 268

moral regulation, 27–28

morning, 3, 15, 21, 52, 100–4, 106, 122,
181–82, 185, 223, 240, 243

motivation, 24–25, 29–31, 36–37, 45, 69,
95, 110–11, 135, 154–57, 162, 207,
216–17, 227, 258

motor ability, 11, 15–16, 20, 28, 161, 180,
203, 231, 246, 268

development, 74

tics (*see* tics)

movement, 15–16, 23, 45–47, 63, 74, 121,
146–47, 201, 230, 241

movies, 13, 23, 126
moving, 42, 238
MSG, 32
multidisciplinary, 41, 54, 163, 256
multilevel support, 23
muscle spasms, 201

N

nagging, 3
name-calling, 81
naps, 106
natural remedies, 196–98
nefazodone, 204
neglect, 121, 123–24, 190
neighbors, 16, 31, 42, 44, 51–52, 56–559,
    64, 93, 125, 127, 142, 158, 164, 171,
    215
nerve cells, 34–36, 39, 271
nervous habits, 46–47
neural bridges, 35
neurobiological, 11
neurodevelopmental, 9, 14, 31, 37, 52, 66,
    71, 79, 97, 154, 206, 234, 258
neurogenetic, 39
neuroleptics, 35
neurological, 9, 31, 37, 47, 186, 254, 261
neurologist, 41, 46
neuron-synaptic, 35
Neurontin, 201
neuropsychological, 30, 42
    evaluations, 42
    functions, 25
    process, 25, 30
neurotoxic chemicals, 32
neurotransmitters (*see also* dopamine; nor-
    epinephrine; serotonin), 32, 34–36,
    201
nicotine (*see also* smoking), 188
noises, 14–16, 23, 26–27, 146, 240–41
noncompliance, 17–18, 21, 24, 84–85,
    87–88, 90–91, 95–97, 117–18, 127,
    143, 168, 214, 218–19, 221, 223, 244,
    259, 268
noradrenergic enhancer, 201
norepinephrine, 35–36, 201
Norpramine, 200
nortriptyline, 191, 200

notes, taking, 14, 18, 115, 132, 135, 160
nursing *(breastfeeding)*, 21
nutrition, 37

O

obscene gestures, 46
obsessing, 18, 106, 220–21
obsessive-compulsive disorder, 46, 202
Office for Civil Rights (OCR), 142, 166,
    253
olanzapine, 187, 201
one-upsmanship, 3, 121
oppositional, 17–18, 38, 44, 97, 105, 158,
    168, 172, 214, 258, 267, 269
oppositional-defiant disorder (ODD), 17,
    190, 202–3, 209, 272
optimism, 155, 157
Orap, 187
organizational skills (*see also* disorganized;
    executive function), 1, 3, 27, 26, 95,
    98, 115, 131, 135–37, 145, 148, 151,
    153, 155–56, 161–62, 172, 229, 236,
    242, 252, 258, 267
Other Health Impairment (OHI), 164–65,
    167
outings (*see also* traveling), 97–99, 233
overinvolvement, 3, 121
overprotecting, 3
overreacting, 24, 143, 212, 222, 225

P

pain, 15, 29, 51, 59, 74, 138, 143, 152, 220
Pamelor, 200
paranoia, 189, 192, 194–95
parenting, 7–8, 38, 52–53, 58, 62, 103, 112,
    114, 123–24, 174, 206–7, 225, 263
    books, 13
    class, 53–54
    physician, 2, 12, 16, 38, 40–43, 45,
        47–50, 52–57, 59, 62–63, 70–72,
        78, 80, 100–2, 104, 107, 116, 122,
        125, 128, 132, 142, 144–45, 150,
        175–76, 182–84, 192–93, 197,
        200–1, 204, 207–9, 229, 234, 236,
        254–57, 259
    poor, 9, 31, 37, 40, 58, 261

paroxetine, 202
passionflower, 204
passivity, 19, 80
Paxil, 202
pediatrician (*see also* physician), 49, 133,
    186
peers, 9–10, 17, 20, 24, 26, 74, 109, 135,
    157, 157–59, 167–68, 170, 177, 180,
    210, 219, 224, 236–38, 250
pemoline, 179, 275
performance, 9, 12, 14, 20, 24–26, 28–30,
    44, 58, 100, 131, 155–59, 162,
    164–65, 177, 230, 232, 235–39, 251,
    256
Periactin, 184
persistence, 14, 19, 30, 37, 187
personality, 12, 35, 44, 61, 123, 192, 238,
    268
pervasive developmental disorder (*see also*
    developmental), 190, 268, 273
pessimism, 48
pharmacotherapy (*see also* drugs; medica-
    tion), 49
phenobarbital, 191
phone calls, 42, 64, 135, 141–42
physical examination, 54, 183
physiological, 1–2, 35, 168
pimozide, 187
pine bark, 197
pinworms, 33
pity, 3, 60–61
Pittman, Frank, 51, 219, 221
placebo, 33, 178, 186, 197
planning, 1, 28, 30, 36, 52, 64, 71–72, 86,
    97–99, 101, 105, 118, 120, 129, 136,
    143, 149, 154, 166, 168–70, 239–42,
    251–53, 263
play, 14–15, 17–18, 21–22, 45, 70, 73, 75,
    82–83, 85, 94, 97, 99–102, 106, 114,
    126, 135, 141, 146–47, 150, 154, 156,
    159, 166, 168–69, 210, 244, 267–68
point system, 216–18, 251
polygenic, 10, 34, 46
positron emission tomography (PET), 30
potential, 36, 44, 131, 260
power, 22, 24, 33, 48, 61, 215
praise, 75, 81, 86–90, 101, 103–4, 111,
    119–20, 129, 147, 157, 170, 211, 216,

241–44, 248
pregnancy, 32, 37
prematurity, 34, 37
preschool, 21–22, 238, 269
preservatives, 32
preventative, 1–3, 10, 32, 34, 51, 90–91,
    185, 261
Primidone, 191
principal, 16, 26, 68, 72, 76, 116, 132, 139,
    141–42, 144–45, 151–52, 157, 166,
    168–71, 250, 255
problem solving, 28, 69, 71, 89, 95, 115, 269
procrastination, 43, 156
productivity, 27, 29, 31, 52, 61, 115,
    155–56, 194, 231
progress reports, 152–53, 172
projects, 29, 31, 96, 101, 113, 131, 134–35,
    146, 148–50, 154–56, 229
promiscuity, 44
protein, 33, 104
Prozac, 202
psychiatric1, 11, 20, 31, 62, 128
psychiatrist, 41, 49–50, 59, 203
psychiatry, 56
psychoeducation, 238
psychoeducational assessment, 20, 41
psychological, 9, 177, 238, 254
    suggestion, 33
    test, 11, 193
psychologist, 27, 49, 254
    clinical, 41, 49
psychopharmacology, 49–50
psychosis, 219
psychostimulants (*see* stimulants)
psychotherapy (*see also* counseling), 50, 72,
    207–8, 262
psychotic, 189–90, 192, 201, 268
psychotropic drug, 49
punishment, 25, 30, 67–69, 76, 82, 86,
    88–90, 108, 110, 119, 125, 152,
    169–70, 205

Q

questionnaires, 42

R

rage, 65, 81, 118
rating scales, 42
reactionary, 90–91
reactive attachment disorder, 273
readiness to respond, 14
reading, 12, 19, 86, 107, 136, 138, 146, 163, 203, 230, 232–33, 240, 251, 260–61
rebound effect, 101, 184–85, 188, 193–94
recess, 2, 17, 135, 141, 159, 167–70, 210, 216, 236, 240–41, 249
recklessness, 18, 21, 269
reconstitution, 25
regret, 75
regulatory-disordered, 105
Rehabilitation Act of 1973, 44, 142, 165, 252–53
reinforcement, 28, 30, 70, 83, 87, 89–91, 94, 98, 103–4, 107, 110, 113, 118, 127, 129, 153, 162, 206, 208, 211, 213, 215–17, 243–44, 248–49, 251
rejection, 177
relationships, 3, 17, 24, 51, 59–61, 65–66, 88, 113–14, 117, 124, 127–28, 136, 157, 172–73, 206, 214, 219–20, 222, 228, 231–32, 255, 262–63
relatives, 31, 58–59, 64, 127–28, 138
remembering, 13–14, 29, 60, 83, 86–87, 89–90, 94–97, 129, 132–33, 138, 144, 146, 148, 151–53, 160, 169, 172, 206, 212, 223, 234, 242, 245
Remeron, 204
reminders, 3, 15, 27, 29, 52, 71, 78, 83, 85–90, 94–98, 101, 105–7, 115, 117, 129, 131, 135, 137, 149–50, 152–53, 157, 169–70, 216–17, 223, 234, 240–41, 243–46, 248, 251, 257, 263
research, 1–2, 9–11, 17, 19–20, 30–34, 36, 41, 132, 154, 162, 181, 197–98, 207–8, 230–32, 237, 239
resentment, 18, 60, 65, 104, 108, 122, 168
response pattern, 25
responsibility, 57, 60–61, 73, 80, 111–16, 123, 125, 129, 142, 144–45, 149, 166, 211, 215, 223, 229, 234, 253, 255
restlessness, 15–16, 23, 43, 86, 100, 180, 268–69

Restoril, 204
restraint, physical, 83, 88, 118, 141, 219
rewards, 19, 25, 30–31, 71, 75, 79, 81, 96, 105–7, 110, 115, 119–20, 125, 131, 134–35, 147, 149, 154, 156, 162, 169–70, 174, 205–7, 215–18, 242–46, 248
Rief, Sandra, 114–15, 135, 161
Risperdal, 187, 201
risperidone, 187, 201
Ritalin, 35, 56, 100–1, 103, 133, 175–83, 185, 188–89, 191, 193, 195, 198, 202–3, 232, 235–37, 259, 275
ritual, 18, 105, 107
rocking, 16, 21, 45, 88
routine, 13, 29–31, 45–46, 65, 94–97, 103–7, 115, 118, 127, 129, 131, 150, 154–55, 179, 203, 210, 223
rules (*see also* behavior, rule-governed), 18, 24, 28, 67–68, 70–71, 79, 85, 87–89, 91, 98, 102–4, 106–7, 117–20, 126, 129, 190, 202, 221, 223, 240, 242–43, 249
running, 12, 15–17, 22, 50, 67, 78, 84, 88, 100, 117–19, 142, 147, 150, 159, 168, 210, 241, 268

S

salicylates, 32
schizophrenia, 11, 31, 189–90, 192, 268
school, 9–10, 12, 14, 17, 20, 22, 27, 31, 38–41, 44, 134, 155, 170, 172–74, 236
  accommodations (*see* accommodations)
  activities, 10, 17, 19, 45, 95, 106, 159, 251, 260
  administrator/staff, 17, 24, 32, 38, 41–42, 46, 64, 125, 131, 133, 137, 141–42, 144–45, 158–59, 167–68, 170, 172, 229, 238, 249, 252, 260–61
  consultation, 42
  curriculum, 132, 210, 230–33, 261, 262
  difficulty/problems, 2, 19, 23, 134, 136, 158, 170, 227, 229, 235, 237–38, 261, 268
  elementary, 15, 22, 79, 148, 238, 269

expectations, 160, 261

high school, 18, 26, 38, 80, 93, 136, 146, 152, 157, 172–73, 227, 234

intervention (*see* intervention)

middle, 80, 146, 151, 157, 234, 252

nurse, 144–45, 166

performance (*see* performance)

psychologist, 41, 116, 145, 164, 228, 246, 255

skills, 163, 227, 238

work, 13, 19, 45, 95, 97, 106–7, 116, 134–36, 138, 141, 146–47, 154–57, 160, 172, 210, 231, 233, 236–40, 244–46, 248, 250, 267, 269

science, 9–10, 31, 33, 148, 176

Section 504, 44, 142, 162, 165–67, 171, 252–53, 261

seizures, 33, 107, 192, 200–1, 273

left temporal lobe, 33

selective serotonin reuptake inhibitors (SSRIs), 202

self-

awareness, 79

blame, 63

care, 3, 130

centered, 18, 73, 126

conscious, 219

consoling, 105

control, 24–25, 28–29, 35, 74, 105, 168, 206, 215, 242, 248, 269

criticism, 52

determination, 98

directed, 153, 210, 260

discipline, 30

esteem, 24, 61, 159, 188, 194, 208, 241, 260–61, 269

expression, 79

image, 22, 26, 74

monitoring, 80, 83, 94, 147, 246

motivation, 29

questioning, 28

regulation, 25, 27, 30, 38, 45–46, 136, 249

restraint, 27

starters, 129, 134, 148, 150, 172, 239, 244, 248

talk, 28, 70–71, 77–78, 216

selfishness, 17–18, 126, 220

sensory deficits, 273

sensory integration disorder, 273

sensory premonitions, 47

separation anxiety disorder, 273

sertraline, 202

Serzone, 204

sex (*see also* behavior, sexual; promiscuity), 36, 44, 48, 195, 220

siblings, 3, 12, 28, 34, 38, 44–45, 52–53, 60, 64, 66–69, 73–74, 77–83, 90, 93, 96, 100–2, 106–11, 131–32, 149, 205–7, 209, 213, 217, 254, 262

side effects, 47, 56, 72, 103, 107, 132, 134, 140, 145, 175, 177–79, 181–84, 187, 193, 198–201, 204, 234, 257, 259

sister (*see* siblings)

skills (*see also* coping skills; organizational skills; social skills), 61, 74–75, 77, 86, 90–91, 113, 131, 135–36, 158, 160–61, 163, 214, 227–28, 232, 238, 247, 249–51, 269

Skills for Success, 135

sleep, 15, 21, 36, 48, 100, 102, 104–6, 109, 184, 194–95, 203, 269, 273

sluggishness, 19, 100

smoking (*see also* tobacco), 201

smoking, maternal, 37

snacks, 45, 103, 106, 125

soaps, 32

social

agencies, 10

class, 37

development, 39, 159

functioning, 14

skills, 3, 24, 42, 76, 158, 173, 188, 227, 269

status, 38

support, 38

worker, licensed, 41

society, 10, 22–23, 40, 62, 67–68, 72, 91, 204

soda (*see also* caffeine), 193

software, 247–48

special education, 38, 116, 136, 141, 163–67, 171, 207, 230–31, 252–53, 261

speech, 25, 28, 44, 70, 74

spelling, 14, 80, 138, 145, 155, 161, 230–31,

247, 250

sports, 14, 147, 168

spouse (*see also* marriage), 53, 123, 211, 224

state laws, 142

stars, 75, 89, 98, 103, 109, 216–18

stickers, 98, 241, 243–44

stimulants, 35, 47, 100–1, 103–4, 107, 133, 147, 154, 175–204, 231–32, 235–38, 246, 257, 275

   and growth, 185–86

stimuli, 36, 231, 267

stomachache, 184

STOP, 95–96

Stop, Look, Think and Do, 36, 77–78

stopwatch, 87, 90, 129, 146–47

store, 13, 17, 67, 71–72, 88, 93, 98–99, 111, 117–20, 129, 139, 210

stress, 3, 17–18, 38, 41–43, 46, 52, 62–63, 65, 93, 97, 113–14, 116–17, 121–27, 130, 140, 143, 149–50, 154, 181, 186, 207, 210–11, 229, 238, 248, 255, 260, 263

structure, 31, 38, 54, 58, 88, 102–3, 106–7, 116, 118, 129, 150, 168, 208, 210, 251

student study team, 116, 166, 170–71, 253

studies (*see also* research), 9–10, 17, 20, 30, 32–34, 36–37, 47, 56, 104, 172, 176–78, 180, 185–87, 189, 193, 198, 201, 230, 232, 235–39

study buddy, 152, 243, 245–46, 250

stuttering, 79, 152

sugar, 32–33, 197

suggestions, 1–3, 16, 29, 40–41, 43, 50, 53–54, 57–59, 64, 73, 75–77, 80, 82–83, 85–87, 91, 95, 97, 105, 107, 113, 118, 121–22, 128, 139–40, 146, 151, 173, 177, 183, 205, 214, 221, 223, 227–28, 233, 236, 243–44, 148–52, 255–56, 259–60, 262–63

suicide, 26, 48

supplements, 103

support groups, 59, 65, 123, 128, 140, 175–76, 217

suspension, 26, 38, 68, 78, 160, 172, 229

swearing (*see also* coprolalia), 18, 46, 168, 213

symptoms, 1, 10–15, 17–18, 20–23, 27,

32–35, 37, 39, 41–46, 48–49, 54, 86, 94, 132, 145, 153, 176–78, 180, 182–203, 232, 237, 258–59, 267–69

synapse, 34–35

syntax, 74

T

talking (*see also* self-talk), 15, 20, 26, 30, 70, 159, 169, 194, 216–17, 221, 240, 268

tantrum, 64, 73, 104, 119, 159

tape recorder, 161, 251

tardive dyskinesia, 187, 201

task completion (see also attention, sustained), 13–14, 25, 27–31, 43, 80, 86–87, 94–96, 129, 180–81, 207, 233, 237, 243–44, 246, 252, 256, 267, 269

Taylor, John F., 1–3, 12, 15, 23, 32, 35, 69, 79

teachers, 2, 7–8, 10, 12, 14–16, 19–20, 23–24, 26, 29, 31, 34, 36, 39, 42, 46, 55, 58–59, 73, 76, 93–94, 100, 105, 113–17, 122, 125, 132–345, 148–53, 155, 159–62, 164, 166, 168–74, 176, 181–82, 191, 202, 204, 207–8, 210, 214, 216, 227–58, 261

teasing, 18, 81

teen (*see* adolescence)

teeth, 33

Tegretol, 195, 201

temper, 17–18, 64, 77, 80, 83, 119, 134, 159, 168, 202, 212

temperament, 12, 44, 123–24, 139, 158, 173, 273

temperature, 36, 203

Tenex, 187, 193, 199

test-taking, 17–18, 20, 131, 155–56, 160–61, 163–64, 193, 231, 236–37, 247

thefts, 18

The Hyperactive Child, 3

therapist (*see also* psychotherapist), 38, 41, 55, 59, 67–68, 73, 81, 127, 132, 139, 152, 175, 209, 219, 221, 224

thioridazine, 201

thought, 18, 20, 23, 25–30, 35–36, 48, 51, 58, 69, 76, 78, 82, 94, 98, 106, 109, 131, 136, 146, 154–55, 160–61, 164,

167, 194, 206, 216, 231, 246–47, 249
three-legged stool, 208–9
Three R's, 95
thyroid dysfunction, 107
ticket-to-talk, 87
tics, 46–47, 186–87, 199
time-keepers, 101, 103
time management, 103, 109, 131, 172, 252
time-out, 71, 88–89, 109, 118–20, 169–70, 205, 219, 224, 241
tobacco, 34, 201
toddlers, 15, 21–22, 64, 105
Tofranil, 200, 204
tokens, 75, 101–3, 120, 127, 170, 205, 211, 216–18, 242, 248–49
tolerance, 18, 22, 40, 44, 54, 68, 84, 86, 91, 109, 138, 159, 167, 177, 179, 183, 188, 192, 196, 199–200, 224, 260
tomoxetine, 201
touch, 3, 15, 71, 117–18, 240
Tourette syndrome (TS), 43, 46–47, 50, 186–87, 199, 201, 273
toys, 19, 21, 27, 45, 66, 78, 82–83, 86–88, 98–99, 101–2, 104–5, 117, 119, 126, 210, 213, 217, 267
traits, 1, 12, 61, 73, 80, 97, 99–100, 123, 146, 154, 157, 168, 170, 205, 209, 212, 245, 259, 260
transitions (see also change, resistance to), 43, 77, 99, 105, 107, 129, 211, 240, 252
trauma, 32, 190, 238
traveling (see also outings), 98
Trazodone, 204
treatment, 9–11, 24, 33, 35, 37–43, 47, 49–50, 54–57, 71, 80, 132–33, 145, 176–78, 180, 183, 185–90, 192–94, 197–204, 208–9, 231, 234–35, 237–38, 256–58, 262
treats, 71, 81, 98, 117, 120, 127, 216
tutor, 117, 134–37, 160, 162
TV, 45–46, 50, 69, 71, 77, 95–96, 99, 101, 103–7, 114, 122, 146–47, 211
twin studies, 37, 187

U

underachievement, 19, 22–23, 34, 38, 43,

230–31, 260
unhappiness, 60, 63, 76, 81, 83, 108, 131, 144, 169, 214, 219, 227
upbringing, 55, 124
urination (see also bedwetting; bladder; enuresis), 200

V

Valium, 188, 204
valerian root, 204
vascular damage, 183
victimization, 26, 28, 60, 62, 65, 77, 81, 128, 213–14, 228, 241, 249
video game, 13, 45, 154, 210, 217
vigilance, 14
violence (see also hostility), 81–84, 86, 108–9, 128, 195, 219
vision, blurry, 200
visualization, 98–99, 213, 215, 221
visual-motor coordination, 161, 231
vitamins, 192, 197
vocal tics (see tics)
volunteers, 136

W

Wechsler Individual Achievement Test (WIAT), 163
weight, 12, 48, 182, 186, 194, 201
Wellbutrin, 187, 200–1
withdrawal (see also headaches), 20, 60, 64, 182, 188, 191–92, 194
Women Escaping A Violent Environment (WEAVE), 128
work habits, 29, 155, 172, 251
worrying, 106, 171, 189, 198, 215, 234, 252
worthlessness, feelings of, 194
writing, 17, 19–20, 22, 98, 113, 115, 135–36, 146, 160–64, 230–61
W-W Theory, 30, 205

X

Xanax, 204

Y

yelling, 46, 59, 67, 72–73, 76, 81–82, 88, 96, 100, 102, 108, 119–20, 134, 138,

170, 212–15, 218, 221–22

Z

Zip My Lip, 83, 88
ziprasidone, 187, 201
Zoloft, 202
Zyban, 201
Zyprexa, 187, 201